A STOCK INVESTMENT BOOK FOR THE 99%
BY A 99%

BT Tan (CFA, FRM)

I0505719

ISBN:9798637671144

tbt444@gmail.com

Cover
Koesen Wong

For
Renee
Reese

CONTENTS

Disclaimer

Resources, References, and Recommended Reading

PREFACE

This book was completed at the beginning of 2020, when the S&P 500 Index and other stock markets were scaling new heights. As it went through the process of editing, the coronavirus struck. Now, at the time of publishing, the world faces the unprecedented, simultaneous threats of a health crisis, economic turmoil, and financial meltdown—a global challenge unlike any other in our lifetime. The coronavirus downturn was as sudden as it has been severe. Many thousands of people have lost their lives; millions more have been infected; tens of millions have become unemployed; billions have been placed in some form of lockdown; trillions of dollars have been unleashed by governments and central banks; oil prices have plunged, and stock markets have fallen into bear markets at record speed.

The suffering to humankind, whether directly from Covid-19 or indirectly from the economic impact, is unmeasurable. Investors do not wish upon such great human suffering. But for those who are lucky enough to be able to invest for the long term, this may prove to be a good opportunity. Many people all over the world have already taken action. The Japanese are opening stock trading accounts at a quickening pace, and Singaporeans are pouring billions of dollars into the stock market.

While I was revising this book countless times amid the ongoing catastrophe, I found that what's written within it is absolutely valid to stand the test of this bear market. Many lessons can be drawn and many mistakes avoided by following the advice given while navigating this latest crisis. A number of chapters are, in fact, more relevant than ever: "Federal Reserve," "Booms and Busts," "History," "Forecasts," and "Picking Bottoms" to name but a few. The chapter "Free Lunch," gives investors a much bigger treat than usual amid the elevated volatility.

The Covid-19 pandemic has created heightened risks and great opportunities in equal measure. At such an uncertain time, the insights in the following pages are needed more now than ever before. I set out to write a book that was timeless and universal. Whether my lofty goals have been achieved, only history will tell, but it definitely withstands the challenges of this trying time.

As a trader who spent 20 years in some of the biggest and most reputable global banks on both sides of the Atlantic, and as a full-time investor now, friends have been asking me a lot of questions lately. Is this the right time to buy? Should I buy Zoom (Video Communications Inc)? I inevitably replied; "If only my book had been ready." I thought this project would take me a year to complete at the most. It took nearly two. Now it's finally ready.

Unless otherwise stated, all dollar values quoted refer to US dollars.

INTRODUCTION

Benjamin Graham (1894–1976), "the father of value investing," once said: "To achieve satisfactory investment results is easier than most people realize; to achieve superior results is harder than it looks." Many fail miserably when trying to navigate the stock market; others have moderate success. Only a few triumph spectacularly.

Rest assured, however, that avoiding failures in the stock market is not a herculean task. *A Stock Investment Book For The 99%* is for regular people and average investors who are looking to achieve satisfactory results with a moderate amount of time and effort. Its objective is to help you invest your money profitably so that you can afford your dream holidays, college fees for your children, a good retirement, and whatever else money can buy.

In this age, with everyone living longer and more people are facing career disruptions, learning how to invest is more important than ever.

Many believe that a system as complicated as the stock market, which has numerous dynamic factors at work, requires investors to adopt complicated strategies and solutions in order to make money. In fact, the opposite is true: less is more. There is a simple solution to the complex stock market, and it's absolutely possible for the average "common" person to make their money work for them.

This book is intended for novice and experienced investors alike who are looking to find a consistently profitable way of investing. It covers a wide range of topics to equip you with the information, knowledge, and tools necessary to navigate the stock market. It provides suggestions and ideas, clarifies areas of confusion, misconception, and misunderstanding, and answers a number of common investment questions. It separates the essentials from the non-essentials and explains how to avoid pitfalls and mistakes. When facing the challenges of the stock market, common sense goes a long way.

The decision to make both the chapters and the book as a whole relatively short, simple, and concise was a deliberate one. Your time is precious—it's not be wasted on information that's easily available online. Nevertheless, in the pages to come, you'll find plenty of dos and don'ts, mistakes to avoid, and lessons to learn. You'll be enlightened by the wise people mentioned throughout and entertained by the follies of the author.

Among the plethora of investment books for beginners, this one probably covers the widest range of topics and strategies to provide investors with the skills and tools required to invest profitably. Most chapters can be read in isolation as an article, meaning you can use the book as a quick reference guide whenever you have questions or doubts about a certain topic. It's almost impossible to absorb everything by reading the book just once; of much greater benefit would be for you to read it again and again over your long investment journey.

This isn't a get-rich-quick guide, and it doesn't offer a secret recipe, but it does offer a free lunch. Yes, it may be hard to believe, but there is a free lunch in the stock market. It's not a trick; it's a treat for finishing the book. Just don't expect Michelin-starred cuisine. The lunch is modest, but at least it's free.

Most investment books are written by the rich and famous—the 1 percent: Benjamin Graham, Peter Lynch, George Soros, John C. Bogle (1929–2019), Robert Kiyosaki, and the like. I am an average Joe, neither rich nor famous. I have never run a big company or big money; I only run for a bus or train. I gained my financial independence with average intelligence, an average work ethic, average luck, some common sense, and investment honesty.

I have huge respect for what the big shots have achieved in the financial world. I admire them for not forgetting the 99 percent and wanting to help us financially. I believe they wrote their books with the best interests of regular people at heart. The problem is while they know the right course of action from an intellectual and conceptual perspective, they don't understand that we folks are mere mortals. Their success is a hard act to follow. These investors are extremely smart, and they work exceptionally hard. While they endeavor to make their books simple, the majority of us find their advice too difficult to implement. I've tried Warren Buffett's way. I've tried Peter Lynch's way. I concluded that I have to sing Frank Sinatra's (1915–1998) "My Way." It's the 99 percent way.

Investing isn't a one-size-fits-all proposition. Each person must find their own approach. The best—and the only—way to learn about investing is to "just do it." Try things out, and see what works for you. When it comes to finding out how you'll react when facing bull and bear markets, there's nothing like committing your own money. After a bit of trial and error, you'll discover what works for you and which investment approach suits your personality.

What's unique about this book is that it accepts everyone is different. We all come from different backgrounds and have different needs, risk appetites, aspirations, considerations, and concerns. We're all biased and see the world through our own tainted glasses. We can't simply follow someone else's principles and processes blindly. That's why there's no top-down approach here telling you exactly what to do each step of the way. What you will learn about are the numerous ways that regular people invest, with observations and opinions on what works and what doesn't, what you should do, and what you shouldn't do.

The majority of investment books by the 1 percent offer the reader a set menu. This book offers a buffet meal. The dishes include high dividends and low price-to-earnings (P/E ratios), value and growth, fundamental and technical analysis, and much more. There's a must-have "signature dish," which will be revealed in the chapter "Game Plan." Other than that, you're free to mix and match whatever dishes you fancy.

Be selective though—pile your plate too high and you might get indigestion. Though the buffet dishes in this book are plentiful, all the ingredients have been chosen carefully and some are hard to find, maybe even unique. The cooking is based on many years of mistakes and failures, experiments and experience. By the end of the meal, you'll discover which dishes you like and which you never want to touch again. You may find you like the simple signature dish so much that you want a bigger portion.

It's not all just theory though—this is a practical book too. It's a culmination of my decades of experience both as a professional trader for large, reputable, global banks and as a private investor. I've tried many methods over the years and made countless mistakes; I've paid my tuition fees and learned valuable lessons. My hope is that by sharing my knowledge and experience with you, you'll make fewer mistakes and pay out less than I did as you learn to invest profitably.

My first foray into investing was at the age of 10, a year ahead of the sage of Omaha, Warren Buffett. It was based on a recommendation from the most trustworthy of people: my dad. I used up all my savings to buy a 10-gram gold bar. The timing and price were perfect. There was only one slight problem: I was on the wrong side of the trade. We'll come back to this tiny gold bar and gold as an investment in a bit.

Fast forward to my college years. Together with some friends— or you could say brothers-in-arms—I had moved on from gold gambling to stock speculation. We were long on enthusiasm and short on capital and experience. But who needs experience when you have the inexhaustible energy of a raging bull and the youthful optimism that the bear is an extinct animal? It was a great time. We had fun; we skipped classes; we did mighty well.

Our accounts began to accumulate. We knew we were astute; we thought we were geniuses.

Then something happened. Stocks started to go down, and down, and down. It was 1994. We turned from geniuses to fools, from heroes to zeros. We lost our money along with pretty much everyone else. We didn't even know why the market direction had changed. We had no idea that a raging bull market could turn into a bear market at the flick of a switch. We were at that age when nobody knows much of anything.

It wasn't until years later that I found out it was the fault of one man: Alan Greenspan, chairman of the Federal Reserve from 1987 to 2006. The story of Mr. Greenspan and why he mattered so much is a long one, and I'll tell it later in its proper place. For now, the point is the road to success—even moderate success—is often paved with failures. I had my first financial failure before I even stepped out of school.

After graduation, I landed a job as a trader in a bank. I hadn't known such jobs existed. To me, banking jobs were just tellers and bored-looking, middle-aged managers sitting behind them.

For years, a combination of inexperience, insufficient capital, and my banks' restrictions on personal trading saw my investments go nowhere. There were some hits, there were some misses, and there were even more losses. My regular spankings from the markets taught me to fear and respect them. Sometimes it felt like the market god was taunting me, but luckily my career as a trader started to take off.

Six years after Mr. Greenspan's hammer blow, I was wiser—or so I thought. I was a genius again. Everything I touched turned to gold; every initial public offering (IPO) I applied and allotted brought big profits on the first day of trading. Making money was easy. Borrowing money was easy. It doesn't take a genius to figure out that lots of easy money can be made with borrowed money.

On March 10, 2000, the Nasdaq peaked, and it went down, and

down, and down. History repeats itself, so the old hands like to say. I realized I was six years older but not one bit wiser. My banking career as a trader hadn't helped. My losses in 1994 hadn't helped. Just like many other investors in the late 1990s, I'd been swept up by the internet bubble.

Over the next two decades, my trading job offered me a privileged front-row seat to the financial crisis and the many dramas that unfolded. I got to understand how banks work and how financial products are created and sold. I got to learn about trading principles and rules that I could go on to apply to my personal investments years later.

I can't exactly sit here and boast that I had a stellar trading career, but neither can I complain about the job or the pay. Traders get a good bonus at the end of each year if they make good money for the banks. Banks don't really care much about how money is made. To them, money is money.

The same, in fact, applies to us. You've picked up this book for one reason and one reason only: through one method or another, you want to make money. If you bought it with the expectation of avoiding work altogether, you'll get little benefit from it. It's been written for people who work to earn money and who want their money to work for them.

To start investing, you need two things: spare money and spare time. Only ever invest with surplus cash—the money that you have left over after you've taken care of your basic needs. That includes cash for rainy days. Investing isn't a laborious process, but it's also not quick and easy. How much time you spend on pursuing a return is something you have to decide for yourself in relation to the time and capital you have available, as well as your interests and capabilities.

You don't need to work at it round the clock. Just look at Robert Rubin and Hank Paulson—both rose to the top of Goldman Sachs before moving on to public service as US Treasury secretary, and both wrote that they had to have a solid eight hours of sleep a night.

According to Malcolm Gladwell in his book *Outliers: The Story of Success*, it takes roughly ten thousand hours of practice to achieve mastery in a field. We learn a craft by repetition. The top investors are passionate about their craft. They're highly competitive, and they possess certain traits that make them successful. Those who believe otherwise have their fortunes wrecked.

The good news is that earning a satisfactory return in the long run is absolutely within the reach of the average person. The key is to keep your expectations moderate. With time and experience, all of us can grow our investment capabilities; you don't need mastery to achieve good results.

In Jack D. Schwager's excellent series of Market Wizards books, we read how legendary traders Richard Dennis and William Eckhardt got into an argument about whether trading could be taught. Dennis bet that it could, and they agreed to conduct an experiment. People from all walks of life would be taught how to trade and then given a sum of money to trade with. Dennis's assertion was right—trading success could be taught.

Many top investors believe you don't have to be highly intelligent in order to invest successfully. More important, they say, is having the right character and temperament. An average IQ is good enough. Many intelligent people actually make lousy investors because their temperaments don't suit investing. The ability to honestly admit our mistakes and take responsibility for our own results is more important.

Not convinced? When one of the smartest men ever, Isaac Newton (1643–1727), wasn't looking up at the sky for new scientific discoveries, he liked to engage in earthly pursuits. In 1720, as stocks of South Sea Company were rising and hysteria was sweeping London, he found himself in a dilemma. He'd sold his investment in the company after it had doubled in price. As he watched the price rise further, he began to regret his decision. The stock climbed higher and higher until it eventually rose eightfold in less than six months.

Newton found it too painful to stand on the sidelines and watch people around him make much more money than he had. The only way to avoid missing out on further profits was to jump back into the stock. He bought again, this time right at the peak. The bubble burst, and the stock price dropped by three-quarters in just four weeks. Newton lost £20,000. The incident led him to say: "I can calculate the motion of heavenly bodies, but not the madness of people."

It's not possible to make a sweeping generalization as to who will succeed in investing. Some people possess more helpful traits than others. Some investors are calm, while others are energetic; some are aggressive, while others are defensive. The traits that make a good investor are hard to pin down. The key is having a well-balanced combination. Too ignorant or too knowledgeable, too slow or too quick, too pessimistic or too optimistic, too relaxed or too tense, too greedy or too conservative, too prudent or too courageous—a deficiency or surplus of one quality can destroy the effectiveness of them all.

Probably the greatest economist of the last century, John M. Keynes (1883–1946), began his investment journey in currencies. He made good money in just a few months. Encouraged, he set up a syndicate to manage money for family and friends. This also got off to a good start. The currencies he shorted, however, soon began to move against him and wiped out not only his profits but also his capital. His father bailed him out. Keynes never gave up though. He continued his speculation and built up capital of $120,000 by the end of 1922.

Next, he moved on to speculate in commodities. When the 1929 crash came, the commodity markets were decimated. This time he didn't lose all his money—just 80 percent. Eventually, he turned to studying companies. He'd gone from macro speculator to micro stock picker, from top down to bottom up. He gave up trying to forecast interest rates and currencies and became a long-term value investor who bought "securities where I am satisfied as to assets and ultimate earning power and where the market price seems cheap in relation to these."

Just like Keynes, you have to find your own way—one that suits your personality and will eventually benefit your bank account. The investment journey is a long, slow one, with many struggles and challenges. Sometimes it's uncomfortable; other times it's hazardous. Occasionally you'll feel like you're on a roller-coaster ride that's both exhilarating and terrifying at the same time. It's not just a journey of ups and downs though—it's also a jolly journey of discovery and learning.

Investing can be a hugely rewarding activity, both financially and intellectually. You'll reap the benefits for decades. When Abraham Lincoln (1809–1865) was young, he wrote: "I will study and get ready, and perhaps my chance will come." You too will get yourself ready. Your chance in the stock market will come.

PART I: THE BASICS

GAMBLING, SPECULATING, AND INVESTING

Speculating and investing are as old as the hills. Many early politicians, including US founding fathers George Washington (1732–1799), Benjamin Franklin (1706–1790), Thomas Jefferson (1743–1826), and Alexander Hamilton (c. 1755–1804), were land speculators. Many other famous and intelligent people have also dabbled in the financial markets: Isaac Newton, Winston Churchill (1874–1965), Charlie Chaplin (1889–1977), Mark Twain (1835–1910), and John M. Keynes, among others. And while the Dutch tulip bulb run of the sixteenth century is often cited as the earliest recorded "mania," we can safely assume that speculating and investing go back much further than that.

How does speculating differ from gambling? It's all about the odds. Gamblers are willing to take a bet even when the odds are against them. They're drawn by the possibility rather than the probability of winning. They hope to get lucky and get rich quick. Speculators—or at least the successful ones—look for trades where the odds are stacked in their favor. The more favorable the odds, the heavier they bet. And though luck plays a big role in both speculating and gambling, in the long run, it's not important for good speculators. A good speculator operates like a casino, only betting when the odds are in their favor. A casino might lose a single bet or have a bad day due to poor luck, but it always gets ahead over weeks or months because the odds are in its favor.

The terms speculating and investing can both be defined as the purchase or sale of stocks, bonds, commodities, or any other assets in the expectation of profiting from fluctuations in their prices.

Generally speaking, investors are rather conservative and place safety of capital first and returns second. Speculators, on the other hand, are interested in quick returns and are less concerned about the safety of their capital. Speculations also have a shorter time horizon than investments, although there's no clear definition to separate one from another. Holding a position for weeks is considered an investment for currency traders but a speculation for stock investors. The line between speculator and investor is a fine one. When a short-term trade turns bad, a speculator might choose to hold on to his losing stock and make it a long-term investment. Conversely, when a quick gain presents itself, an investor might not be able to resist the temptation to grab a speculative profit.

Speculating is actually inseparable from investing. An investment always has some degree of speculative risk. For example, an investor who buys a stock with the intention of holding it for years faces speculative risk every three months during its earnings announcements.

The most successful speculations and investments require broader knowledge and sounder judgment than your average business endeavor. Just like Olympic medalists, top speculators and investors are few and far between, and they all put a great deal of effort in to get to the top of their field. For those of us who aren't concerned with aiming for the podium, the good news is that just a few hours a week are sufficient to get a good investment result.

This book isn't for gamblers, and it's not for speculators; it's for investors. That's not to say you shouldn't seek speculative profit, but rather that you should only do it when the odds are in your favor. To quote China's former paramount leader Deng Xiaoping (1904–1997): "It doesn't matter if a cat is black or white; as long as it catches mice, it is a good cat."

CASH AND BONDS

Any person who earns more than they spend is automatically an investor. Most people don't realize this and consider themselves to be savers, with money sat in the bank rather than invested elsewhere. The truth is that cash is an asset class just like stocks and bonds are.

Because the value of cash doesn't fluctuate from one day to the next like stocks—except in countries such as Venezuela and Zimbabwe—most people consider it to be safe. It's true that cash is unlikely to lose its value drastically in the short run like stocks can, and it's also true that it can earn a bit of return, albeit a very low one. The problem with cash is that it's almost certainly going to lose value in the long run, unless there is persistent deflation, like in Japan. Inflation is pretty much a given. Remember how much you paid for a hamburger or a movie 20 years ago? Only a fraction of what you would pay now. A dollar that you keep safely under your pillow or in the bank is going to buy a lot less in 20 years' time than it would today. Being conservative and keeping all your money in cash is a losing strategy in the long run.

Other investments, such as short-tenor time deposits or investments in money market funds, are considered to be cash as well, as they can be converted to cash quickly. Their value doesn't fluctuate much, although at the height of the global financial crisis, money market funds in the US "broke the buck" (dropped below $1). Some stockbroking accounts actually pay interest on cash. Generally speaking, these interest rates are linked to money market rates, which are much higher than the interest rates in savings and current accounts.

We need cash for rainy days; we also need cash for bear markets. If we're fully invested, our capital loss during a bear market will be substantial, but if we keep everything in cash, our return will be lower than inflation. We therefore each have to decide what we think is a good mix, according to our personal risk appetite and our opinion on the current markets. Timing the market is difficult, so you might want to invest over a number of years—when the bear market hits, you want to have cash so that you can take advantage of it.

To earn a return that's higher than inflation in the long run, we have to look at asset classes other than cash. Two of the most common financial asset classes are stocks and bonds. The long-term average annual return of US bonds (coupons and price appreciation) is between 5 and 8 percent. For stocks it's about 10 percent (dividends and price appreciation). The average inflation rate in the US over the past 100 years is just above 3 percent. While the main focus of this book is stock investments, it's worth having an understanding of bonds, as they're important to many investors. In a typical investment portfolio, a financial advisor's recommendation is usually a 60/40 split between stocks and bonds respectively.

For those who know their James Bonds better than their government or corporate bonds, bonds are basically "I owe yous" (IOUs). The sellers of bonds are mainly governments or companies, and the buyers are institutional or retail investors. The sellers get to use the borrowed money, and the investors get some return in the form of coupons—regular interest payments, usually annually or semi-annually. The borrowers promise to return the principal at the end of the bond's tenor, which can be a number of months but is mostly measured in years.

Bonds are debt securities under which the borrower is obliged to pay back principal, while stocks provide part ownership of a company. Bonds are the less risky of the two. First, bondholders have priority claim of assets over shareholders when a company goes bankrupt. Second, bond prices are less volatile than stock prices. Less volatility is widely considered to be less risky in the financial markets, though this is disputed by some. Bonds have lower risks with lower returns, while stocks have higher risks with higher returns. Knowing the risks and returns in each asset class helps you decide how to allocate your money among them.

Some people are surprised when they find out the bond they've bought has a fluctuating price. They buy with the expectation that they'll get their principal back in the end and meanwhile just collect the coupons. They feel "safe" in their investment—come rain or shine, coupons will be collected. In actual fact, every bond has a secondary market, though some bonds have illiquid secondary markets.

Bond prices usually start at 100, or par, when they're issued. They have an inverse relationship with interest rates. When interest rates go up, bond prices decline to 98, 95, or lower; when interest rates go down, bond prices advance to 102, 105, or higher. A 3 percent, 20-year bond will sell at 100 if the current interest rate is 3 percent, but will decline to 86 3/8 if yields for a similar bond's coupon increase to 4 percent. It's true that if a bondholder doesn't sell, they can just collect the 3 percent coupon for the next 20 years and see this as not losing. They could, however, have got a higher coupon of 4 percent—there's a real opportunity cost in committing to the earlier 3 percent bond.

Among the most popular bonds with conservative investors are government bonds, as they're considered to be the safest. Not all government bonds are safe though. Only a dozen or so countries, such as Australia, Canada, Germany, Singapore, and Switzerland, are rated AAA by Standard & Poor's, one of the big three credit rating agencies. The US was downgraded from AAA to AA + in 2011. The list of countries that never default on government debt to foreign creditors is even shorter, comprising just Australia, Denmark, Singapore, and the US. Most countries have defaulted at some point, and some of them, including Greece, Russia, and Argentina, are "serial defaulters."

Government bonds serve as a reserve against deflation and hard times. Interest rates are low during deflation, so bond prices are high and the coupons earned give investors more purchasing power. During inflation, bond prices do badly—when interest rates rise, bond prices head in the opposite direction. If an investor bought too early with a low coupon bond, not only would his bond lose value but his coupon might not be able to cover the rising inflation.

Since the US interest rate peaked at around 20 percent in 1980, the US bond market has been experiencing a long bull market. When interest rates were low in the mid-2000s and most of the 2010s, many investors were "forced to chase yields." They wanted high returns for their money and had to look further and at more exotic bonds—the longest US government bond is 30 years, whereas Argentina, Austria, Belgium, and Ireland all issued 100-year bonds in recent years.

Austria's "century bond," issued in 2017, offered what was considered a paltry yield of 2.1 percent. In 2019, a new century bond was issued at 1.1 percent. The investors who bought the earlier bonds are doing very well, the bond price having almost doubled in two years. In 2016, Argentina, a country with a long history of bond defaults and currency crises, also issued a century bond. It was snapped up by yield-hungry international investors, despite Argentina's chronic problems of high inflation and a weak currency. It's hardly surprising that these investors saw this 100-year bond drop way below par just a few years later.

As unbelievable as it may seem, there are investors who buy bonds at negative yields. Instead of receiving interest for lending money, they pay interest to the borrowers. This means they are certain to get back less than what they paid if they hold the bond to maturity. The belief that zero would act as a floor for interest rates was shattered about two decades ago when negative yields started in Japan. Nowadays, the governments of Germany, France, Sweden, Denmark, and Japan are borrowing at negative yields. Swiss bank UBS and the Danish Danske Bank are charging clients for simply holding cash in their bank accounts. In Denmark, there are even "negative mortgages," with borrowers being paid interest when they take them on!

Globally, negative-yield debt has ballooned in recent years, amounting to well over $15 trillion by the summer of 2019. It's hard to understand why anyone would want to pay interest to lend money. This topsy-turvy phenomenon has some explanations, but none of them are good. The main culprit is huge quantitative easing in Europe and Japan—the central banks bought so many bonds that they drove interest rates below zero. As a result, pension funds and insurers, who need liquid, non-volatile assets, have no good alternative to buying bonds, even at negative yields. Another explanation is that some are taking a speculative view that interest rates will head even further into negative territory and that they'll be able to sell their bonds later at higher prices.

P/E RATIOS

Price-to-earnings (P/E) ratios are calculated by dividing the price per share by the earnings per share (EPS). If a company is trading at $20 per share and its EPS is $2, the P/E ratio is 10. It's the most widely used and understood ratio in the stock market. Many investors use P/E ratios as a measure of how cheap or expensive a stock is. A high P/E ratio means a company stock is expensive, and a low P/E ratio means it's cheap. P/E ratios aren't as simple as they seem, however, and they convey more information than the average investor may realize.

The way to think of P/E ratios is the number of years it will take a company to earn back your initial investment, assuming the company earnings remain the same. If you buy a stock for $10 and its EPS is $1 per year, it will take 10 years for the company to earn your $10 purchase price. P/E ratios are also a measure of how fast a company's earnings can grow. If a company has a P/E ratio of 10, the expectation is that the company's earnings will grow at 10 percent per year. If the P/E ratio is lower than the actual growth rate, it's a bargain.

When choosing between a company with earnings growing at 20 percent per year with a P/E ratio of 20 and a company growing at 10 percent per year with a P/E ratio of 10, the former is clearly the better choice, even though it's more expensive to buy. The compound effect of growing at 20 percent will greatly offset the current high price in the long run. Generally speaking, a big, established company is happy to have annual earnings growth of 10 to 15 percent, while a newer, smaller company may be able to grow at 25 to 30 percent. A stock with a P/E ratio of 40 or above is dangerously high priced, and there's little room for error. It's rare for a company to be able to sustain such high growth. Of course, there are exceptions, and some great companies can sell at a high P/E ratio and sustain high growth for much longer than most people expect—sometimes years or even decades. Just look at Walmart and Amazon.

It goes without saying that a company that has a high P/E ratio and is growing quickly will outperform one that has a low P/E ratio and is growing slowly. Often the P/E ratio of a company or a sector shifts not because the facts and numbers have changed much but because there has been a different appraisal of the same facts—a change in sentiment. When a company's earnings increase, the share price increases at a faster pace. Say a company's earnings are $1 per share and it's selling at $10 with a P/E ratio of 10. When the company's earnings jump to $2, the share price is usually more than $20. What happens is the market, after seeing a big jump in earnings, turns bullish about the stock and has higher expectations. Instead of still assigning a P/E ratio of 10, it assigns a ratio of 20. With earnings of $2, the share price becomes $40. Now investors are willing to pay a premium for the company's future prospects. The increase in P/E ratio is often an even more important factor in raising stock prices than the actual increase in earnings per share. When the P/E ratio of a company goes up, we shouldn't jump to the conclusion that this stock has become too expensive—the higher P/E ratio at which it's now selling may be a reflection that its intrinsic quality has improved and that the market is giving it a better appraisal.

When we buy a company that's "in vogue" and has an astronomically high P/E ratio, we may have to wait a long time before we can make any money, even if the business is doing well. This was what happened to McDonald's and a number of other "Nifty Fifty" companies in the early 1970s. The market wisdom at the time was that some companies are so good you can just buy at any price and hold them forever. Between 1973 and 1980, the earnings of McDonald's jumped 400 percent. Did the shareholders make money? The P/E ratio, which was at an astronomical level of 75 in 1973, dropped to just 8 by 1980. So, despite the big increase in earnings, the shareholders lost about half their investment in those seven years.

For cyclical stocks, with fortunes dependent on the wider industry's business cycle, a low P/E ratio doesn't necessarily make it a bargain. It usually means a stock is at the end of a prosperous cycle, with high earnings pushing the P/E ratio low. A high P/E ratio with low earnings is much better news. Often it means the company has passed the worst of the cycle and signals that business will soon greatly improve; earnings will beat analyst expectations, and fund managers will start actively buying the stock, causing its price to jump.

Some investors base their decisions solely on P/E ratios. They look for stocks with a low ratio without necessarily understanding the limitations and dangers. They should take care and investigate before diving in though—a company usually has a low P/E ratio for a reason. It may be that the company is facing financial difficulties or that the industry is out of favor due to some recent bad news. Either way, the issue is unlikely to go away in the near future, which means it's doubtful the stock will head north any time soon. These investors are not value investors; true value is based on much more than a low P/E ratio. They want to buy low and sell high but often end up buying low and selling lower.

People who buy at high P/E ratios are the so-called momentum traders. Some of these proponents, like William O'Neil, have a great long-term track record. These traders look to buy high and sell even higher. They understand that such a market is volatile and that the success rate isn't high. They often have a success rate of less than half, with some well below that. If that's the case, how do they make money? The key is they let the profits run and cut the losses fast. They limit losses for the many losers and maximize gains for the few winners, with an overall positive result. For those who thrive on the excitement of momentum trades, the difficult part is having the discipline to cut their losses when needed.

The takeaway from all of this: There's no consensus among top investors and academics as to whether it's better to invest in companies with low P/E ratios or high ones. The key lies in understanding each method well and choosing the one that suits your own personality.

When you look at the P/E ratios of the same market from various sources, such as Standard and Poor's, Barron's, and Bloomberg, you usually see different figures. Some market P/E ratios include companies that lost money, and some don't. The important thing is to pick one reputable source and stick to it for consistency.

Another complication of P/E ratios is they've morphed into different varieties. These days there's the forward P/E ratio, which uses forecasted earnings instead of realized and historical earnings. The problem with this is that financial market forecasting isn't an exact science; it contains lots of guesswork and flimsy assumptions. Another variety is the cyclically adjusted P/E ratio, which adjusts and smooths out volatile seasonal earnings. This ratio can be interpreted in different ways, however. I once read an article in the *Financial Times* that used it to say the US stock market was a bargain. The opposite view was given in *The Wall Street Journal*, which ran an article saying it was still expensive.

Whether these more complicated P/E ratios are actually useful to investors is debatable. They definitely create confusion and add complications for the average investor, but then the investment community has a perverse tendency to make simple things difficult for ordinary folks. The ultimate renaissance man, Leonardo da Vinci (1452–1519), was believed to have said: "Simplicity is the ultimate sophistication." These ratios certainly don't follow that mantra.

The other thing to realize is that it's not just individual companies that have P/E ratios—countries' stock markets do too. To complicate things further—and there's no good and clear explanation as to why—each country's P/E ratio has its own range and average. Analysts like to compare the P/E ratios of different nations to justify whether a country is cheap and worth a buy. It's like betting that the average height in a country with a short population will overtake that of another country with a tall population—such a bet needs decades to have a chance of winning.

More relevant is to track the P/E ratio of a single country over a period of time. Over the last 100 years, the S&P 500's P/E ratio has mainly ranged between 10 and 20, with an average of 16, and a top of around 40 in 1999. When there's a bubble, P/E ratios can reach astronomical values. Both the Nikkei and the Nasdaq's P/E ratios peaked at around 80 at the height of their respective bubbles in 1989 and 2000. It's important to realize that interest rates have a significant effect on the prevailing P/E ratio. Never look at the P/E ratio of a country without looking at the interest rates. If the interest rates are below the historical average, the P/E ratio should be higher than the historical average and vice versa, all else being equal.

Also bear in mind that despite being the most widely followed ratio, using the P/E ratio of a stock market to time investments is actually quite difficult. Historically, if you'd bought US stocks whenever the S&P 500 P/E ratio dropped to 10, you would have been too early, losing 30 percent in 1982 (P/E ratio 7), 40 percent in 1974 (P/E ratio 6), and 50 percent in 1932 (P/E ratio 5) before seeing any rebound. Only those who could sit through those big losses were able to reap big rewards years later. In June 2007, the P/E ratio of the S&P 500 was right at the long-term average of 16, yet the stock market entered a big bear market one year later during the global financial crisis. By June 2009, the P/E ratio had jumped to a high of 23, despite much lower stock prices, because earnings had dropped even more. A simple buy-and-hold strategy beats using P/E ratios to try to time the stock market.

DIVIDENDS

A dividend is a payment made by a company, mostly in cash but occasionally in stocks, to shareholders. It's seen as a "reward" for their investment in the business. In the US, dividends are usually paid quarterly, while in other countries, they're often paid annually or semi-annually. Most dividends are paid from a company's net profits, however sometimes they come from reserves. This explains why a company's dividend payments can be higher than its net profits and why even a loss-making company can pay dividends.

Dividends paid to shareholders are like coupons given to bondholders. The difference is coupons are fixed and dividends aren't. The distribution of dividends is entirely at the discretion of management and can therefore vary from year to year. Most companies don't issue a clear dividend policy, meaning payments can be erratic and hard to understand. Companies that do have clear dividend policies may state they will pay a percentage (say 50 percent) of net profits. Some even give future dividend guidance like stating that the dividend is progressive, i.e. that management will strive to increase the dividend payments yearly. These companies might or might not explain the rationale behind the policy.

The significance and importance of dividends can be confusing to the average investor. Some market participants claim there's no correlation between dividends and a stock's performance. Others are proponents of either high- or low-dividend-yield stocks, with both sides counting famous, successful market participants among their numbers and citing credible studies to support their views.

Some studies claim that high-yield stocks provide a better total return (dividends + capital gains) with lower volatility. Others show that low-yield companies have a faster increase in capital gains over the years, which is enough to offset the lower dividend. Moreover, they show that given enough time, the dividend of low-yield growth stocks will increase until a high yield is offered. There have also been studies that show stocks that pay no or high dividends seem to have above-normal returns. It's stocks that pay low dividends that have low returns.

The decision as to whether a company's dividends are right for an investor is a matter of personal circumstance and choice. Retirees, who need a regular, immediate income, generally prefer high, stable-dividend stocks. They like the certainty—although no company's dividends are ever completely certain—that they'll get the same or more dividends regularly, regardless of ups and downs in stock prices. Alternatively, they may choose a low-dividend-yield stock that offers higher capital gains. They can then sell a small portion of this stock to cover any income shortfall from the low yield.

Let's say a retiree has $10,000 to invest. Their first option is to buy a high-yield stock that offers a 5 percent yield and no capital gains. Every year, they collect a $500 dividend. Their second option is to buy a 1 percent, low-yield stock, the price of which is going up 5 percent annually. In this case, after one year, they collect a $100 dividend and the stock has gone up to $10,500. They sell $400 worth of stock, taking their stock holding to $10,100. Either way, their total income is $500, but the stock value increases to $10,100 if they choose the low-yield option (note that this illustration doesn't take tax into account). Even though option two offers a higher total return, many investors still prefer option one. It's a psychological decision rather than a logical one—many people feel that the dividend they get is "real" and the appreciation of the stock price isn't.

For investors who don't need income, dividend yield shouldn't be a major consideration. The truth is that no matter how high the dividend, a company won't prosper without growing its earnings. Don't buy into companies with a dividend payout that's so emphasized it restricts growth. Companies that pay a generous, regular dividend usually can't find good investments for the money. These companies are mostly low- or no-growth businesses, and the stock price is unlikely to go up by much.

That being said, high-dividend stocks are considered safe by some investors. They reason that since the companies are able to pay high dividends, the earnings and cash flow can't be too bad and the stock price should be able to hold better than the general market in a downturn. During the 1987 crash, high-dividend companies performed better than no-dividend companies, suffering less than half the decline of the general market. It's important, however, to be aware that individual high-dividend stock performances vary widely. Some high-dividend-yield stocks are in industries that always pay generous dividends, such as utilities and real estate investment trusts. These stocks are generally safe, though their prices can be more volatile than many assume. Other high-dividend stocks are low grade, affording high yields because their future is uncertain and dividends are in doubt. This pushes the price down and the yield up.

Some people propose buying these stocks as a contrarian play; they believe the stocks offer both higher dividends and higher capital appreciation. Such a strategy can easily backfire. If a stock goes down due to financial difficulties, the chance of a dividend cut is significant. This can then cause the stock price to collapse—it's not uncommon for stock prices to drop a fifth or more on the news of a dividend cut. The second issue is that the stock might go down even further, in which case a few percent higher in dividend isn't going to be enough to offset the much bigger loss in the stock price. There are many examples of high-dividend stocks and funds that perform poorly.

By mid-2018, L Brands, whose brands include Victoria's Secret and Bath & Body Works, was offering a dividend yield of more than 6 percent. This followed a drop in its stock price of around 50 percent in just half a year. Those who were enticed by the high yield were to see the dividend cut by half in November 2018 and the share price continued to slide. Some companies are able to pay high dividends despite worsening earnings and financial health. This can be a deadly trap for investors who are attracted to the high yield but ignore the weakening earnings and balance sheets. Examples of such companies are numerous and include some big names: Blockbuster, General Motors, Lehman Brothers, Washington Mutual, and Fannie Mae, among others. In my US stock portfolio, which wasn't chosen based on dividend yields, all the high-dividend stocks performed very poorly compared to the low- and no-dividend stocks.

Another example of why choosing high-dividend stocks can be detrimental to investors comes from an exchange-traded fund (ETF)—specifically the SPDR Portfolio S&P 500 High Dividend ETF (stock code SPYD), which tracks an index of the 80 highest yielding stocks in the S&P 500. The fund's dividend yield is about 4 percent—double that of the S&P 500. It's total return, from its inception on October 21, 2015 up until the end of 2019, was about 40 percent, while the SPDR S&P 500 ETF (code SPY's) was about 70 percent. Many similar examples can be found in other high-dividend-yield ETFs.

What should you do when a company you own cuts or increases its dividends? Studies show that stocks that had dividends cut underperformed the market over both one- and three-year periods. Conversely, stocks that increased dividends outperformed the market in the same time frames. Psychologically, it's difficult to sell stocks when the price plunges due to a dividend cut, but an immediate sell is probably the best course of action in this scenario.

Say a stock that's trading at $100 pays an annual dividend of $6. If the dividend was cut by 60 percent to $2.40 and the stock price plunged 20 percent to $80, that would bring the dividend yield down from 6 to 3 percent. The main reason investors own the stock—for the high yield—is gone. Dividend cuts are never taken lightly by any management team, and they're usually only made after all other options have been exhausted. The subsequent chance of dividend increases in the coming years is slim, and the chance of further cuts is pretty high. Rather than stick with this stock that's yielding 3 percent and has a grim immediate future, investors would be better off finding another stock with a 3 percent yield that offers better prospects, or another high dividend stock.

Another common and, this time, happy question facing investors is what to do if a high-dividend stock they've bought has risen substantially in less than a year—let's say four times the dividend yield. From my experience, it's probably wise to sell the stock, or at least half of it. Companies that pay generous dividends aren't high-growth companies. The dividends have been earned in a matter of months instead of the expected four years, and the chances of their stock prices multiplying in the years to come are very slim. Holding out is a risky strategy— four years is a long time in stock market, and a lot of things can happen. Plenty of other opportunities should arise in that time to put the cash to work. Another benefit of taking the profit in this situation is that it reduces the size and volatility of your portfolio. Turbulent times may be coming. This isn't a case of being too eager to profit take—the reasoning is sound and rational.

Some companies, while not having high-dividend yields, still consistently increase their dividends over a long period of time. Tiffany is one such company. Even in 2009, in the aftermath of the global financial crisis, its dividend was growing. If you buy into one of these companies and hold on to the shares long enough, a dividend yield at cost price would be very satisfactory. ExxonMobil's dividend, for example, has grown at about 6 percent annually since 1982. And if you'd bought shares in the ETF SPY, which tracks the S&P 500, since its inception in 1993, you'd have received $1.10 of dividend in its first year, with the yield at 3.8 percent. By 2018, the dividend, which compounded at an average annual rate of 6.1 percent to reach $5.10, would have given you an overall yield of almost 18 percent.

The dividend yield on the S&P 500 has been one of the most watched indicators of the stock market's generosity. It's also one of the oldest market-timing tools. For over 100 years, stock markets were generally considered to be near a top whenever the yield was below 3 percent and near a bottom when the yield rose to about 6 percent. In both 1973 and 1987, the S&P 500's yield had dropped to below 2.7 percent, however this was mainly due to high stock prices and not lower dividends. By the end of 1974, the S&P 500 had dropped by almost half. Similarly, on October 19, 1987, the Dow Jones Industrial Average (Dow Jones) crashed 508 points, or 22.6 percent.

Yields also dropped below 2.7 percent in 1994, but while stocks fell, a bear market didn't materialize. Indeed, the market went on breaking records for the next six years until 2000, when the yield dropped to 1.1 percent. The internet bubble then burst. In the late 2010s, the yield also dropped to well below 3 percent and since then has mostly been hovering around 2 percent without having any impact on the stock market. The main reason for this is that interest rates have been very low during this period. Just like P/E ratios, when we look at the general market dividend yield, we have to take interest rates into consideration, as both move in the same direction in the long run.

The last thing to mention is special dividends—additional payments that are outside the standard dividend payment cycle. Investors love them—it's like Santa Claus has come to town! It is always nice to have extra money, especially when it's unexpected. One-time special dividends can pump up shares until the ex-dividend date—the date when the new buyers of the stock are not entitled to the dividend—but they usually fail to leave a permanent impact on the price in the long run. Buybacks and progressive dividends are more likely to have a long-lasting, positive impact on a stock's price.

MARKET CAPITALIZATION

Market capitalization, often simply known as market cap, is the number of shares issued multiplied by the share price. This is the most common measure of how big or small a company is. There are other ways to measure the size of a company, such as revenue, profits, assets, and so on. Market cap is an important criterion for some investors when choosing a stock. Some prefer big-cap companies, which are perceived to be safer and more likely to provide stable dividends than smaller ones. Others like small-cap companies, which they believe can grow faster and offer multiple returns.

There's no denying that the big, famous market cap companies, otherwise known as "blue chip" companies (the term is believed to originate from the highest value chips—blue—in Monte Carlo's casinos), are safer than most smaller companies. But having blind faith in these companies isn't always the best course of action. Being termed blue chip doesn't make a business immune from losing value in the long term or even from going bankrupt. Eastman Kodak and Sears Roebuck, both part of the Dow Jones for nearly 100 years, went bankrupt in the 2010s.

Blue chips can be more volatile than you think. It's not uncommon for these supposedly steady companies to move 30 percent or more within a year. Even something as big and diversified as Berkshire Hathaway has dropped by half three times in its 50-year history. Another big business, Kraft Heinz Company, dropped almost 30 percent in a single day in 2019 after it issued a profit warning, announcing the write-down of two of its biggest brands by $15 billion, cutting more than one-third of dividends, and confirming that its accounts were under investigation by the Securities and Exchange Committee (SEC). Who would have thought that a big, boring company that sells ketchup and cheese, and counts its biggest shareholder as none other than Warren Buffett, could have such a drastic drop in just one day? Others have fallen too. General Electric, which boasts Thomas Edison (1847–1931) as its founder, was kicked out of the Dow Jones in 2018, after spending almost 100 years in the index. Many other famous blue chips have been dropped from the venerable index over the years too, including American Can, United States Steel, and General Motors.

The Dow Jones is perhaps the most famous stock index in the world. It's definitely one of the oldest, having been founded in 1896. It's made up of 30 US companies. The other famous US index is the S&P 500, which is made up of the 500 biggest market cap companies in the US. The two indexes use different weighting methodologies—the Dow Jones is price weighted, while the S&P 500 is weighted on market cap. Most days, their movements are pretty much identical, despite their differences. Over the decades, the ratio of Dow Jones to S&P 500 has been amazingly stable—roughly 10 to 1. This ratio dropped to about 9 in the late 2010s, however, as the S&P 500 performed better than the Dow Jones due to the relentless rise in technology stocks, which came to dominate the top 10 in terms of market cap. Alphabet (the parent company of Google), Amazon, and Facebook are all constituents of the S&P 500 but not of the Dow Jones. Apple and Microsoft are constituents of both.

Small-cap companies are measured by different indexes, one being the Russell 2000, which measures the performance of 2,000 companies that are ranked in market cap from 1,001 to 3,000. Just like the S&P 500 and many other famous indexes, such as the UK's FTSE 100 (FTSE) and Japan's Nikkei 225 (Nikkei), the Russell 2000 is weighted on market cap.

Investors who prefer small-cap companies need to keep in mind that for every successful small-cap that grows to be a big-cap there are many more that become tiny cap or get buried under a tombstone. The Russell 2000 can outperform or underperform the S&P 500 by as much as 90 percent over a few years. In the long run, however, the performance of the two indexes tends to be similar. If you'd bought Russell 2000 in 1979 when it was launched, the performance after four decades wouldn't have been much better than if you'd bought S&P 500. One reason why the Russell 2000 doesn't outperform the big-caps is that many of its best companies "graduate" from the index.

The overall market cap of a country's stock market is calculated by adding up all the listed companies' market caps. The US tops the list, with a total market cap of more than $20 trillion. In the late 1980s, when Japan was experiencing a big bubble and the Japanese yen was appreciating strongly, the country's market cap briefly overtook that of the US. At the height of Japan's bubble, its banks dominated the top ten biggest market cap companies in the world. Japan held on to number two for almost three decades, until it was overtaken by China in 2015.

When it comes to individual companies, the late 2010s saw technology companies top of the leaderboard in terms of size, with Apple, Amazon, and Microsoft each having crossed the $1 trillion mark. They're no longer the biggest in the world though. That crown was taken in December 2019, when Saudi Arabia's state oil company, Saudi Aramco, listed and briefly crossed the $2 trillion mark. To put that figure in perspective, it's significantly larger than the market cap and gross domestic product (GDP) of most countries.

The domination of technology companies has also happened in emerging markets. By 2019, Samsung Electronics, Tencent, Alibaba Group, and Taiwan Semiconductor Manufacturing Company made up almost 20 percent of the Morgan Stanley Capital International Emerging Markets Index. In 1965, AT&T and General Motors made up 14.5 percent of the S&P 500. From 1990 to 2018, the weight of the top 10 companies in that index ranged from 17 to 26 percent. In 2010, the biggest companies were ExxonMobil, Microsoft, Apple, Procter & Gamble, and Johnson & Johnson. By 2019, Apple and Microsoft had retained their positions and had been joined by other technology giants —Amazon, Alphabet, and Facebook.

When the market caps of companies hit astronomical figures, it's a sign we're in a bubble. In 1987, Nippon Telegraph and Telephone (NTT) had a market cap of $350 billion—more than the entire German stock market. The Japanese bubble continued to inflate for another two years. In 1989, the biggest banks in Taiwan had a market cap greater than Chase Manhattan Bank and Citigroup combined. The Taiwanese stock market bubble, which rose almost 20 times in five years, popped the following year. In November 2007, the market cap of PetroChina topped $1 trillion. China's stock market bubble burst soon after.

Another warning sign is when a sector is too dominating. In 1980, energy stocks made up 28 percent of the S&P 500, but they came off hard in the following two years. Technology made up a quarter of the S&P 500 in late 1999, and the five biggest technology companies at the time—Microsoft, Intel, Cisco, Dell, and Sun Microsystems—accounted for a third of Nasdaq market cap. The internet bubble burst a few months later. Fast-forward to 2007, and financial stocks made up one-fifth of the S&P 500. Lehman Brothers went bankrupt one year later and ushered in the global financial crisis. Financial stocks were hit the hardest.

Until 1996, the market cap of US companies had never risen above GDP. At the 1929 peak, the ratio of market cap to GDP was 80 percent, but by March 2000, when the Nasdaq peaked, the ratio had hit 180 percent. This ratio is seen by some as a measure of whether a country's stock market is undervalued or overvalued. Way above 100 percent is considered overvalued, and around 50 percent is considered undervalued.

FUNDS

For investors who look for safety in blue chips, funds are probably a better proposition than individual stocks. Many investors buy funds, whether mutual funds or ETFs. When an investor buys a fund, they are buying into a basket of companies. For example, an investor who buys a Dow Jones ETF (stock code DIA), is buying all 30 companies in the index. The company that runs DIA, State Street Global Advisors, will buy stock of each company on behalf of the investor. In the US, there are thousands of mutual funds and ETFs—maybe even more than the number of stocks.

Mutual funds gained popularity in the US in the 1960s, when many aggressive funds were launched to take advantage of the craze in the hot stocks of the time, such as Polaroid and Xerox. One fund manager in particular—Gerald Tsai Jr. (1929–2008)—became a mutual fund star during this period. When he left Fidelity Investments to set up his own fund, investors poured in much more money than he was planning to raise. Stocks often moved on the news that Tsai was buying and selling—or was thought to be buying and selling. His star status faded by the end of the decade, however, when the go-go era ended. The next mutual fund star was Peter Lynch, who during his 13 years running Fidelity Investments' Magellan fund gave its investors a compound return of almost 30 percent per annum, meaning that $1,000 invested in the fund for the 13 years up until his retirement in 1990 turned into almost $30,000. He beat the market by 13 percent annually. One reason for his legendary reputation, other than his outstanding performance over a long period of time, was he chose to retire at the height of his career to spend more time with his family. He never returned.

One type of mutual fund—the index fund—was not a smashing success right out of the gate. When John C. "Jack" Bogle first launched the Vanguard 500 fund in 1976, he couldn't raise enough money to buy all of the S&P 500 stocks. However, his relentless fee cuts for the benefit of investors won him both market share and great respect. By the time he died in 2019, the company he'd founded, The Vanguard Group, was a colossus, with more than $5 trillion worth of assets under management (AUM). As Warren Buffett once said: "If a statue is ever erected to honor the person who has done the most for American investors, the hands down choice should be Jack Bogle."

ETFs started much later than mutual funds, in the early 1990s. Since then, they've grown exponentially in terms of both size and shape. Other than stock and bond versions there are also commodity, currency, and real estate ETFs. There are thousands of them, the biggest being SPY, which has assets worth hundreds of billions of dollars. Run by State Street Global Advisors, the fund invests in S&P 500 companies.

Over the last three decades or so, the ETF market has attracted huge amounts of money, and the companies who run the funds are getting increasingly creative to attract even more. Now, as well as the traditional long-only ETFs, we have short ETFs, with which investors make money if the stock market is going down and lose money if it's going up. This is attractive to those who are bearish or want to hedge their longs. There are other ways to go short or to hedge, like using futures and options, but there's an advantage to choosing a short ETF, at least for the nonprofessional: there's no margin call (a demand from the broker for the investor to make up the shortfall in a margin account). The flip side: the costs associated with short ETFs are higher than those of normal, long ETFs.

Another form of ETF is the leveraged ETF, which doubles or triples the daily movement of the underlying asset or index it tracks. For example, if the S&P 500 is up 1 percent, a 2x S&P 500

ETF will be up about 2 percent. The key word here is "daily," and this is where the confusion comes in. Some investors assume that such ETFs will double their returns irrespective of the time frame. This is far from the truth. In fact, the longer you hold on to a leveraged ETF, the less correlation there is between the long-term underlying movement and the ETF price. For a manager to be able to promise an ETF that can double the underlying, they can't just buy the stocks and hold them—they have to either borrow money to buy double the amount of stocks or use derivatives like options and futures. Whatever they do, it costs money, and all the costs are passed on to the investors. Leveraged ETFs bleed you to death very slowly. They should only be bought sporadically, when you're sure about your timing. And remember: never hold them for too long.

Overall, funds can be categorized into two styles: active and passive. Managers of active funds try to pick a basket of companies that can beat a benchmark index like the S&P 500. Passive funds, however, simply mimic an index with the aim of performing no better or worse than it. Many studies have shown that active funds, with a more active turnover and therefore higher costs, underperform passive funds in the long term.

Peter Lynch's record as an active fund manager is unparalleled. Unfortunately, most managers don't perform half as well as Lynch. Many don't beat their benchmarks. Others outperform the index, but when investors rush in, they underperform it. A few active managers over the years managed to outperform for a decade or two but eventually faded away at the end of their careers. Neil Woodford, one of the most celebrated stockpickers in the UK, had a great 25-year track record at investment management firm Invesco. He couldn't follow that up after leaving in 2014. By 2019, hundreds of thousands of retail investors had their money trapped in his fund, and his reputation was tarnished. Another well-known UK investor, Anthony Bolton, enjoyed 28 years of superb performance at Fidelity Investments, retired, then returned to blemish his record in the early 2010s by investing in China. Over in the US, "Bond King" Bill Gross, who co-founded PIMCO in 1971, attained rock star status with a stellar performance that attracted hundreds of billions of dollars to the company. In 2014, he was abruptly and acrimoniously ousted in an office coup. Gross subsequently joined Janus Henderson but couldn't outperform the bond market and retired quietly in 2019.

So, if passive funds clearly outperform active funds, why do active funds still attract trillions of dollars? One reason is the "star fund manager effect." The marketing effect of such managers is worth more than the many millions of dollars spent on advertising. What Peter Lynch did for mutual funds, George Soros and Ray Dalio are still doing for hedge funds. There will always be investors who dream of investing in the next Lynch, Soros, or Dalio.

While it's true that passive funds typically outperform active funds, there are times when active funds outperform passives, sometimes by a wide margin. The managers of these funds are either skilful, lucky, or a bit of both. Active funds are attractive to active investors who like quick money and chase the latest fad. The market is constantly coming up with new funds that it knows the investing public will be interested in. The primary goal of some of these funds is to gather as much money as possible. This clearly benefits the fund companies, however it's usually at the expense of investors.

The perceived performance of active funds is boosted by a concept known as "survivorship bias," which ignores funds that do badly in their early years and that get shut down quickly. As a result, the performance of active funds appears better than it actually is because it only aggregates the performance of the survivors.

In terms of differences between mutual funds and ETFs, one of the main things is the fee structure. Mutual funds charge an upfront fee, which can be as high as 5 percent. For an investor who puts $100 into the fund, that means only $95 is invested in the stocks, with the other $5 going to the fund manager and fund distributor (usually banks or insurance companies). With ETFs, there's no upfront fee. Indeed, you can buy and sell an ETF just like a stock and pay the same commission and fees. Both mutual funds and ETFs do charge a yearly management fee, but with strong competition, these fees are driven lower and lower to the benefit of investors. By today's standard, any management fee above 1 percent is expensive. One of the lowest fees is an incredible 0.03 percent. Nowadays, some funds even have no fee.

The benefits of funds to investors are numerous. Diversification is maybe the most important one. As in every field of human activity, chance plays its part, but diversification reduces the importance of luck when it comes to investing. In a fund that holds many stocks, when one stock is down due to an unlucky event, another is up due to a lucky one. Overall, the good luck and the bad luck even out. Diversification allows an investor to achieve a certain return with lower risks and to ensure the fund's prices don't reach zero (unless, for example, you bought into a fund that invested solely in Kuwait and then Saddam Hussein (1937–2006) successfully annexed the country).

Investors should be wary of funds with less than $50 million of AUM. The problem is twofold. First off, the fund has a good chance of closing down—it may be uneconomical for the company to run it, the fund manager may retire, or it may lose its popularity—on average, there were 100 ETF closures each year of the 2010s. If you don't sell before it closes, your money will be stuck for weeks or months while the fund manager is liquidating the stocks. The second problem is that these funds usually have poor liquidity. You have to pay a high spread to get in and out, which increases your transaction costs substantially. You also need to wait longer for your limit orders (orders to buy at below current price or sell at above current price) to be executed.

Be careful though: while diversification over different industries and asset classes is definitely warranted, over-diversification is far from desirable. The main reason is that past a certain point, the returns are reduced more than the risks are. Over-diversification guarantees a mediocre result but isn't a guarantee against a poor result in a crisis. Hedge funds were touted as an asset class that was less correlated with stocks and bonds —even inversely correlated—however this claim was proven to be wrong during the global financial crisis, when investors found that their hedge fund investments lost them money just like stocks and bonds did.

Another advantage of funds is their simplicity. It's much easier to buy and sell one fund than many stocks, though this benefit is hardly appreciated by investors until the stock market turns volatile. There's also no need to monitor each company's earnings and dividends. A fund aggregates the dividends from each company and pays the fund holders either quarterly or semi-annually. Some funds—those that place emphasis on providing high dividends—even pay monthly, while others pay annually or not at all.

Bear in mind that it's impossible for an investor with limited capital to buy all 30 companies in the Dow Jones. To buy one share in each company at the start of 2019 would have set you back about $3,700. Buying a single share of Dow Jones ETF (stock code DIA) would have cost in the region of $250.

Finally, it's important to realize that although funds are generally less volatile than individual companies, some industry and country funds can drop or rise substantially. XLF, an ETF that includes all of the financial stocks in the S&P 500, lost 83 percent from its peak in 2007 to its nadir in early 2009. The rebound, from the low of 2009 through to June 2011, was almost 160 percent. Another ETF, XOP, which consists of oil- and gas-exploration-and-development companies, hit a high of $71 in mid-2008 before free-falling almost 70 percent in the next five months to $23. By June 2011, it too had recovered 160 percent. COPX, which is made up of copper mining companies, was trading below $10 at the beginning of 2016 but rose to almost $30 in the space of two years. Elsewhere, EWZ, an ETF that invests in the Brazilian stock market (BOVESPA), saw its price drop from almost $55 in September 2014 to less than $18 in January 2016 and then rebound to above $47 by January 2018. And in August 2019, ARGT, a country ETF that invests in Argentina, lost a quarter of its value in one day when the opposition surprised the market by winning a primary election.

PART II: THE NEXT LEVEL

BUYBACKS

Other than paying shareholders dividends, a company can choose to reward them by buying back its own stock in the open market, thereby reducing outstanding stocks in the process. The shareholders are rewarded, not by a dividend paycheck, but by holding a higher percentage in the company. If you hold 1 percent of a company and the company buys back 50 percent of its stock, your holding is now 2 percent. Since your stake in the company has doubled, you enjoy a double share of the company's future earnings and dividends. Key financial ratios also improve. The earnings per share have now doubled, even though the earnings are still the same. This is highly positive for stock prices. In addition, if dividends tax is at a higher rate than capital gains tax, investors enjoy a tax advantage when a company chooses buybacks over dividends.

The other benefit of buybacks is harder to measure but can be just as important over time. By making repurchases when their company's market value is well below its business value, management clearly demonstrates that it is enhancing shareholders' wealth rather than expanding its own domain or doing nothing for—or even harming—shareholders' interests. Seeing this, shareholders and potential shareholders increase their estimates of future returns from the business. This upward revision, in turn, produces market prices that are more in line with the intrinsic business value.

Despite the benefits of buybacks, they still have their critics. Some believe the money should be invested in the business, while others think it should be paid to the workers instead of only benefiting the shareholders. There are also voices that claim buybacks distort earnings per share without increasing earnings. These cynics believe buybacks benefit company management but not the shareholders. Are buybacks bad for shareholders? Both Warren Buffett and Peter Lynch are big fans, but only if the buyback is done at below intrinsic value.

In theory, when companies buy back their own shares, all else being equal, the share price should head higher. But share buyback isn't a magic wand that can move a stock's price up. IBM has spent more than $100 billion buying back almost half its own shares since 1995, however the share price has only gone up 30 percent over the same period, greatly underperforming the S&P 500. When buyback is done below the intrinsic value of a company, the value of that company increases significantly. However, many buybacks nowadays are used to push up or support share prices. When repurchases are made above intrinsic value, the value of shareholders' holdings is destroyed. It's like buying a $1 bill for $1.10. The continuing shareholders are penalized. It's not good business for those who choose to stick around.

While companies might announce they intend to buy back a certain number of shares, they often don't follow up to inform shareholders how much they've actually bought back. Some companies issue shares to their employees as an incentive or issue shares instead of cash for dividends. These newly issued shares dilute the shareholders' stake in the company. The buyback needs to be bigger than the new shares issued in order to have a positive effect on share prices and shareholders' holdings. HSBC, the bank with the global footprint, is one such company issuing shares as dividends and buying back its own shares at the same time.

The amount of money US companies spend on buybacks and dividends remained similar up until the mid-2000s. Buybacks then surged, surpassing dividends and only dipping below them during the global financial crisis. From 2010 to 2016, US companies bought back almost $3 trillion worth of shares, while dividends stood at nearly $2 trillion. The total was around one-fifth of the S&P 500 market cap. The bumper year came in 2018, when US companies took advantage of President Donald Trump's tax cuts to spend more than $800 billion on buybacks. The long bull market after the global financial crisis certainly benefited from US corporations' big buybacks. Companies that have regularly bought back their own shares over the years include Microsoft, Cisco, IBM, and Apple. As a result, these companies have typically been able to reduce their outstanding shares by more than 30 percent over the decades.

Companies sometimes choose to borrow in order to buy back their dividend-paying shares. This might seem irresponsible and unsound, however it makes good financial sense. This action has two advantages: First, the interest expense on the borrowing is tax deductible. Second, with less outstanding shares, the company pays less dividends. Apple, for example, takes advantage of its great balance sheet (with hundreds of billions of dollars in cash) and high credit rating to borrow money cheaply so that it can increase its share buyback. It's important to get the balance right though, as too much debt can lead to a downgrade and higher interest rates on the debt. Oracle fell foul of this when its credit rating was downgraded in 2019 by Standard and Poor's because of debt-fueled buybacks.

BANKRUPTCY AND RECEIVERSHIP

In the US, chapter 11, also known as receivership, is a form of bankruptcy that companies usually file for when they have a cash flow problem yet their assets are still worth more than their liabilities. Companies that file for chapter 11 are protected in a bankruptcy court, which appoints a receiver to oversee the company's business. A major financial reorganization inevitably takes place to enable the company to generate revenue from its assets so that it can pay off debts and get on a firmer footing. Receivership usually requires some capital injection from shareholders and from bondholders swapping their bonds for shares. In the process, shareholders' interests in the company are greatly diluted. The receivership terminates when the company is restored to sound financial health. This usually takes several months or, in the worst cases, a few years. With chapter 7, on the other hand, it's game over—bankruptcy. This happens when liabilities exceed assets. The business ceases operation, employees are sent home, and assets are sold off.

Bankruptcy is a disaster for shareholders and bondholders, but it's a boom for lawyers and advisory firms. When Toys "R" Us and Lehman Brothers filed for bankruptcy, the advisory firms had a bonanza, collectively earning hundreds of millions of dollars. Why would the shareholders and bondholders willingly pick up such a big bill? The argument is you pay more, you get more. By engaging highly paid firms and lawyers, shareholders and bondholders can extract more money from the bankruptcy process.

Companies that have just emerged from chapter 11 bankruptcy often trade at a premium to their intrinsic value because of their low price along with unwarranted optimism by some investors, who believe that buying these companies is not only a safe bet but can offer multiple returns. After all, the worst has already happened and things can only get better. But there are cases where companies that have just emerged from bankruptcy go into bankruptcy again. American Apparel is one such company, having filed for its second bankruptcy in as many years in 2016. Gymboree, which sells children's clothing, filed for its second bankruptcy in January 2019, just eighteen months after its first.

Some industries see lots of bankruptcies. Many US railroad companies have been through receivership at least once, while a considerable number have been through the process twice. US airlines have also seen many bankruptcies over the decades. As a result, there have been a number of mergers, and there are now three major airlines. On the bright side, Kmart emerged from bankruptcy around mid-2003 and saw its value increase by more than 400 percent in just one year, though it went on to file for bankruptcy once again in 2018.

One of the most famous case studies of a great company emerging from near death is Apple, which nearly filed for chapter 11 in 1997. According to Steve Jobs (1955–2011), the company was just a few weeks away from running out of cash. Its savior was its fierce competitor Microsoft. Steve Jobs and Bill Gates had an acrimonious rivalry at the time, but Gates swooped in to save the company because he was worried the regulators would regard Microsoft as a monopoly if Apple failed. Many people have this "big miss of a lifetime" in mind when they are looking for the next Apple—the next dying company. Overall, however, there are more cases of failure than success when buying a recently bankrupted company, and there's no historical evidence to support the theory that stocks that have just emerged from bankruptcy will outperform the general market in the long term.

CORRELATIONS

Correlations measure past price relationships and are a favorite tool in the financial markets for predicting future price movements. Any pair that has a meaningful correlation is a good candidate to trade. Correlations trading could be in gold and silver, oil and the US dollar, General Motors and Ford, the S&P 500 and the Russell 2000, etc. Gold and silver are an example of a positive correlation. That means that in the past, when the price of gold was up, the price of silver was likely to be up too. Traders will buy silver if the gold price has gone up but silver has yet to move. Correlations trading is also popular with foreign exchange (FX) traders, who observe currency correlations and trade accordingly. For example, if the Japanese yen and South Korean won are positively correlated, a jump in yen will attract buyers in won.

Using correlations as a trading strategy is risky. First of all, correlations are a measurement of the past price relationship. They're backward looking; they don't predict the future. Correlations traders seem to forget the disclaimer: past performance is not indicative of future results. Second of all, correlations are never static; they're fluid and always changing. A good example of this is Japan, where the yen and the stock markets are usually negatively correlated—when the yen goes up, stock prices go down. Why? Japan is a big export country, and a strong yen is bad for exports. This is bad for the stock markets, which include big exporters such as Sony and Toyota. However, in the 1980s and 90s, the opposite actually happened. The markets reasoned then that a weak yen meant high import prices and high inflation, and the stock markets dropped as a result. The correlation between the yen and the stock markets has changed, despite Japan having always relied heavily on exports.

Going back to gold and silver, yes, they have a positive correlation, though sometimes they're highly correlated and sometimes they're hardly correlated. The gold-to-silver ratio, which is calculated by dividing the gold price by the silver price, has spanned a very wide range over the last 20 years, from a low of around 30 to a high of around 90. Some traders will buy gold when the ratio is near to 30, as gold is cheap relative to silver, and buy silver when the ratio is near to 90. But 30 and 90 are not lines in the sand—they can be broken. 20 years isn't a long enough period to make the top and bottom range statistically significant and reliable. Many things can go wrong with a simple correlation-based strategy such as this, and hedge funds that trade successfully on correlations tend to use big data and computer programs to generate buy and sell signals. My experience and observations of the FX market show that if you want to trade on correlations, you need a more sophisticated strategy than basing decisions purely on a simple number.

Why are correlations so fluid? Ray Dalio, an original thinker who founded investment management company Bridgewater out of his tiny New York apartment and built it into the biggest hedge fund in the world, says it's all about market drivers. He sees correlations as an unreliable indicator and stresses the need to understand what "drives" the prices. Drivers are the causes, and correlations are the consequences. So, in the case of Japanese yen, Dalio would look at what drives the currency up and down—trade balance, interest rates, and so on. He would also try to figure out what drives the Japanese stock market—earnings, policies, etc. He looks at each market separately and completely ignores correlations.

The correlation between the two most important asset classes —stocks and bonds—is widely and keenly observed by the financial markets. This correlation is more fluid than the one between the Japanese yen and the Nikkei, which has only changed once in the last few decades. Sometimes stocks and bonds move in the same direction; sometimes they move in opposite directions. There's no proper correlation, and no one knows in advance when it will change, yet many investors still trade on it. What drives change in the correlation between stocks and bonds? One scenario is when interest rates rise as a result of inflation. In this case, both stock and bond prices drop as investors pull money out from both asset classes. Another scenario is when interest rates rise due to a growing economy with no worries about inflation. In this case, bond prices will still drop but the growing economy and increased earnings will cause the stock market to rise, with some investors moving money from bonds to stocks. Correlation. It works until it doesn't.

LEVERAGE

To some people, leverage is a dirty word, and they vow they'll never use it. The truth is that leverage is almost unavoidable. Nearly all of us leverage in one way or another, irrespective of whether we're aware of it or whether we like it. When you buy a stock with cash, you may not necessarily consider yourself to be leveraging, but the company you're buying into almost certainly uses leverage—most companies borrow money for their business operation. On a more personal level, unless you're born with a silver spoon in your mouth, you borrow money to buy a house. Regardless of whether the property is for investment or to live in, this is leverage. Most people who buy a property with sensible leverage and hold it long enough make money in the end. This shows that leveraging, if used well, isn't as dangerous as some people think.

In the financial markets, leverages are easily available. You can buy stocks on margin; you can buy and sell leveraged products like futures and options. You can also invest in a leveraged ETF or a contract for difference (CFD), which allow traders to profit from price movements without owning the underlying asset. Investors need to be very careful of leveraged products—not only are they risky, they're addictive. Once investors have a taste of good profits from their wonders, however, very few can resist going for it again. In the worst cases, just like drug addicts, some investors take higher and higher doses of leverage in a bid to make outlandish returns. It doesn't end pretty.

You may have heard stories of relatives and friends losing their shirts in futures and options markets. Indeed, the undisciplined use of leverage is a big reason why most people lose money in those arenas. If you buy an index future that requires a 5 percent margin and the index moves up by 5 percent, you double your money. This mouthwatering return can blind the greedy. They forget that the risk is much higher—a 5 percent drop will wipe out all the money in the margin account.

A leveraged product by itself isn't dangerous; it's how you use it that makes it risky. A Lamborghini with a top speed of 200 miles per hour is as safe as a Volvo if you always stick to the speed limit. Likewise, a future that requires a minimum 5 percent margin doesn't mean a trader can't put in 10 percent, 50 percent, or even 100 percent if they choose not to leverage in a leveraged product. Futures prices are no more volatile than the underlying cash prices. The high-risk reputation of futures is mainly due to over-leverage, driving at 200 miles per hour on every road all the time.

You can't look at leverage in black-and-white terms—it's a double-edged sword with both high risks and high returns. You can't just dream of the high return it brings and forget about the high chance of losing, but you also can't allow the high risks of leverage to put you off taking a better investment.

In fact, contrary to what most people believe, leverage can, in some cases, actually reduce risks. A moderately leveraged, well-diversified portfolio is actually less risky than an unleveraged, undiversified portfolio. Say you have a typical recommended portfolio of $6,000 of stocks and $4,000 of bonds. Using leverage, you can borrow $2,000 to buy more bonds. Now you've changed your portfolio from a 60/40 split between stocks and bonds to a 50/50 one. This new portfolio is less volatile than the unleveraged portfolio, as bonds are less volatile than stocks. It's also possible to borrow at an interest rate that's lower than the bonds' yields—some banks are willing to lend at a good rate if you pledge your portfolio as collateral. This moderate borrowing—20 percent of your portfolio—can enhance your return slightly while reducing your portfolio's overall volatility.

SHORT SELLING

The main focus of this book is long-term investing, however a chapter on "short selling" is still warranted, as novice investors can find the concept confusing. In fact, many experienced investors still struggle with it. In financial jargon, investors are "long" when they have bought stocks and they are "short" when they have sold stocks they don't own. Herein lies the confusion: most people can understand how investors can sell a stock they own but are confused about how they can sell a stock they don't own. How can someone sell an orange if they don't have one? The answer is to borrow an orange. An investor can borrow a stock from banks and brokers to sell short. Once the investor "buys back" the shorted (borrowed) stock, they return it to its owner. Some banks and brokers allow retail investors to lend stock to short sellers to earn supplemental income. The shareholders are still entitled to their dividend, but the voting rights go to the borrower.

Why short sell? The obvious reason is to make money. Speculators can profit handsomely if the stock they sell falls sharply. By buying it back at a lower price than they sold it, they can pocket the profit. Another common reason to short sell is hedging. An investor who owns Visa might short sell Mastercard to hedge. Why wouldn't the investor simply sell Visa? One possibility is they like Visa so much they're afraid to miss the price advance. At the same time, they're worried about a correction. The solution is to short sell Mastercard, which the investor thinks of as an inferior company. This way, they keep their long Visa but hedge their risk of a correction with a short Mastercard.

Before deciding to short sell, investors need to do their homework—not all stock exchanges allow short selling, and not all stocks are available for short selling. The cost of short selling varies too. When investors borrow stocks to short sell, they need to pay a stock loan fee ranging from 0.25 percent to over 10 percent per annum. Generally speaking, big companies' stocks are cheaper to borrow than small companies' stocks, but a company's borrowing fees can vary over time, depending on factors such as changing volatility of the stock, the availability of the stock to lend, and so on. Japan's public pension fund—the world's biggest—struck a blow against short sellers in 2019 by declaring it would no longer allow overseas shares to be lent from its $737 billion global equity portfolio.

In 1949, Alfred W. Jones (1900–1989), was credited with launching the first-ever hedge fund. He bought the best companies he could find for his fund, and at the same time, he short sold the worst companies. In other words, he hedged his best companies with his worst companies. The idea was that if the general market was down, the shorted stocks would go down more than the long stocks; if the general market was up, the long stocks would go up more than the short stocks. It was a groundbreaking idea. The term hedge fund was born, and the name stuck, even though most hedge funds today don't actually hedge; instead, they take directional bets, trade on algorithms, and buy and sell in nanoseconds—everything but hedge.

Even for investors who never short sell, it's a good idea to seek short sell data on individual stocks and general markets. The information is easily available. Some believe that if a stock is heavily shorted, there's probably a good reason for it—there's no smoke without fire, as the saying goes. Typically, short sell interest of 10 percent or more is considered high, however it can go above 50 percent. One of the most common reasons a bear market rally is strong, say up by more than 20 percent over a period of days or weeks, is because when stocks rebound, short sellers lose money and are forced to buy back their shares indiscriminately. During a bear market, if the short interest of the general market is high, some believe the market is near a turning point.

Investors who do want to short sell need to keep a few important things in mind. One key consideration is that shorting a stock opens investors up to potential losses far beyond the original capital commitment. Say you have a $1,000 short position in a stock. The maximum profit, if the stock goes to zero, is 100 percent ($1,000), as the stock is now worthless. If, however, the stock falls by half, your position size is reduced to $500 with $500 profit. As the stock falls, professionals will sell more to maintain the same exposure. In our scenario, that would mean selling another $500 worth of position. The maximum loss, on the other hand, is as high as the stock can go. If the stock price doubles, the position size is $2,000 and the loss is $1,000; if the stock goes up 10 times, the position size is $10,000 and the loss is $9,000.

As shown in the example, short sells lose money as the position size increases. In other words, with a short position, your risk exposure increases as the trade goes against you, whereas with a long position, it decreases. Investors also need to bear in mind that as a short seller borrows from shareholder A and sells to shareholder B, when there is a dividend, the company will pay it to shareholder B and the short seller will be obliged to pay dividends to shareholder A.

Arguments about the merits and morals of short selling are endless. The proponents of short selling believe it serves some vital, useful functions, such as improving market liquidity and pricing efficiency, highlighting dubious accounting, and exposing fraud. They see short sellers as the boy who calls out that the emperor has no clothes. Short selling, they say, can also temper overpriced companies and market bubbles and keep the market rational and efficient.

Others believe short selling should never be allowed and even go as far as to claim that it's evil or sinful; they believe short sellers profit off others' misery. Some American investors feel that short selling is unethical and "un-American." It's true that some short sellers make money dubiously or even illegally. For example, after short selling a stock, some speculators spread false rumors to make the price fall, however dubious or illegal ways of making money can also be employed by unscrupulous investors who long stocks.

Whenever the general market or an individual stock is falling fast, short sellers are a favorite punching bag. They're an easy scapegoat for investors who are long in stocks and losing money. Occasionally, when there's turmoil in the market, regulators ban short selling. For example, the US and some western countries limited or banned short selling during the global financial crisis. The argument is that short selling causes short prices to fall or that it at least exacerbates the fall. The history of short selling bans shows that it fails to stem a further fall in prices. A 2012 report published by the Federal Reserve Bank of New York concluded that short sell bans have "little impact on stock prices", and that they "lowered market liquidity and increased trading costs."

Almost all "market wizards" incorporate short sells in their trading. A favorite short sell is a one-product company because if that product fails, the company is in deep trouble. A common recommendation is to only short sell if a stock is astronomically expensive. These traders understand that short selling can enhance profits and reduce portfolio risk. As an armchair investor, what should you do? Should you short sell? My answer would be no. You're not a professional. The skill set needed for short selling is more demanding than for long stocks; the risks are much higher, and you need to monitor a short position much more closely than a long one. There are inherent disadvantages in short selling. The costs are high, it goes against the long-term trend of high stock prices, losses can be far greater than your position size, your timing needs to be near perfect, and so on. If, after carefully considering all of this, you still want to short sell, make sure you only do it sporadically and selectively.

PART III: KNOWLEDGE IS POWER

GOLD

What happened to my tiny gold bar? I still have it to this day.

Gold has been a popular investment for humankind since civilization began and has been used as money throughout history. It's a symbol of wealth and power. This precious metal has a mesmerizing appeal to some cultures, notably Indian, Chinese, and Vietnamese, and gold jewelry is very fashionable in the world's two most populous countries: China and India.

As most people know, gold comes in varying degrees of purity. A carat (ct) is defined as being $^1/_{24}$ of pure gold by weight. 18ct gold therefore consists of $^{18}/_{24}$ (75 percent) pure gold, with the remaining 25 percent made up of an alloy of silver, copper, zinc, and nickel. 24ct gold is, in theory, 100 percent gold, but in reality it's about 99.9 percent. The reason for this is that gold's actually a relatively soft metal and is therefore very fragile. The 0.01 percent alloy in 24ct gold helps keep it from turning into fairy gold dust. Other types of gold include rose gold and white gold. Rose gold is a mix of gold and copper, while white gold is a mix of gold and at least one white metal, usually nickel, silver, or palladium.

In 1699, Isaac Newton became the UK's Master of the Royal Mint and fixed the price of gold to the pound. The UK officially adopted the gold standard in 1816. Its success prompted other countries in Europe to follow suit. By the late 19th century, most European countries, along with the US, were on the gold standard.

There have been many gold rushes over the centuries, each bringing great wealth to a few but exploitation and shattered dreams to the rest. California gold was discovered in early 1848, before the age of telegraphs and telephones. It took months for the news to reach the northeast US coast. It was finally announced by President James K. Polk (1795–1849) in an address to Congress in December of that year. The gold rush had begun —it was intense and epidemic. The rush brought hundreds of thousands of gold seekers from as far away as China to the then thinly populated California. It wasn't just the gold diggers who made money. Levi Strauss (1829–1902) actually made his first pot of "gold" by selling durable jeans to the workers.

In 1933, in the depths of the Great Depression, President Franklin D. Roosevelt (1882–1945) halted the convertibility of US dollars to gold at $25 to 1 ounce, thus abandoning the gold standard. He also banned the export of gold and made it illegal for Americans to own gold for investment purposes. During World War II, it was decided that the US dollar would be convertible into gold at $35 an ounce. This lasted until 1971, when President Richard Nixon (1913–1994) declared the end of fixed convertibility—gold prices were to be determined by market forces. On January 1, 1975, in anticipation that Americans could once again buy gold, the price shot up to $200 per ounce—an almost sixfold increase from its previous fixed price. It was typical "buy the rumor, sell the fact." Those who bought in advance, in the hope of selling to the American public, got carried away. They bought too much, and they bought at prices that were too high. When the expected strong demand didn't materialize over the subsequent few months, the price duly crashed to $100.

What is gold? The obvious answer is it's a commodity, just like copper, cotton, and coffee. In actual fact, gold is a multi-faceted entity. To many people, it's a store of value. This has been the case for thousands of years, with some believing that there's none better. The Vietnamese boat people who fled the Vietnam War understood this. They didn't get into the boats with Vietnamese dong in their bags; they carried gold bars and coins. Gold is widely considered a safe haven. In times of great uncertainty or war, people want to own gold. During the Iran hostage crisis in 1979, when 52 Americans were held in the US embassy in Tehran, the price of gold surged. Soon after, in early 1980, after the Soviet Union's invasion of Afghanistan, it reached around $850 per ounce. Gold also jumped by $15, or around 5 percent, on September 11, 2001—the day planes brought down the twin towers of the World Trade Center in New York.

To some people, gold is a currency—one that can only be minted and can't be printed by central banks. In countries that have experienced high inflation and hyperinflation, citizens understand the importance of holding gold instead of paper money. Gold is an inflation hedge. Some people have a firm belief that whenever there is inflation, gold prices will go up. Gold isn't the only option though. In the past few decades, new financial instruments, like Treasury bond futures and inflation-linked bonds, were created. These can also hedge inflation risks—gold is losing its role as an inflation hedge. Still, over the last two decades, when cash has offered almost zero return, more and more people have been willing to switch to gold, as the opportunity cost of holding it is low. The all-time peak of gold, nominally, was $1,918 an ounce on September 6, 2011—a time when both inflation and interest rates were low.

Gold isn't a productive asset, however. Properties collect rents, stocks provide dividends, and bonds pay coupons. Gold doesn't generate income and has no intrinsic value. Indeed, investments in gold have a negative cash flow. If you invest in a gold ETF, there's a management fee. If you keep a gold bar in a bank's safety deposit box, there's also a fee. An investment in gold is profitable only if the price, determined by supply and demand, has gone up. Unlike other commodities, production and consumption are not important factors to the price of gold.

The industrial use of gold only makes up a small part of its demand. Most gold is mined from underground then minted and stored in an underground vault. One unique feature of gold is that investors and speculators provide both the main supply and demand. Also unique is the fact that demand can swiftly turn into supply and vice versa if the prevailing sentiment changes. The price of gold is heavily dependent on sentiment or the fundamentals that drive that sentiment. The US dollar, inflation, and big events such as wars have a strong influence on sentiment and, in turn, gold prices.

Gold is a chameleon—its role is changing constantly. Sometimes it's mainly a currency, other times it's a safe haven or an inflation hedge. The changes come unannounced, and no one is sure what its main role will be at any particular point in time—we can only guess. If there's a war and prices go up, it's probably playing the role of a safe haven. If there's inflation and prices go up, it's probably playing the role of an inflation hedge. If it's going up when the US dollar is going down, it's probably playing the role of a currency. The quick switch between speculative supply and demand and the multiple roles that gold plays makes forecasting its price almost impossible. Nevertheless, these facts don't stop people from making predictions on gold prices all the time.

What happened when the Dow Jones crashed on Black Monday, October 19, 1987? Did the price of gold go up because of uncertainties and fear? Yes, but only for a short while. After surging over 4 percent initially, it fell for the rest of the day. The following day, it dropped further. Instead of playing the role of a safe haven, it suddenly had a new role as the ATM (automated teller machine) for investors who'd lost heavily in the stock market. They had to turn gold into cash to pay for their losses. The other explanation went like this: as the market was expecting a depression, there was no need to fear inflation. Investors who bought gold as an inflation hedge were selling it, and those who expected it would surge in a crisis were given a rude awakening.

Gold will always have its die-hard fans—the so-called "gold bugs." They'll always advocate buying gold for one reason or another, and they'll always find plenty of reasons why an investor should own gold. But when we look back, we find many instances when the price didn't go up like these gold bugs would like us to believe. Many wars, including the Falklands War, the Iran-Iraq War, the two Gulf wars, and the War in Afghanistan only had a minor, temporary effect on the price.

Gold is fine for a short-term trade, but it's not a good long-term investment. It doesn't give its owners an income. The only gain that can be made is when someone is willing to buy it at a higher price—the greater fool theory. We might see gold losing its luster in the coming decades as cryptocurrencies gain popularity. The new generation—millennials—are also less obsessed with it, both as jewelry and as an investment. For the super-rich, it makes sense to diversify and use gold as a store of value and a hedge against Armageddon. For most of us, however, who have limited capital, unless we live in a country where the currency value is in doubt, gold probably has no place in our long-term portfolios.

OIL

Oil is by far the biggest commodity traded in US dollars, with coffee a distant second. The biggest oil tanker in the world can carry two million barrels of oil—in monetary terms, that's worth over $100 million, assuming the oil price is above $50 a barrel. Oil's importance to the world economy is huge, and its impact on politics, monetary policy, and financial markets is way beyond that of any other commodity.

Just like diamonds, the quality and price of oil varies. The two benchmarks most commonly quoted on the news are Brent oil, which is "sweet" (low sulfur content), "light" (low density), and extracted from the North Sea; and West Texas Intermediate (WTI) oil, which is also sweet but is of "medium" density and is extracted from the US. The sweeter the oil, the easier it is to refine. Most of the time, Brent trades at a premium to WTI.

The first US oil was discovered and drilled in Pennsylvania in the mid-19th century. Drilling had originally been developed in China around two thousand years earlier, allowing wells that could go down thousands of feet. The news that oil had been discovered and promised instant wealth spread like wildfire and started a mad rush to get drilling. But while oil was plentiful, barrels were in short supply, and they soon cost twice as much as the oil inside them. At that time, oil was mainly being used to produce kerosene, which was in big demand as a cheap, clean fuel for lighting homes. Gasoline was an almost useless by-product. Oil prices were as volatile then as they are now. Supply could come in quickly, as everyone was trying to drill as much and as quickly as possible, which meant prices could drop fast.

One of the most synonymous names with the rise of the US

oil industry was that of John D. Rockefeller (1839–1937). He masterfully and ruthlessly consolidated the industry under his company Standard Oil, a name chosen to give consumers confidence that his oil had a uniform consistency and wasn't of the dubious quality that was common at that time. By the end of the 19th century, Rockefeller had become the richest man in the US. He would recall later, however, that this came at a price, as he seldom got "an unbroken night's sleep."

As the years went by, the way in which oil was used started to change. By the early 1900s, electric light bulbs were gaining popularity, and kerosene lamps were increasingly restricted to rural areas. As the lighting market started to slip away, a new one was opening up: gasoline-powered automobiles.

Up until 1952, oil production in the US accounted for more than half of the world's total. It was enough to sustain the home market for a while. The American boom, after World War II, changed that, however, as US citizens bought more—and bigger—cars than ever before. By 1971, demand for oil had outstripped supply and the US could no longer be purely self-reliant—it had to start importing. Oil became an important part of US politics and foreign policy. By the 2010s, with the advance of technology, oil companies were able to drill horizontally for oil. This created a shale oil boom in the US. Production shot up by a few million barrels a day, and the US turned into a net exporter once again.

Right from the beginning, oil has been an international business. The wells in Baku (now the capital of Azerbaijan) were first drilled in 1871, making Russia the biggest producer outside the US at the time. This changed after oil was discovered in Mexico in 1910, which started a boom. Within 10 years, Mexico had become the second-largest oil producer in the world. Petróleos Mexicanos (Pemex) was nationalized in 1938 to become one of the first-ever state-owned oil companies.

In the same year, oil was discovered in Kuwait and Saudi Arabia. It swiftly became the main source of revenue for the Saudi government, overtaking the income that came from Muslims making the pilgrimage to Mecca. In 1940, the Middle East was still a minor player in the oil market, producing less than 5 percent of the world's oil. This would change drastically in the coming decades. The two oil shocks of the 1970s went on to cement the Middle East's central role in the world's oil market.

Next to make a play was Africa, with the oil majors turning their attention to the continent in the 1960s. Nigeria, Angola, and Libya were all to become oil-producing countries. The UK would join their ranks in the 1970s when North Sea oil started to flow to the market.

Since its foundation in 1960 by five member nations—Iran, Iraq, Kuwait, Saudi Arabia, and Venezuela—it has become hard to find an article about oil that doesn't mention the Organization of the Petroleum Exporting Countries (OPEC). Today, OPEC has 14 members, mostly from the Middle East and Africa. In 1967, tensions in the Middle East flared as a result of the Third Arab-Israeli War—also known as the Six-Day War—when the Arab allies launched an oil embargo "weapon" on countries including the UK and the US. The embargo was short lived, however, and supplies were redistributed to countries on the embargo list. The Arab countries had lost revenue without having managed to hurt the embargoed countries. In footballing terms, OPEC had scored an own goal.

In the early 1970s, with the oil supply problem becoming chronic, the media started to report an "energy crisis." Things intensified in 1973 when war broke out between Israel and the Arabs once more. This time, Israel was caught off guard, the Arabs mounting a well-coordinated attack on the holiest day of the Jewish calendar—Yom Kippur. Israel had thought their clear military supremacy and crushing defeat of Arab forces just six years prior would be enough to stop the Arabs from even thinking of an attack. This complacency led Israel to dismiss some telltale signs, such as the Soviets suddenly airlifting dependents out of Syria and Egypt.

This time, the oil market was already tight, and the oil weapon worked perfectly. Oil prices quadrupled, and Americans queued in long lines to fill their cars' tanks. The reason the embargo worked second time round was that US oil fields had already begun to decline. In the meantime, during the late 1960s and early 1970s, the developed world's economy had grown rapidly, and oil demand had soared. Furthermore, price controls introduced by President Nixon's administration in 1971 discouraged investment in oil production while at the same time encouraging Americans to consume more.

The catalysts of the "second oil shock" (the first took place in 1973) were the American hostage crisis in Tehran and the Soviet invasion of Afghanistan. Once again, Iranian output had fallen, which set off a new round of panic buying. Prices more than doubled in the year to April 1980. Oil companies remained focused on their vulnerabilities and continued to buy more oil by way of "insurance." They were gushing in cash, and went on a buying spree to scoop up department stores, copper plants, and even a circus! But it was the management teams who ended up being ridiculed as clowns when these investments turned out to be unnecessary distractions that lost the oil companies many millions of dollars.

The general outlook was bleak. The Iranian Revolution and the Iran-Iraq War had crippled the oil exports of the countries involved and captured the headlines of international newspapers. At the same time, the oil market was unaware of rising production in Mexico, Alaska, and the North Sea. Egypt, Angola, Malaysia, and China—yes, China—were all becoming oil exporters too. The collapse of demand brought about by high oil prices as well as the inventory dump by oil companies and the relentless non-OPEC supply turned the feared shortage into a massive glut in the 1980s. OPEC heavyweights Iran and Iraq fighting for eight years didn't stop the slide in prices.

By 1986, the price had collapsed by around 70 percent from $32 to $10. Saudi Arabia continued to lose market share, only to recover with the collapse of the Soviet Union in 1991 (Russia's oil production dropped sharply when the Soviet Union dissolved but its production is now compatible to Saudi Arabia and the US). Later on, during the Asian and Russian financial crises of 1997 and 1998 respectively, oil prices dropped around 60 percent to $11. OPEC was powerless to stem the decline when demand dove. The US shale boom in the 2010s and the emergence of Russia as a top producer rivaling Saudi Arabia went on to further reduce OPEC's influence in the global oil market.

The strategic importance of oil as a commodity is second to none. The success or failure of wars depends on oil; the attack on the Soviet Union by Germany in World War II was about oil; the decision by Japan to attack South East Asia instead of Siberia, Russia was about oil; the invasion of Kuwait by Iraq and the subsequent quick, forceful repulse by the US and its allies was about oil.

Oil is a major consideration for every nation's economy and national security. The US made the decision to build up its Strategic Petroleum Reserve after the "first oil shock" of 1973. And Japan, which imports almost all its oil, didn't welcome prices dropping in the 1980s, as it was worried lower oil prices would weaken its resolve and commitment to other energy sources, and it didn't want to go back to the days when the country was highly dependent on oil. In addition, at that point in time, Japan was running a huge trade surplus against America, and a big drop in oil prices would only have widened the surplus further and attracted more political pressure from the US. Coming to the present day, China is one of the world's biggest importers of oil and is building up good relationships with a number of oil-producing countries, from Russia to Saudi Arabia, Angola, and Venezuela. Oil—like money—really does make the world go round.

But if the oil market is so deep and big and so important to the world, why do prices fluctuate so much? To answer that, we need to look at OPEC. OPEC's oil production quota is based on each country's oil reserves. Naturally, each country wants to claim a higher reserve than a lower one. For most OPEC countries, oil is the most important source of revenue. Economic theory tells us that when prices goes down, supply will also go down. However, in the case of OPEC, members all rush to produce more in order to maintain the same revenue, which pushes prices down even further. To oil producers, it's only sensible to cut supply if the price falls below the production cost. Even so, they're reluctant to do this, as it can be costly and complicated to temporarily shut down operations.

When prices are going up, oil companies react by buying more of today's cheaper oil than tomorrow's more expensive oil. They build up inventories. Drivers want to top up their fuel tanks too. Then there are the people who hoard oil in a rising market. All of these extra, "unreal" demands push the price up even further. This causes more panic buying, and the problem becomes self-fulfilling. This was what happened in 1979 when oil prices were surging. There's also the issue of how long it takes supply to respond to demand. It takes many years to go from discovery to production. Alaska North Slope oil was discovered in 1968 and North Sea oil a year later, however production in both places only started in 1977.

The price of oil has a huge global impact, affecting everyone. Higher oil prices mean higher gasoline and electricity bills. Businesses pass on the higher cost to consumers by raising prices of goods and services. Central banks watch the oil prices like a hawk. Any sign of inflation brought on by higher oil prices is responded to with higher interest rates. Many see high oil prices as a form of higher tax, as consumers spend more on oil and its related products and have less to spend on other things. This is bad for the economy, and it's bad for the stock market. Generally speaking, low oil prices are good for the stock market overall, but they're obviously bad for the oil sector.

In the late 1970s and early 1980s, when oil prices and inflation were high, investors were told they had to have oil companies in their portfolio; if not, their savings could be eroded by inflation and rising oil prices. However, since the 1970s, the effect of oil prices on the stock market has been minimal. When prices surged in the mid-2000s to a peak of around $145 per barrel in 2008, it didn't bring inflation to major economies or panic to financial markets. The 2008 global financial crisis had nothing to do with high oil prices.

FOREIGN EXCHANGE

The biggest financial market in the world isn't the stock or bond market; it's the currency market—more widely known as the foreign exchange (FX) market. Trillions of US dollars' worth of currencies are traded every day, mostly between banks, in the interbank market—a 24-hour market, which literally follows the sun around the world.

Every week, the market starts on Monday morning in New Zealand and ends on Friday evening in New York. Every currency is assigned a three-letter acronym—the US dollar is USD, the euro is EUR, the Japanese yen is JPY, the Chinese yuan is CNY, and so on. The US dollar is the omnipotent currency in the FX market, and all currencies are quoted against it, mostly in terms of how many units of currency there are per dollar. For example, USD/JPY is currently quoted at around 110. This means that 1 US dollar can be exchanged for 110 Japanese yen. In a few cases, it's quoted the other way round. The euro against the US dollar is currently quoted as EUR/USD at around 1.1000. This means that one euro can be exchanged for 1.1 US dollars. The British pound (GBP), the Australia dollar (AUD) and the New Zealand dollar (NZD) are all quoted this way.

In 1944, Allied powers met at Mount Washington Hotel in Bretton Woods, New Hampshire to discuss post-war orders. They decided that the US dollar would be convertible into gold at $35 an ounce and that other currencies should be pegged to the US dollar. Known as the Bretton Woods Agreement, this system lasted until 1971, when President Nixon declared the end of the $35 gold conversion rate. Banks were looking to convert their holdings into gold, and the US no longer had enough gold to cover its obligation. This was a monumental event for the global financial markets—many developed countries' currencies and gold became "floating," with prices determined by market forces.

In recent years, FX trading has become more mainstream, with FX now touted as a new asset class and a way to diversify. The issue with this is that developed countries' currencies generally take years to move a third or more. For ordinary folks who don't have lots of zeros in their bank accounts, diversification into other currencies is both unaffordable and unnecessary. Diversifying into foreign currencies like NZD and buying a house by a lake in New Zealand in preparation for World War III is best left to the rich.

As a 24-hour market, FX trading is one of the most liquid markets in the world. For us folks, our FX trade sizes are likely to be in tens of thousands or hundreds of thousands of dollars unless we use crazy leverage. In FX markets, this can be up to 100 times the account balance. That means that with $10,000 in your FX margin account, you can buy and sell $1 million worth of currency. However, even if you use high leverage and trade in millions, that's still a tiny amount in a trillion-dollar market. The deep liquidity of the FX market is good, but it's pretty irrelevant to most of us—a small fish doesn't need a big pond.

How does the 24-hour market benefit FX traders? It allows them to react to real-time news. If something happens overnight, a stock market investor has to spend a sleepless night until the market opens the following morning. An FX trader can react immediately and go to bed with peace of mind. The assumption is the faster we can react, the better. As a professional FX trader who spent years staring at FX prices for many hours a day and got the latest news faster than most retail traders, I concluded that this is a fallacy. It's really hard to know how the FX market will react to news. Sometimes the market reaction can be violent to start with and then reverse just as quickly. Other times the market hardly moves, even though you think it should.

Then there are the cases of "buy the rumor, sell the fact," when an anticipated piece of news hits the wire and the market does a boomerang. The possibilities are numerous, but you get the picture. The 24-hour market that offers that quick reaction isn't a good reason for you to trade FX.

Another draw for traders is how the thin spread of the liquid FX market lowers transaction costs, though together with a high-leverage, 24-hour market, this tends to encourage overtrading. The key question on FX trading isn't about liquidity and costs, it's about whether the FX market offers a better chance to make money than the stock market. The answer is negative.

A good reference point for this is *The Wall Street Journal*, which used to produce a daily table showing the best fund performances. When the table was showing FX funds, it was hard not to notice that the top FX funds regularly performed worse than the top stock and bond funds. This was despite FX funds using leverage whereas stock and bond funds don't.

Which fundamentals affect the FX market? Most economists agree that GDP, interest rates, and trade balance are some of the more important elements. What's not so clear is which ones are more important or how they affect a currency's value. The fundamentals that FX traders focus on are a moving target. There are times when traders pay attention to interest rates and monetary policy; there are times when they watch trade figures closely; there are times when they focus on political developments. No one knows when the focus will switch, and it's often not immediately obvious that a switch is happening. Sometimes there's no clear focus on fundamentals at all. Instead the market concentrates on other issues, such as technical support or resistance, or where the big stop-loss orders are.

In an economics textbook, if a country raises interest rates, the currency will strengthen, but in reality, it's not uncommon for an emerging country to raise interest rates only to see its currency weaken. Perhaps FX traders were disappointed with a tepid hike; perhaps they were spooked by a sharp rate increase; perhaps it came down to pure panic, and nothing could stop traders from selling the currency. Interest rates alone have many permutations that can move the FX market.

The FX market is extremely complicated. A currency's value isn't determined purely by its country's fundamentals; it has to be measured against another country's fundamentals and currency. It's all relative. If a country's fundamentals are bad, the currency won't necessarily weaken. US economic fundamentals were bad in the 1980s, with record-high budget and trade deficits, and the market consensus was that the dollar would decline. George Soros, the hedge fund legend and philanthropist, had a contrarian theory. He thought that a huge trade deficit, expansionary fiscal policy, and tight monetary policy would be bullish for the US dollar. He was right; the dollar strengthened instead.

Soros became famous worldwide in 1992 by "breaking the Bank of England." His $10 billion wager that the pound would weaken made him and his hedge fund investors a cool $1 billion. With a career spanning more than five decades, Soros has made tens of billions of dollars for himself and his investors over the years, although as successful as he is, he was probably wrong more often than he was right in the FX market. Soros made money from Thai baht during the Asian financial crisis of 1997. He went on to bet that the Indonesian rupiah and Korean won would strengthen, but as the crisis spread from Thailand to other Asian countries, these currencies fell steeply and he lost more than he had made in Thai baht.

According to Soros, the FX market is a seven- or eight-factor market, unlike the stock market, which is a two-factor market. Clearly the man who made a killing in the FX market understands just how complex that market is.

Julian Robertson, another hedge fund titan in the 1990s, lost his shirt when the Japanese yen strengthened at an unprecedented speed in 1998. What separates these billionaire traders from us isn't that they get it right most of the time—indeed, they often get it wrong; the difference is they're never stubborn and they don't argue with the market. They readily admit when they're wrong, cut their losses, and move on. When the odds are greatly in their favor, they pile on hard and score a gigantic win.

It's clear that currency has an important effect on the stock market. What's not so clear is how the two interact with each other and how a currency effect can be offset by other factors. A weak currency due to the printing of money is good for the stock market—the currency is losing its value, and everyone wants to convert it into other assets. When President Nixon took the US off the gold standard in August 1971, the US stock market surged. If a country is facing a crisis, however, a weak currency and weak stock market can run hand in hand. Foreign investors sell their stocks and convert the proceeds to US dollars, thus weakening both the stock market and the currency. Locals who want to preserve the value of their money sell their own currency and convert it to US dollars or other sound and stable currencies. This happened during the Asian financial crisis, when countries such as Thailand and Indonesia saw both their currencies and stock markets fall sharply.

There's no clear relationship between the FX market and the stock market. On September 22, 1985, representatives from the US, the UK, West Germany, France, and Japan met at the Plaza Hotel in New York to sign an agreement aimed at weakening the US dollar, which had doubled in the previous five years. The historic Plaza Accord, named after the hotel where it was signed, halved the US dollar over the next two years. Despite the extreme volatility of the US dollar, the bullish US stock market that started in 1982 went charging on until the 1987 crash. The lowering of interest rates from the early 1980s through to 1986 seemed to have a bigger impact on the stock market than the dollar.

Since China loosened its peg to the US dollar in 2005, a weak currency has been bad for the Chinese stock market and a strong currency has been good for it. When the yuan appreciated by

2 percent on July 21, 2005, the Shanghai stock market jumped by 15 percent. Profits at Chinese companies had been boosted, as the raw materials they needed to import were priced in US dollars and had therefore become cheaper. Ten years later, on August 10, 2015, China shocked the world with a 2 percent devaluation. The Chinese stock market slid over the next few months until early 2016.

The FX market can be volatile at times, especially when it comes to some emerging market currencies. If a currency isn't free floating, it can be subjected to a sudden devaluation and revaluation. This happened to the British pound and the Swedish krona in 1992, the Mexican and Argentinian pesos in 1995, Asian currencies in 1997, the Russian ruble in 1998, the Brazilian real in 1999, and the Argentinian peso once again 2002. Some currencies saw devaluations two or even three times within the space of just one or two years: the Finnish markka in 1991 and 1992, the Kazakhstani tenge in 2014 and 2015, the Egyptian pound in March and November 2016, and the Azerbaijani manat in 2015 and 2017. In January 2015, the Swiss franc jumped more than 20 percent in less than an hour when the central bank unexpectedly gave up defending the ceiling.

When calculating a currency gain and loss, things can get a bit confusing. Currencies always come in pairs—mainly the US dollar versus another currency. Using USD versus JPY as an illustration, when the exchange rate moves from 1 USD = 100 JPY to 1 USD = 150 JPY, the US dollar has appreciated 50 percent against the Japanese yen. However, to a Japanese tourist in America, their spending power hasn't decreased by 50 percent. Previously, it took 100 JPY to buy 1 USD. Now, the same 100 JPY can be changed to (100/150) = 0.666 USD. The tourist's purchasing power has dropped by one-third rather than one-half.

The same goes for overseas investing, and it's important to keep the issue of currency risk in mind whenever you invest elsewhere. If you choose not to hedge the FX risk, the FX movement can either enhance or reduce your stock returns. Let's do some simple math on the total return you can expect if you invest overseas.

If the foreign stock you bought has gone up by 50 percent and your currency has gone down by 10 percent, your return isn't 40 percent but rather $[(1 + 0.5)*(1 - 0.1)] - 1 = 0.35$, or 35 percent. If you make a 100 percent return on your overseas investments but your currency loses 50 percent, you break even.

FEDERAL RESERVE

Unlike Britain's central bank—the Bank of England, which was founded in 1694—the US Federal Reserve, commonly known as the Fed, is relatively young, having been established in December 1913. The foundations for the modern Fed were laid in March 1951 though, when the US Treasury and the Fed reached an agreement under which the Treasury would look after government debt management and the Fed would focus on monetary policy.

Today the Fed has a dual mandate: price stability, which means low inflation—near 2 percent but not over—and maximum employment. To achieve its mandate, it has two tools to conduct monetary policy. First, the Fed sets the discount rate and the fed funds rate. The discount rate is the interest rate at which the Fed lends to banks, while the fed funds rate is the interest rate at which banks lend their reserve balances to one another on an overnight basis. These two rates generally move in lockstep. Second, the Fed conducts open market operations by buying and selling government bonds and bills. When the Fed buys bonds and bills, it injects money into the banking system. Selling bonds and bills has the opposite effect of soaking money up from the banking system.

The discount rate and fed funds rate are decided by the Federal Open Market Committee (FOMC), which meets eight times a year. The FOMC is made up of seven board governors and the presidents of the twelve regional federal reserve banks. The twelve presidents have a rotation among them, as only five can vote at any one time. The FOMC makes decisions by majority rule, but in practice, the Fed chairman usually leads, and the others mostly fall in line. Ever since Alan Greenspan became chairman in 1987, most of the meetings have ended with a unanimous vote or just one or two dissents.

All Fed governors are appointed by the US president for a 14-year term. The long-term appointment of Fed governors is to ensure they can focus on making the right decisions without worrying about political pressure. Fed chairs, on the other hand, only serve a four-year appointment.

The Fed is subject to oversight by Congress, and the Fed chair is required to submit a semi-annual report on monetary policy. Officially, the Fed is set up as an independent institution to make its own monetary decisions, however that didn't stop a number of US presidents, including Ronald Reagan (1911–2004) and Donald Trump, from trying to meddle with its policies. Whether the Fed is truly independent has been a contentious issue ever since its formation.

In terms of influencing financial markets, the Fed is arguably the most important institution in the world. Some investors go as far as to say that only the Fed matters. It's not an exaggeration to say that the Fed's firepower in financial markets is more potent than US military might. Other big central banks, such as the European Central Bank (ECB), the People's Bank of China (PBOC), and the Bank of Japan (BOJ), simply pale in comparison. In property investing, the key is "location, location, location." In stock investing, it's "Federal Reserve, Federal Reserve, Federal Reserve."

Ironically, though the Fed's focus is domestic, its actions often have a greater effect on foreign countries than they do on the US itself. One of the main reasons the Fed matters so much internationally is that the US dollar is the world's reserve currency and most commodities, from oil to gold, are priced in US dollars. The Fed's words and actions have a direct effect on the value of the US dollar and in turn affect all other countries' currencies and economies.

In December 1996, Alan Greenspan, Fed chairman at the time,

gave a speech in which he uttered the now famous phrase "irrational exuberance," which he coined while in his bathtub. Japan's stock market—the first to be able to react to the two words—promptly dropped 3 percent. Hong Kong's market followed with a similar 3 percent drop, and Germany's with 4 percent. The Dow Jones opened 2 percent lower but recovered almost all by the end of the day. The warning from Mr. Greenspan was soon forgotten. The US stock market, irrational or not, continued its climb until 2000.

Years later, in May 2013, then chairman of the Fed Ben Bernanke hinted at an end to quantitative easing, a monetary policy through which a central bank increases the money supply by purchasing government bonds from the markets. Panic swept across emerging markets, from South Africa to Turkey, Brazil, and Thailand. The concern was that a reduction in stimulus would create a vicious cycle in which the stronger US dollar would lead even more money to flow the US's way. Both the currency and stock markets of these countries plummeted in the following months—an episode now known as "taper tantrum."

There's no doubt that the Fed's actions on interest rates have huge impacts on financial markets, but how big and how long the time lag is isn't clear. It's hard to predict how the markets will react to rate changes, and it's even harder to try to time the market. In 1928, the Fed started to raise interest rates, but the huge stock market bull run continued until the following September. The same thing happened in 1987: the Fed tightened monetary policy early on in the year, but the big crash didn't come until October. More recently, the Fed hiked rates from 2015 to 2018 but reversed them in 2019. The stock market kept breaking new highs regardless.

In general, both the stock and bond markets will head lower if a fast and furious rate rise, prompted by inflation, breaks the economic boom and earnings. To combat inflation, in 1973, the Fed tightened monetary policy and brought about what was then the worst bear market since the Great Depression. The Fed also responded to the second oil shock by raising interest rates in 1979 and 1980. The stock market only bottomed in 1982.

If a rate rise is slow and measured, it is still negative for bond markets—higher interest rates always cause bond prices to go down—but it is usually positive for stock markets. The rises in interest rates from 2003 to 2007 and 2015 to 2018 are good examples of this. If a measured rate rise is due to an expanding economy and higher earnings, it is positive. Alan Greenspan observed that incremental tightening reinforces the perceived power of the boom and is therefore likely to raise stock prices rather than lower them.

When the Fed eases interest rates, this helps the stock markets. It doesn't necessarily mean the stock markets will go up; sometimes it just slows down or lessens the severity of a bear market. Investors shouldn't just jump straight into the stock market when the Fed first lowers interest rates.

In May 1921 the Fed lowered interest rates. The Dow Jones reacted with a 20 percent drop before it bottomed on August 22. In March 1949, interest rate easing caused the index to decline by 10 percent before it hit bottom on June 13. In August 1982, Mexico defaulted. The stock market responded with a big rally because the Fed introduced massive interest rates easing. That was the beginning of a long bull market, which lasted until the 1987 "Black Monday" crash. On January 3, 2001, after six rate increases and in between its scheduled meetings, the Fed cut interest rates unexpectedly. The Nasdaq responded with its biggest upward move ever of 14.2 percent on a record volume. It was a bear market bounce. The bear market carried on until the Nasdaq hit bottom in late 2002, losing around 80 percent from its peak in March 2000. When the Fed came to the rescue and cut rates in late 2007 and early 2008, the stock market responded with enthusiasm, however the situation deteriorated quickly in the coming months, and those investors who bought at the first sign of easing were to regret it later when the S&P 500 crashed by about 50 percent from its peak.

Warren Buffett, who would prefer to be remembered as a good teacher than the best investor, understands the importance of interest rates and their effect on both the economy and the earnings of companies. To help folks like us understand interest rates better, he uses the analogy of gravity—the higher the interest rates, the higher the gravitational force. The economic plane can still fly with higher gravity, but it needs a more powerful engine. Earnings can also rise with higher gravity but only up to a point. When gravity is too high, everything crashes back to earth. He's a good teacher indeed.

"Fed put" is a term that has frequently appeared in financial articles over the past few decades. It's thought to have come about after Alan Greenspan became Fed chairman in 1987. The "put" refers to put options, which allow the option buyer to sell an underlying asset at a predetermined price. Put options offer buyers protection against a big drop in prices. Say an investor owns a stock that's currently trading at $80. To protect themselves, they buy a put option with an exercise price of $75. No matter how low the stock price goes—even if it hits zero—the investor is able to sell the stock at $75 before the option expires.

The Fed put concept means that investors are protected by the Fed against a big drop in stock prices. Whenever there's a crisis, investors can count on the Fed to come to the rescue by cutting interest rates, like in 2001 after the internet bubble burst and in 2008 when Lehman Brothers went bankrupt.

As powerful as the Fed is, however, it can't stop a bear market or prevent a crisis. Investors still have to shoulder the losses. Some claim that Fed put creates a moral hazard and leads investors to be less careful with their money than they otherwise would be. This is probably true, but the Fed is given a mandate to act as the lender of last resort and has authority in an emergency. Firefighters must fight a fire—they can't watch and debate whether extinguishing a house fire might make the neighbors less careful.

INVERTED YIELD CURVES

Yield curves are graphical representations that show the interest rates of similar bonds of varying maturities. We can plot a yield curve by using the y axis for interest rates and the x axis for maturities. In most cases, we see an upward-sloping graph, which shows that as the tenor gets longer, the interest rate gets higher. This makes good sense—the longer the tenor, the higher the risk. Borrowers are more likely to renege on a debt over a longer period, and investors are right to demand higher interest rates for higher risks. Investors also want some compensation for the erosion caused by inflation. Such upward-sloping yield curves don't happen all the time though. Occasionally, the curve is "inverted," when the shorter-tenor interest rates are higher than the longer-tenor.

The most watched yield curve is US government bonds. Short-term US interest rates are set by the Fed. Longer-term interest rates are set by market forces and are based on the collective economic and inflation outlook of millions of investors. When market participants think economic clouds are gathering, they tend to buy bonds, which are considered safer than stocks. Remember how bond prices have an inverse relationship with interest rates? They move in opposite directions, which pushes yields lower. When the longer-tenor yields fall below the shorter-tenor, we get an inverted yield curve. It's widely believed that this is the bond market's way of "signaling" short-term interest rates are too high for the deteriorating health of the economy. This can precipitate a recession, which forces the

Fed to cut short-term interest rates.

It's also widely believed that an inverted yield curve is a great predictor of recessions and bear markets—there's been one before every US recession since World War II. Some argue that they actually caused the recessions because an inverted yield curve dampens the willingness of banks to lend—banks' borrowing costs (based on short-term interest rates) are higher than its lending rates (based on long-term interest rates), therefore they'll lose money if the yield curve is inverted. They'd rather keep the money than lend it at a loss. This drop in lending and credit then slows down economic activities.

Despite its widely cited "100 percent record" in predicting recessions, there are a few problems with using an inverted yield curve to predict a bear market. Some countries, including the UK, Germany, and Japan, have all seen inversions in the past without suffering a recession. On top of that, market commentators, have struggled to agree which inversion is more important—three months versus 10 years or two years versus 10 years? The majority seem to go for two years versus 10 years, as this appears to give less false signals.

The next question is how long the inversion needs to last in order to make it a good predictor. Some studies have shown that the 10-year interest rate needs to be half a percent or more lower than the three-month rate and that the inversions need to last a few months. Then there's the problem of the time lag between inversions and recessions. The shortest lag is around one to three quarters, while the longer is two to three years, with the average lag lasting about five to six quarters. Finally, the relationship between recessions and bear markets isn't clear. There have been times when a recession wasn't followed by a bear market. The time lag between a recession and a bear market is, again, hard to predict.

The first time there's an inversion, whether it's three months versus 10 years or two years versus 10 years, the media will report this widely followed indicator extensively. From there, we have to wait to see whether it lasts and just how inverted the curve is. The longer it lasts and the more inverted it is, the more likely it is that a recession is coming. We also need to wait and see when the recession is going to happen and when the bear market is going to arrive. Historically, while waiting for all of this to play out, the US stock market has risen by 15 percent on average. So, despite the 100 percent prediction record, using inverted yield curves to make investment decisions is full of uncertainties and no one can be 100 percent sure that the 100 percent record won't be broken in the next inversion.

INFLATION AND DEFLATION

Most of us understand inflation well. Things get more expensive year after year, whether that's food, rent, entertainment, or transportation. To people all over the world, inflation is as certain as death and taxes. But prices can also go down. The Great Depression of the 1930s saw many countries facing deflation, and Japan has been experiencing deflation since its property and stock market bubble popped in 1989. What causes inflation and deflation? It's partly psychological—the fact that people expect prices will advance or decline contributes to price movements; it becomes self-perpetuating.

Inflation is a form of partial defaulting, as it allows all debtors, governments included, to pay their debts in a currency that has less purchasing power than when they took their loans out. When politicians have to decide between the next election and the next generation, the choice is clear. Governments can print money to fund their spending or pay their debts. The temporary prosperity brought on by more fiat money might just buy enough time to get the politicians reelected.

Regardless of the intentions behind it, the action of printing money can lead to inflation. Asset prices rise, as everyone realizes their money would be safer in material goods. The prices of property, gold, stocks, and even stamps can all go up. However, if inflation is due to a rise in the cost of materials such as oil and other commodities, and not the printing of money, the impact on stock prices is opposite.

The cure for cost-push inflation is higher interest rates, which can bring all sorts of negative consequences to the financial markets. Higher interest rates slow economic activity and lower corporate profits. Prior to the 1970s, market wisdom in the US was that stock was a hedge against inflation. It was believed that many companies had pricing power to pass on the higher costs to consumers and that some companies were even able to increase their profit margin by raising prices more than the cost increase. The truth was that companies were not able to pass on the higher cost—or at least not the full higher cost—to consumers, who were naturally more selective in what they bought and who balked at higher prices.

Another issue is that higher interest rates during periods of inflation mean higher interest expenses for companies. The belief that stocks were a good hedge against inflation was totally discredited when oil prices and inflation jumped in 1973 and again in 1980, bringing the stock market to its knees each time. Inflation in itself doesn't cause the stock market to head lower; it's the cure—higher interest rates—that become the straw that breaks the camel's back.

Why is inflation so devastating to stock prices? The "teacher" Buffett called it a giant corporate tapeworm. In his 1981 shareholder letter, he wrote: "That tapeworm preemptively consumes its requisite daily diet of investment dollars regardless of the health of the host organism. Whatever the level of reported profits (even if nil), more dollars for receivables, inventory and fixed assets are continuously required by the business to merely match the unit volume of the previous year. The less prosperous the enterprise, the greater the proportion of available sustenance claimed by the tapeworm. Under present [high inflation] conditions, a business earning 8 or 10 percent on equity often has no leftovers for expansion, debt reduction or "real" dividends. The tapeworm of inflation simply cleans the plate."

On August 6, 1979, Paul Volcker (1927–2019) was appointed Fed chairman by President Jimmy Carter. His determination to tame inflation saw him push the fed funds rate up sharply to 20 percent. As a result, the economy went into recession. Volcher is forever remembered as the towering Fed chairman (he was two meters tall) who slayed the inflation dragon. Indeed, inflation in America has been low ever since. Many explanations have been put forward as to why it has remained low for so long. Some think it's due to an increase in productivity brought on by new technology and the rise of cheap labor in countries such as China and India.

A weak currency, it's widely believed, will bring about inflation, as imports become more expensive. There was no such surge following the 1985 Plaza Accord, however, the US dollar weakening by nearly half in the subsequent two years. The US dollar has, in fact, moved up and down in big waves over the years with little effect on inflation. The Japanese yen has also seen big moves up and down over the last three decades and weakened by about 30 percent in the three years from 2012 to 2015. Despite this, it's still mired in deflation. On the other hand, some countries, such as Argentina and Egypt, do experience inflation surges when their currencies weaken.

Even more concerning than inflation is hyperinflation. Put simply, hyperinflation is inflation on steroids. It's of modern vintage because it can only happen with paper money. When gold and silver were used as currency, there was no way these precious metals could be produced in huge quantities in a short space of time. Paper money, on the other hand, can be printed quickly. During hyperinflation, everyone wants to hoard goods —any goods—because of how fast prices are rising. This in turn sends prices even higher. It becomes a vicious cycle. Savings become worthless, and no one wants to put any money in the bank. Banks have no deposits, and businesses have no capital. Governments, deprived of revenue, turn to printing more money, which adds further oil to the fire of rising prices. There are some winners in this dire situation though—debtors, who can pay down debts easily with the ever-increasing money, and exporters, who receive hard foreign currency, which increases in value as the local currency falls.

One of the most absurd episodes of hyperinflation happened in Germany in the 1920s. At its height, workers were often paid twice a day, as prices were rising hourly! Legend has it they would load up wheelbarrows full of money just to buy a loaf of bread. This unfortunate economic hardship contributed to the rise of Adolf Hitler and the German people's paranoia about inflation and the use of credit.

Hyperinflation also occurred in many South American countries from the 1960s through to the 1980s and, more recently, in Venezuela and Zimbabwe. In 2008, the Zimbabwean dollar plunged from a rate of 10 to the US dollar in August to 1,000 in October. The country's stock market gained 500 times its value as locals rushed to turn the fiat money into assets and goods. By 2009, the South African rand and the US dollar were being used, as Zimbabwe had started printing 100 billion dollar notes.

So, that's inflation. What about deflation? For most people, who only experience rising prices in their lifetime, it's somewhat of an alien concept. If inflation is bad, shouldn't that mean deflation is good? The short answer is no—it can be just as negative, sometimes even worse.

During deflation, stocks naturally decline—as the value of money rises, both earnings and balance sheet values are reduced. Businesses suffer from excess capacity and tepid demand. As a result, a dividend can be cut or even totally eliminated.

One of the most famous instances of deflation is the Great Depression, when stock prices were decimated. Between 1929 and 1932, the Dow Jones plunged 89 percent—by far its worst-ever drop. But while it's clear that stocks are affected by deflation, its effect on bonds is less clear. Interest rates are low during deflation, and this is positive for bond prices in general. But when investors are worried about the ability of corporate bonds to pay coupons and even principal, bond prices will decline. Deflation makes bond payments more difficult each year, as they become more expensive.

So, if both stocks and bonds are affected, what can you do to prosper in a deflationary environment? An easy, good hedge is to live off cash. It's a better solution than buying stocks and bonds, as the income they produce isn't enough to cover the decline in their values. This logical course of action can be psychologically challenging, as many people don't like the idea of living off capital and having no income. In reality, cash can be invaluable during periods of deflation, as you can pick up some good companies at bargain prices.

Generally, deflation is less disastrous for individuals than infla-tion, provided people still have a job. It usually occurs during hard times when factories have too much capacity. This tends to lead to a jump in unemployment. Deflation is less painful to turn around than inflation, largely because the methods used, such as lowering interest rates, have less political resistance. In 2003, when Alan Greenspan, Fed chairman at the time, cut interest rates to almost zero in the aftermath of the internet bubble burst, he argued the low rate was partly to insure against the US falling into deflation. Lowering interest rates to zero and introducing massive quantitative easing measures hasn't stopped entrenching, persistent deflation in Japan, however. It's been going on there for 30 years and counting.

HISTORY

"If past history was all that is needed to play the game of money, the richest people would be librarians." This witty quote from Warren Buffett seems to dismiss the importance of history. Sure, knowing history alone won't make us rich, but for investors, the wisdom it can impart is invaluable. If I'd known the history of gold and financial markets better, I wouldn't have bought my tiny gold bar or participated blindly in the dot-com bubble. Knowledge of history expands our life experiences and helps us view current news and events with the right perspective. It reminds us not to extrapolate what's happening currently or to assume that either doom and gloom are here to stay or the party will never end.

If you've read Ray Dalio's books and articles, you'll know that he's a great believer in history. The timeless, universal principles and lessons he derived from history were the key to propelling his hedge fund, Bridgewater, to its status as the biggest in the world.

Many investors are wary of major world events. They choose to stay on the sidelines of the stock market whenever there are uncertainties. They'd rather be safe than sorry; they're always waiting for a better time when confidence is higher. Other investors are fearful of uncertainties and dump their stocks when geopolitical tensions or natural disasters hit. But if there's one thing that's certain in the stock market, it's that there'll always be uncertainties. The fact remains that while the world experiences many setbacks, disasters, crises, and wars, the progress of humankind, the growth of the economy, and the rise of stock markets are unstoppable. After reading this chapter, I hope you'll be able to look at the big picture—at history—and know that stock markets are resilient; I hope it will give you enough confidence that you aren't easily shaken out of good stocks and funds and that you'll have the courage to hold on to them for years or even decades.

Over the course of US history, the sitting presidents have found their lives endangered many times. Some sadly perished. In 1955, President Dwight D. Eisenhower (1890–1969) suffered a heart attack. The stock market plummeted 6 percent. Fortunately, he recovered quickly, and so did the market. On Friday, November 22, 1963, President John F. Kennedy (1917–1963) was assassinated in Dallas. The stock market fell around 3 percent that day. On Tuesday, November 26, after closing on the Monday for the funeral, the stock market wiped out all the previous week's losses and then some. On March 30, 1981, President Ronald Reagan was shot at close range. He was wounded but recovered. The stock market only dropped 1.2 percent.

The story is similar when it comes to natural disasters. While they can be devastating to lives, livelihoods, and the local economy, the effect on global stock markets is usually minimal and temporary, even in the most serious cases. The tragic tsunami that swept across many Asian countries on Boxing Day 2004, which cost more than two hundred thousand lives, is a case in point. One year later, Hurricane Katrina caused huge damage to the Gulf Coast, making it the costliest natural disaster in US history in terms of human impact. With the exception of insurance companies, the US stock market hardly reacted. And while Japan's Kobe earthquake in 1995 and tsunami in 2011 caused the Nikkei to plunge in the following days, the negative impact on the global financial markets didn't last long.

Another constant in human history is terrorism. We often see protesters around the world wearing Guy Fawkes masks that feature a sly grin, mustache, and goatee. Fawkes (1570–1606) was, in fact, a 16th century terrorist. Terrorism isn't a new phenomenon, and it didn't start after 9/11—there were just as many terrorist acts before. In 1972, 11 Israeli athletes were killed by Palestinian Liberation Organization (PLO) terrorists at the Olympic Village in Munich. In 1983, a terrorist explosion killed 241 US marines in Beirut. In the 1970s and 80s, the PLO and other terrorist groups routinely hijacked commercial planes and also targeted cruise ships. Post-9/11 terrorist acts include the Bali bombings in 2002, the Madrid train bombings in 2004, the London tube bombings in 2005, and the Paris bombings and shootings in 2015. With the exception of 9/11, none of these terrorist acts had a lasting impact on global financial markets.

A great example of how investors can reap rewards in the long term and how those who would rather be "safe than sorry" can actually end up being "safe and sorry" is the history of Hong Kong's stock market benchmark, the Hang Seng Index. The Hang Seng started life on November 24, 1969, closing that day at 158 points. In its half-century-long history, its best year was 1972, when it surged almost 150 percent, and its worst was 1974, when it was down 60 percent. The index was hit hard by the first oil crisis in 1973, which decimated more than 90 percent of its total value in 1973 and 1974.

When Britain and China were negotiating the future of Hong Kong in 1982, the Hang Seng dropped by half in just six months. With talks in 1983 failing to make progress, the Hong Kong dollar plummeted to its lowest value in history. Panic buying of the US dollar turned into panic buying in supermarkets. Wealthier Hong Kong people made plans to migrate to Vancouver or Melbourne. On March 29, 1984, the index tumbled a further 8 percent when Jardine Matheson, a conglomerate with a long history in Hong Kong, announced it was to become a Bermuda holding company because of political uncertainty over the territory's future.

On October 19, 1987, even before Wall Street suffered its biggest-ever daily crash later that day—Black Monday—the Hang Seng dropped 11 percent. When stock markets around the world crashed in the aftermath, Hong Kong decided to close its exchange for the rest of the week. The inevitable crash still came, and when the Hang Seng reopened on October 26, it lost a whopping 33.3 percent in a single day!

The events in China's Tiananmen Square in 1989 brought yet another crash to the Hang Seng. On June 5, the day after the crackdown in Beijing, the index lost about 22 percent of its value. One year later, it had risen by about 50 percent. The best day for the Hang Seng was October 29, 1997, at the height of Asian financial crisis, when it rose by 19 percent, although that didn't cancel out the downward trend that month, the index closing 30 percent lower than it had started.

Overall, the Hang Seng has risen strongly over its history, gaining more than 40 percent in 1986, 1991, 1999, and 2009. In 1993, it soared more than 100 percent, and in 2003, in the midst of the SARS outbreak, it gained 35 percent. A few years later, in 2007, while the credit squeeze saw the index move lower, it rebounded by about 40 percent within just six weeks. It did, however, go on to lose almost half its value the following year during the global financial crisis. The 2010s saw a less volatile index, with five years producing single-digit percentage returns.

How has the Hang Seng performed overall in its 50-year history? On November 25, 2019, it closed at 26,993—170 times higher than when it started! Those who missed the boat or sold based on any uncertainties along the way are truly sorry now. However, while the Hang Seng has performed better than all other major benchmark indexes during this period, it has also been the most volatile. To enjoy a fantastic long-term return, one has to treat the Hang Seng like a roller coaster ride—there are some big ups and downs, and lots of twists and turns, but in the end, it turns out pretty alright.

As investors, we constantly have to deal with big events happening all over the world. Each day and each new year present new challenges, uncertainties, and risks. In the midst of negative events and geopolitical risks, it's tempting for investors to try and "play it safe" by holding cash rather than stocks. But let's rewind a bit and look at what happened to the stock markets during some of the more eventful periods in history. Keep in mind that these events were all headline news in their day. Just like the protracted trade war between the US and China that started in 2018, most of them lasted for weeks, if not months. Stock markets watched each one like a hawk, and short-term volatility spiked as they unfolded. Opinions and predictions were offered by the media as to how the events would develop and what investors should do to protect themselves. Usually that meant selling stocks and holding cash, hedging the stocks, or switching to defensive stocks, like utilities and consumer staples. It sounded like sensible, prudent advice. But was it actually good advice?

Let's start with 1968. North Korea seized a US navy ship and held 83 people on board on suspicion of spying. In the US and the western world, anti-Vietnam War protests were gaining strength and becoming more violent. The US was committing more troops in Vietnam, and the death toll rose sharply. In April, Martin Luther King (1929–1968) was shot dead, and a wave of riots swept across more than 100 US cities. Two months later, Senator Robert F. Kennedy (1925–1968) faced the same fate. In August, Russian tanks were sent to Czechoslovakia to quell protests. At the end of the year, the S&P 500 still edged up 8 percent.

In 1979, the Iranian revolution and the US hostage crisis further weakened the US's stance in the world. This, along with the Vietnam War, the Watergate scandal, the huge budget and trade deficit, and the rise of Japan, contributed to the consensus view that the US was facing permanent decline. Elsewhere, the Soviet Union invaded Afghanistan and China invaded Vietnam. According to some, the world was falling apart. Gold prices vindicated their views, surging to an all-time high of more than $850 per ounce the following January. The stock market didn't seem to worry much though, and the S&P 500 closed 12 percent higher.

The beginning of 1995 saw a massive earthquake in Kobe, Japan. Thousands of lives were lost and economic damages totaled tens of billions of US dollars. The earthquake sent a financial shockwave all the way to Singapore and caused a rogue trader to lose enough money to bring down Barings Bank, one of the UK's oldest financial institutions. In Oklahoma, a terrorist bomb killed 168 and injured hundreds more. A budget deadlock in the US saw federal workers sent home, as the US government had no money to pay them. Meanwhile, in Mexico, the peso suffered a sudden devaluation, which morphed into the "Tequila Crisis." The US government and the Fed, fearing the crisis could spread to the US and the wider world, stepped in to coordinate rescue efforts. The stock market surged by a third.

So, if a single year is too short a time frame to have a significant impact on the stock market, what about a decade? Let's take a look at the media's narrative over the years and how the stock market reacted.

Take the 2010s. What can you remember of the decade? Brexit, Trump winning the US presidency, the trade war between the US and China? What else? Actually, a lot more happened then most of us can recall.

The decade started with a bang—a volcanic eruption in Iceland, which brought air travel in Europe to a standstill for several days. At the same time, the media and investors alike were wondering whether the quick, strong rebound of 2009 could last —the economic recovery was widely considered to be fragile, and the widening US and western world budget deficits brought about by bank bailouts were a big worry.

On March 10, 2011, a tsunami hit Japan. It was the most devastating natural disaster to strike the country for decades, and there were grave concerns about leaks from the Fukushima nuclear plant. Later that year, the US faced a debt ceiling crisis. The financial markets were worried that the US might do the unthinkable and default on its debt. As a result, Standard and Poor's downgraded US government bonds from the highest rating of AAA. Europe was facing difficulties too, marred in a crisis that started in Greece but spread to Portugal, Ireland, and Spain. Collectively—and rather cheekily—the four countries became known by the acronym PIGS. As the eurozone debt crisis intensified, even Italy and France's abilities to service their debts were called into doubt. The crisis that had previously hit Asia was happening all over again in Europe, but this time it was on a much bigger scale.

Two thousand and eleven also saw the Arab Spring sweep across the Middle East, with pro-democracy protests taking place in Tunisia, Egypt, Libya, and other states. In Syria, the uprising turned into civil war. Over the course of the year, the S&P 500 plummeted about 20 percent, and many stock markets, including France, Germany, Brazil, China, and India, turned into bear markets. Gold surged to an all-time high of over $1,900, and US 10-year Treasury bonds fell below 2 percent for the first time in more than 60 years. The financial markets were worried about a "double-dip" recession.

2012 started with Standard and Poor's downgrading France as well as eight other eurozone countries. The agency blamed the move on the failure of eurozone leaders to deal with the debt crisis. Eventually, the eurozone and the IMF backed a second Greek bailout of 130 billion euros, with Mario Draghi, president of the European Central Bank (ECB) at the time, saying: "Within our mandate, the ECB is ready to do whatever it takes to preserve the euro. And believe me, it will be enough." The financial markets agreed, and the eurozone debt crisis abated somewhat.

The following year, the media started speculating as to whether the bull market that had started in March 2009 was aging and wondering whether its valuation was overstretched. By mid-year, global markets had tumbled over concerns about a credit crunch in China as well as the Fed's hint about reducing the size of its monthly bond purchases. Emerging markets were hit especially hard, with countries like Indonesia, India, Turkey, and Brazil seeing their stocks and currencies plunge in the following months. The 10-year Treasury yield jumped from 1.6 to 2.2 percent in a month, and the October deadline to raise the debt ceiling in the US made the markets nervous.

In 2014, Crimea was annexed by Russia. Tensions between Russia and the West rose sharply. As the stock markets continued to hit new highs, many economists and analysts warned that stock prices had been significantly, even absurdly, overvalued for a long time. They felt that investors had been greedy and were acting irrationally. Fed chair Janet Yellen agreed—she was worried that asset prices had reached unsustainable levels. The same year, record withdrawals of junk bond funds and a spike in junk bond interest rates meant stock investors would have been well advised to run for cover—better to be safe than sorry.

The eurozone debt crisis continued to haunt the markets in 2015. Meanwhile, China's stock market was experiencing a bubble, which peaked in June that year and was followed swiftly afterwards by a crash. In August, China shocked the world when it devalued its currency by 2 percent—not that big a move in the currency market but a significant one for the tightly controlled Chinese yuan. The world began to worry about the slowing Chinese economy. The price of copper dropped to its lowest level since 2009, and stock markets the world over fell. They continued to head south for the rest of the year.

Two thousand and sixteen started with China's stock market rout, which in turn rippled through the international stock markets. Many commodities, including oil, hit lows. In June, UK citizens unexpectedly voted for Brexit and duly sent financial markets, especially the UK and European banks, into a tailspin. Spain and Italy's stock markets tumbled more than 12 percent in a day. The financial markets recovered in days. Trump's triumph as the next US president also gave the markets another scare, with the Mexican peso sliding as much as 13 percent. The subsequent recoveries were even quicker than Brexit, and a "reflation trade frenzy" soon took hold.

The following year was uneventful, and the stock market went up 20 percent with barely a peep of turbulence. President Trump passed a major tax cut. Across 2016 and 2017, the S&P 500 didn't suffer anything more than a 5 percent dip.

In January 2018, President Trump started the trade war with China. On February 6, US stocks suffered their biggest drop in 6 1/2 years, with the S&P 500 down over 4 percent due to worries that inflation would force interest rates higher. The last quarter saw US stocks tumble, with the Nasdaq falling into a bear market and the S&P 500 nearly following suit.

The last year of the decade saw the trade war escalate and the hope of a deal dashed before then being revived. The ever-erratic President Trump and his plethora of tweets sent stock investors chasing shadows. The world's financial markets were also watching the drama of Brexit closely. Big, violent protests took place in countries across the world, from Hong Kong to Chile, Algeria to Bolivia, Iran to Iraq. Donald Trump became the third president in US history to be impeached.

With all this turmoil, how did the stock market do overall from 2010 to 2019? The S&P 500 rose by 185 percent, meaning $1 invested had turned into $2.85. The return in the 1990s was even better, with $1 turning into $4 by the end of the decade. The decade in between—the 2000s—is the only one in history that saw the US stock market go down, with the S&P 500 dropping 23 percent. The reason? The period started with the biggest bubble in US history and ended with the global financial crisis—an unfortunate, uncanny combination of the biggest boom and bust since the Great Depression. If the stock market hadn't recovered strongly in 2009, the decade would have ended with a much deeper loss. Those investors who kept the faith were richly rewarded in the subsequent 10 years.

Of course, history isn't all doom and gloom—good news and progress happen too. But Bill Gates is right: "Headlines, in a way, are what mislead you, because bad news is a headline, and gradual improvement is not." This chapter only highlights the negative news because investors don't worry about the positive. It's the big, bad events that cause investors to miss the boat or jump ship. The thing you should take away from all of this is that you don't have to hold stocks for fifty years or more to make money. Hardly anyone can sit tight and do nothing for so long, and it's fine to lighten your stock holdings from time to time. I hope this look at history serves as a lesson not to overreact and overtrade, and to always hold some stocks, as recommended by Benjamin Graham. Most major events—terrorist attacks, natural disasters, geopolitical tensions, even wars—have no lasting impact on the economy or the stock markets. Remember: stock markets regularly "climb the wall of worry" and negative headlines to scale new heights.

WARS

How do wars affect your investments? If your country is at war, that question is probably the least of your concerns, but if the war is elsewhere, there are some lessons you can learn. Generally, stock markets don't take war well—initially, at least. But when a war has started or ended, the markets tend to sell at higher levels than they prevailed at before there was any thought of war.

One explanation of this seeming paradox is that governments have to spend more than they can possibly collect while a war is being waged. This increase in fiscal spending—and the printing of money to fund that spending—is the main driver for stock markets rising. When money is less desirable, asset classes like stock markets go up, as more and more people use their money to buy assets. The American Civil War, from 1861 to 1865, saw the stock market decline sharply after the attack on Fort Sumter, which marked the war's beginning. But after Congress passed the first Legal Tender Act to issue $150 million worth of new paper currency in 1862, the stock market went up. Investors rightly realized that industry and agriculture would be stimulated by the need to ramp up the war effort and that the new money would bring about inflation.

World War I, from 1914 to 1918, was also good for US stock investors. Initially, on July 30, 1914, US markets sank. It was their worst day since the panic of 1907, as Europeans, whose own markets had already been shut down, rushed to sell their US holdings. The fear in the US was that transatlantic trade would collapse and gold would be moved from New York to London. The stock exchange shut its doors the following day and only partially reopened in December for companies that had no international nature. Normal trading didn't resume until the following spring. It was exports to Allied countries that lifted the US from recession, and the stock market duly turned around. The flow of gold actually reversed, and by 1915, European countries were sending their gold to New York for safekeeping. By this time, the whole market sentiment had changed, and rumors that the war would end led to corrections. 1915 became the best year to date for the Dow Jones, which gained a whopping 82 percent, although it went on to lose 22 percent in 1917, after the US entered the war in April.

In September 1939, when World War II started, the Dow Jones rose almost 12 percent in a week. It went on to end 3 percent down for the year. The losing streak continued with a loss of 13 percent in 1940 and 15 percent in 1941. As in 1917, the increased prospect of direct military involvement depressed stock prices. Following the attack on Pearl Harbor in December 1941, the Dow Jones dropped 5 percent in a week. The Fed kept interest rates low to help the government finance the war effort. From the low of 1942 to the top in mid-1946, the Dow Jones more than doubled.

US stock prices were also affected in 1950, when North Korea attacked South Korea. When it emerged that the US and some of its allies would fight for South Korea, prices in the US dropped more than 10 percent. After three weeks of lower prices, it became clear that the conflict could be contained and that World War III wasn't on the cards. The stock markets rallied. The Dow Jones finished the year 18 percent up, and the upward trend continued with further rises of 14 percent in 1951 and 8 percent in 1952. By the time the Korean War ended in 1953, however, the Dow Jones was down 4 percent.

The Vietnam War, the following decade, had little immediate market impact, as it grew without any obvious beginning. Neither the Gulf of Tonkin incident on August 2, 1964 nor the Tet offensive, in which the North Vietnamese mounted a large, coordinated attack on the south, including Saigon, had much impact on the financial markets. The US stock market actually moved higher throughout the fall of 1964, despite the escalating war, as huge personal and corporate tax cuts were passed. In May and June 1965, however, as American troops started moving in, the stock market dropped 12 percent. At the end of the decade and into the early 1970s, the stock market continued its overall bullish mood, despite the US military facing high casualties and making little progress in Vietnam. But as images of helicopters leaving the US embassy in Saigon were broadcast around the world in 1973, the stock market was about to see its worst bear since the Great Depression. The cause wasn't the conflict in Asia though—it was a different war altogether.

The culprit, in fact, was the Yom Kippur War, fought between Israel and its Middle East neighbors in 1973, which saw oil-producing Arab nations impose an oil embargo on the US and the West. While the tactic hadn't worked in the 1967 Six Day War, this time, with the oil market already tight, oil prices shot up from $3 to $12 a barrel. With inflation surging, stock markets the world over tanked. By 1974, the S&P 500 had dropped almost 50 percent.

In August 1990, Iraq invaded Kuwait and provoked Israel by launching Scud missiles. The world was worried that Israel would retaliate with a nuclear attack and that the US might be stuck with another long, costly conflict like the Vietnam War. The US stock market headed south and briefly entered a bear market in October, the Dow Jones down from July's peak of nearly 3,000 to about 2,400. Going into year end, as the US and its "coalition of the willing" began to build in Saudi Arabia, the stock market drew some strength from growing optimism that the conflict would end quickly. Despite this, 1991 saw the second-worst start for US markets in history. The Dow Jones was down 4.7 percent in the first five days of trading, standing at around 2,500.

The First Gulf War was unique in the sense that Saddam Hussein was given a deadline of January 15, 1991 to withdraw from Kuwait. The stock market rose ahead of the deadline and leaped on January 17 when the ground war started. As expected, the price of oil shot up to $40 a barrel. What followed was one of the most unbelievable reversals in oil's history, with the price plunging to $22 the very next day. The Dow Jones, however, continued to rise and broke 3,000 for the first time by April, up more than 25 percent from the previous October's low. The bull market was all the more remarkable, as it happened in the midst of war and recession.

The Second Gulf War happened after the internet bubble burst, when the US was once again deep in recession. By the time the conflict started in March 2003, the Nasdaq was down about 80 percent and the S&P 500 about 50 percent. The potential war had stunted stock markets for months, and the hope was that once it began, it wouldn't last long. The war lasted three weeks and ended with Saddam Hussein being overthrown. March 2003 marked the bottom of the internet bear market, and the stock market went from strength to strength over the next four years until its peak in 2007.

Many more wars have happened than most investors know or remember. All made headline news at the time, but the effects they had on the stock markets—if they made any mark at all—were temporary. In 1956, with the support of the Soviet Union, Egypt's president, Gamal Abdel Nasser (1918–1970), nationalized the Suez Canal to end Britain's military presence in the canal zone. The tensions soon escalated into a full-blown crisis. Britain, France, and Israel joined forces to retake the canal. Soviet leader Nikita Khrushchev (1894–1971) railed against the invasion and threatened to rain down nuclear missiles on Western Europe. The US threatened economic sanctions on the three nations if they didn't withdraw.

In April 1961, Cuban troops drove out US-backed invaders at the Bay of Pigs. In Asia, China and India went to war over the disputed Himalayan border. In 1971, India fought with Pakistan. It was the bloodiest of the many wars involving the two nations. Vietnam invaded Cambodia with the support of the Soviet Union in 1977, and the world worried that the countries of Southeast Asia would fall like dominoes. Two years later, China went to war with Vietnam "to teach Vietnam a lesson."

In 1980, a bitter war started between Iran and Iraq. It lasted eight long years and cost half a million lives. The fear that oil prices would head skyward as a result didn't materialize in the end. In fact, oil was on a downward trend in the 1980s. 1982 saw yet another war break out, this time in the remote Falkland Islands off the coast of Argentina. Britain's quick victory in the war cemented the reputation of Prime Minister Margaret Thatcher (1925–2013) as the "Iron Lady." In the same year, Israel invaded Lebanon to root out the Palestinian Liberation Organization (PLO). The US invaded Grenada in 1983 and Panama in 1989. None of these wars had much of an impact on the stock market.

The Arab Spring, which began in December 2010, led to civil war in Syria. Both Russia and the US were drawn in, and the world witnessed the rise of ISIS. In 2014, Russia raised tensions with the West when it annexed Crimea and threatened the rest of Ukraine. It was one of the worst crises between Russia and the West since the Cold War.

To further illustrate how wars have limited impact on stock markets, let's go back to the Yom Kippur War. One year after the war finished, the S&P 500 was down more than a third. It wasn't the war that had devastated the stock markets though—it was the quadrupled oil prices brought on by the Arab oil embargo that did the big damage. The one-year post-war mark is an interesting one. A year after the Soviet Union invaded Afghanistan in 1979, the S&P 500 was up by a quarter. The first and second Gulf wars, in 1991 and 2003, saw a similar trend, with the S&P 500 up by about 30 percent one year later. One of the few conflicts to seemingly buck the trend was the "War on Terror," which was initiated by President George W. Bush after 9/11. One year after the tensions started, the S&P 500 had dropped 18 percent. The negative return, however, had more to do with the fact that the US was in the midst of a recession after the internet bubble burst in March 2000 than it did with the conflict.

BOOMS AND BUSTS

Financial markets are bound to have booms and busts. Yes, investors have become more knowledgeable over the years, but we just can't seem to shake off the inevitable. After enough time has passed and we've forgotten—or don't even know—the history, we make the same mistakes over and over again. Whenever there's a new technology or fad, the excitement can generate into a bubble. The believers dismiss the naysayers and claim "this time it's different," giving a long list of reasons as to why. But human folly—greed and fear—is never different. During a boom, the public makes money on paper, and it remains on paper. When the bust comes, euphoria quickly turns to panic. Paper profit turns to real loss, and a whole new generation of investors becomes disillusioned with the stock market.

During the internet boom, I had the brilliant idea of creating a portfolio of cheap stocks—cheap in absolute price but not in valuation. There was no study of valuation; I didn't bother to look at P/E ratios; I didn't even care if the companies were making money. This idiotic idea turned into fantastic paper profit right out of the gate. One of the stocks declared itself an internet company, and the price went up twentyfold! I thought it could go even higher! When the bubble burst, everything crashed back to earth and the whole portfolio was in ruins. If only I'd known about stock market booms and busts back then. As Ray Dalio put it, we can't just rely on our experience—we need to learn from the experiences of others.

In the 1630s, a craze swept through the Dutch Republic while it was on its way to becoming a world power. The object of speculation? Tulip bulbs, imported from Central Asia via Turkey. Named after the Persian word for turban—dulband, which it looks like—the flower became known as "tulp" in Dutch and quickly became a symbol of status. Initially, prices were stable and only went up gradually. However, for some reason or another, more and more people were attracted to buying and selling the bulbs for speculation. As the news of people making a killing just by trading tulip bulbs spread, even more investors were drawn to the craze. According to some records, in the end, prices went up twentyfold in one month. It was said that a single bulb could buy a house. The inevitable crash wiped out the speculators but brought little damage to the Dutch economy.

The 1929 stock market crash on Wall Street was different. In fact, the roaring 1920s—the era of "The Great Gatsby"—actually started with a bear market. From the low in 1921, it went up almost five times to a peak on September 3, 1929. When Andrew W. Mellon (1855–1937), one of the richest men in America, became secretary of the Treasury, he cut taxes aggressively. Radio, automobiles, and airlines were fairly new and exciting for the investing public, and using credit to buy consumer goods—mainly automobiles—was gaining popularity. But the rise of the automobile industry had an unintended consequence. In 1900, one-third of cropland in the US was being used to produce fodder for horses. As the number of automobiles exploded in the 1920s, the number of horses dwindled. Farmers switched their cropland to produce food rather than feed, which dampened food prices. This, in part, led to the lowering of interest rates from 1921 to 1927. A recession, which lasted for one year until November 1927, didn't change the direction of the market. By the time the Fed increased interest rates in February 1928, the stock market was too strong and too euphoric to turn around. By August 1929, the interest rate was 6 percent—too low to curb speculation but still too high for the economy.

Estimates indicate that only half a million Americans owned stocks before World War I. By 1929, as many as twenty million, or one in six, had stockbroking accounts. Investment trusts, which were similar to today's mutual funds, numbered less than 40 in 1920, but in 1929 alone, more than 200 trusts were formed. At the height of the bubble, some of the trusts were trading at double their asset value. Many speculators bought stocks on as little as a 10 percent margin. Radio Corporation of America (RCA) was the growth stock of the 1920s, rising from $32 in 1926 to $574 in 1929, while airline Wright Aeronautical saw its stock price surge from $25 to $245 in 19 months after Charles A. Lindbergh (1902–1974) successfully completed the first solo flight across the Atlantic Ocean.

Just like all bubbles, the up move wasn't a smooth or straight line, and there were times when the market broke and dropped sharply. In December 1928, the Dow Jones dropped more than 11 percent in a week. There were several other sharp breaks in 1929, but the market always scaled new heights soon after. Yale economist Irving Fisher (1867–1947) made a jubilant observation at the time that stocks had reached what looked like a "permanent high plateau." This gave investors more confidence, and they became more greedy. They thought the party would last forever.

The market peaked on September 3, 1929 and began to slide, slowly at first before picking up steam after mid-October. On Thursday, October 24, the market collapsed by more than 6 percent on the highest volume ever. Over the next two days, things were a lot calmer—in those days, the stock market was open on Saturdays. But when the market reopened on Monday, October 28, it fell a whopping 13 percent and another 12 percent the next day, breaking the volume record of the previous week's "Black Thursday." On Wednesday, October 30, John D. Rockefeller, probably the richest man in the world at the time, said: "My son and I have for some days been purchasing sound common stocks." That day, the market enjoyed a strong rebound, rising 12 percent. More strong rebounds followed, but the market always ended up with lower lows. The bottom came much later, in 1932, when the Dow Jones was down 89 percent from its peak and 80 percent from the crash. These events ushered in the Great Depression, a time that would cause hardship to millions of Americans as well as millions more people all over the world.

Would the US see another 89 percent drop in the stock market again? On June 17, 1930, ignoring pleas from over a thousand American economists, President Herbert Hoover (1874–1964) signed the Smoot-Hawley Tariff Act. Its heavy tariffs would account for more than half the price of some imports. The day before Hoover signed the bill, the stock market suffered its worst day since the crash of 1929. Initially, the Fed eased interest rates, however it raised them again toward the end of 1930. It was an ill-advised move, and bank failures accelerated as a result. In late 1931, the Fed hiked its discount rate by 2 percent in two weeks.

Reflecting on the era, Dr. Ben S. Bernanke, an academic who specializes in the Great Depression, commented: "The real disaster started in December 1930, with the failure of a private bank with an unfortunate name, the Bank of the United States." Indeed, though the institution had no relationship with the federal government, the story of its collapse helped cause panic among small depositors. Dr. Bernanke describes 1931 as a year of small crises that built into a catastrophe. In April of that year, the largest bank in Austria also failed, helping create financial panic in Europe. Then, in September, Britain abandoned the gold standard, and the subsequent runs on banks restricted the money supply, setting off a round of severe deflation. To balance the budget, the (US) Revenue Act of 1932 almost doubled tax rates.

The Great Depression taught economists some valuable lessons: that the almost religious belief that budget must be balanced is of a different generation and that while trade wars may be happening, they're unlikely to grow to a global scale. In subsequent years, we've learned that the Fed—as seen both during and after Alan Greenspan's tenure—is always ready to cut interest rates to protect the economy. Dr. Bernanke became Fed chairman in 2006, continuing in the role until 2014. His understanding of the policy mistakes of the past was put to good use during the global financial crisis, and as a result, we ended up with the Great Recession, not another Great Depression.

While it seems unlikely that US stocks will see another 89 percent fall, other countries have experienced a drop of similar magnitude. One example is the Hong Kong stock market, which collapsed more than 90 percent from 1973 to 1974, when struck by the first oil shock. A few decades later, Russia's stock market also lost about 90 percent as a result of the 1998 Russian financial crisis and almost 80 percent during the 2008 global financial crisis.

In 1967 and 1968, despite the ongoing Vietnam War and the fact that the country was hugely divided by both the war and by race, the US experienced a big bull market, with small-cap stocks up 150 percent in those two years. Many companies went on a buying spree to become conglomerates. Investors greeted these mergers and acquisitions enthusiastically, sending prices sky high. Company managers used special accounting techniques to make acquisitions look better than they really were. The misconception was that companies should be valued solely on their per-share earnings growth. How that growth was achieved was disregarded. To keep earnings growing, the acquisitions had to get bigger and bigger, and eventually the conglomerates ran into the limits of size. From the December 1968 peak to the bottom in May 1970, the Dow Jones dropped about 36 percent, with 10 particular conglomerates seeing a whopping 86 percent average decline.

Investors had a short memory though, and they soon forgot all about the conglomerate boom and bust. The next boom was in "one-decision" stocks, which investors never had to think about selling. These were the best stocks to own. They were big, well managed, and, most importantly, they grew fast. No price was too high. The Coca Cola Company, IBM, Polaroid, and Xerox were just some of the companies known as the Nifty Fifty. The draw was that these growth stocks would reward investors generously with growing dividends and capital appreciation. At their peak in 1972, the Nifty Fifty had an average P/E ratio of 43 —more than double that of the S&P 500—and a dividend yield of 1.1 percent—less than half that of the S&P 500. Then came the Yom Kippur War, in which the Arabs launched a surprise attack on Israel. The oil embargo imposed by OPEC pushed oil prices up around four times, and inflation surged. The Fed responded by raising interest rates in 1973, bringing on the worst bear market since the Great Depression. The Nifty Fifty dropped 62 percent—more than the 45 percent drop in the Dow Jones.

In 1982, Ronald Reagan became the 40th president of the United States, unleashing bounds of American optimism and spirit. Deregulations were in vogue, taxes were cut, and the stock market went soaring. In 1987, the stock market started with a particularly large roar. The Dow Jones hit record after record in the first 10 sessions and jumped 9 percent overall. It peaked on August 25 at 2,746, up 45 percent for the year and more than 250 percent from the low of 777 on August 12, 1982. Valuations were high, P/E ratios were at their highest in 25 years, and the dividend yield was only 2.6 percent. By September, however, the Dow Jones was drifting lower. The trend intensified in October with a drop of 9.5 percent in one week and 17 percent from the peak. The media began to compare what was happening to the 1929 crash, no doubt sending some nervous investors into panic mode.

On Black Monday—October 19, 1987—the Dow Jones plunged by 508 points, or 22.6 percent. It was the biggest one-day drop ever. Exacerbating the downward move was portfolio insurance—a product that sold stock index futures when the market was dropping in order to "insure" against further drops in portfolio value. What was lost in stocks would be covered by gains made in futures. When the stock market was down heavily, computer algorithms sold indiscriminately in the futures market, causing futures to trade at a deep discount to stocks. This created panic among investors, who sold more in the stock market, while the portfolio insurance sold more in the futures market. A vicious cycle was created. Many individual stocks had overwhelming sellers but no buyers, effectively shutting them down.

The following day, the Fed assured the markets it was ready to serve as a source of liquidity and lowered the fed funds rate from 7.5 to 6.75 percent. Another selling climax was averted. After the White House made a few calls, some big companies announced they were buying back their shares, and the SEC relaxed its rules to allow companies to buy back their shares immediately instead of after making a formal announcement. Though the Dow Jones was weak for the rest of the year, the economy wasn't affected too much in the end.

One of the biggest bubbles ever was the internet—or the dot-com—bubble. This exciting, cutting-edge technology introduced a whole range of new possibilities as to how we communicate and how businesses operate. The potential was huge. Investors started enthusiastically buying up internet stocks, making fat, fast money along the way. It all began with Netscape on August 9, 1995. Having started its first day of trading with a share price of $28, it went on to close at more than double its IPO price.

Another factor contributing to the boom was that most internet companies only floated less than a fifth of their shares. The lower supply and poor liquidity made it easier for prices to surge. Any company that declared its intention to go into the internet business or to simply add ".com" to its name saw its share price rocket. This phenomenon was far from new. The same thing had happened in the 1960s with electronics companies, when companies with "ton" at the end of their names were rewarded with a surge in prices, and in the 1850s, when railroad was a relatively new technology, stocks in rail were all the rage.

It wasn't all plain sailing for internet companies though. The crises in Asia in 1997 and Russia in 1998 rattled things, albeit only temporarily. The boom lasted longer than many expected, with the Nasdaq gaining more than five times from 1995 through to its peak on March 10, 2000.

When the crash came, it was fast and furious, the Nasdaq dropping around a third in just one month. That year, it plunged 39 percent overall. The Dow Jones fared better initially, only losing 6 percent, while the S&P 500 fell just 10 percent. Along the way, there were some strong rebounds, but they were always followed by lower lows. By March 2001, the S&P 500 was down about 23 percent from its peak. This bear market wasn't broad based though, and seven sectors were actually higher than they'd been a year prior. In fact, real estate investment trusts hit a record high in the same year. The Nasdaq was the first index to level out when it hit bottom at 80 percent below its peak in October 2002. The Dow Jones and the S&P 500 bottomed in the spring of 2003, around the time the Second Gulf War was about to start.

Unlike the internet boom, the global financial crisis wasn't an obvious bubble, at least not in the US stock market. The S&P 500 P/E ratio was at a long-term average of 16 in 2007. The bubble was actually happening in the US property market, which was inflated by low interest rates to counter the aftereffect of the internet bubble burst. Before the crisis hit, then Fed chairman Alan Greenspan stated that the US housing market, as a whole, had never fallen, but when it started to drop in 2006, the effects spread to the many financial products that had been created by the banks to ride the property boom. When these products tanked, the banks were forced to write off hundreds of billions of dollars.

By September 2008, the banking sector was teetering on the edge of a cliff. Then Lehman Brothers went bankrupt. The stock market was extremely volatile for the rest of the year. The S&P 500 saw an 18 percent drop in one week—the worst since 1933.

There were three subsequent rallies of roughly 15 to 20 percent, all of which were followed by new lows. The only thing that prevented the banks and the global economy from falling into an abyss was the special measures implemented by the world's governments and central banks. Ciitbank and AIG were saved by Uncle Sam. From its October 2007 peak, the S&P 500 bottomed 57 percent lower in March 2009. It staged a strong rebound for the remaining part of the year and finished about 20 percent up overall. The US economy went into recession in 2009 but swiftly recovered.

In Japan, the major boom happened in the late 1980s. One of the peculiarities of this stock bubble was that the investing public was more interested in the "hidden assets" (land and properties) in the balance sheet of companies than in technology. Short-term capital gains tax of 150 percent had created a market with few sellers. The result had been a spectacular rise in land prices from the mid-1950s to the late 1980s, with some estimates putting the increase at fifty times its starting point. After the Plaza Accord was signed to lower the US dollar in September 1985, the Japanese yen moved from 260 per dollar to 150 in a few short months. In order to mitigate the effect of a strong yen on Japan's huge export sector, the BOJ lowered interest rates. Inflation wasn't an issue, as oil prices crashed in 1986 and imported goods were cheaper due to the strong yen.

In 1987, NTT—Japan's huge government telecom company—was sold to the public. The IPO was significantly oversubscribed, and the price nearly tripled. The company had a market value of $350 billion—more than the entire West German stock market—and its P/E ratio was more than 150. On October 20, 1987, the day after Wall Street's worst-ever crash, Japan's all-powerful Ministry of Finance made a few phone calls to the country's biggest brokers. The brokers then made an unbelievable offer to their big clients—a guarantee against losses. The end result was Japan held up relatively well in the aftermath of Black Monday.

During the Japanese bubble, margin loans for stocks went up by eight times. Making money in the stock market was so easy that even the yakuza gangsters wanted a part of the spoils. It was reported that they colluded with big brokerages to corner some stocks. The strong yen led the Japanese to embark on a huge buying spree, scooping up artwork by the likes of Vincent Van Gogh (1853–1890) and Claude Monet (1840–1926), and iconic buildings in America like the Rockefeller Center in New York. By 1989, the stock market's P/E ratio had risen to above 60, the dividend yield was less than 0.5 percent, and the Nikkei was up 500 percent for the decade.

As with any bubble, the believers had their reasons as to why they thought Japan's stock market wasn't one. They acknowledged the high P/E ratios but put that down to accounting rules that encouraged companies to underreport their earnings in order to keep tax payments low. They justified high share prices by citing the huge, understated land and property holdings in the companies' balance sheets. They also reasoned that most listed Japanese companies had huge "cross-shareholdings," owning a big stake in each other's stocks for long-term investment. This, they argued, reduced the supply of shares and pushed up prices. Furthermore, with the yen appreciating rapidly and most believing it would appreciate even further, Japanese investors were unwilling to invest overseas. The money was therefore put to work in the Japanese stock market.

By 1989, the BOJ had reversed the cycle of easing. Interest rates were raised until they reached 6 percent in August 1990. The Nikkei reached its all-time high at the end of 1989, at nearly 40,000. The continuous rise in interest rates to tame inflation finally brought the stock market down. When the market fell below 20,000 in September 1990, the authorities reduced the margin requirements, life insurance companies were told to stop selling shares, the ban that had been previously imposed on IPOs was extended, and public pension funds were used to buy stocks. Despite all these measures, the slide continued, and by August 1992, the Nikkei had dropped to almost 14,000—about three-quarters off its peak. The hidden assets that were cherished before the bubble burst turned into hidden losses. Land prices in Tokyo crashed more than 60 percent. Golf club membership prices, which went up tenfold in the 1980s, crashed by 50 percent. The Nikkei only reached a bottom of about 7,000 after the global financial crisis. By that time, it had dropped more than 80 percent from its peak in 1989. Since the crash, the economy has hardly grown, yet unemployment rates remain low. And while interest rates were cut to zero and massive quantitative easing was introduced, deflation has continued to persist.

A short hop across the sea, China's stock exchanges, which only opened in 1990, have been singing their own tune for the most part of their short history. The majority of the time, they're barely correlated to the world's stock markets; occasionally, they're negatively correlated. When the majority of countries in Asia were facing their worst-ever crisis in 1997, China's stock markets soared by 38 percent. When the internet bubble burst in 2000, they were up almost 50 percent. According to one study, there are two main reasons why China's bull runs come to an end: either official policies have turned negative or the supply of shares has ballooned because of IPOs or due to big selling by major shareholders.

In January 1992, Deng Xiaoping, the architect of the opening up of China, toured Shenzhen and other cities in the south of the country. He made calls for people to persist in reform, increase investment, and experiment with shares. Chinese investors interpreted his calls as the government wanting to boost the market and bought earnestly to push prices up. Later that year, in August 1992, a riot took place in Shenzhen. It was the worst civil unrest in China since the 1989 Tiananmen protests. The reason? Up to a million people lined up for more than two days to get forms to apply for the red-hot IPOs, allocated by a lottery system, that guaranteed a big profit to whoever was lucky enough to get one. When the forms ran out, some of the late-comers were outraged, and things quickly deteriorated. Many of the rioters believed that government officials were saving the forms for themselves or their families and friends. By February 1993, the benchmark index, the Shanghai Composite Index, rocketed to almost 1,600, from having been at around 100 in December 1991. The government was concerned about this gravity-defying rise and wanted to put a halt to it. The expectation that the government would sell off state-owned shares provoked a panic and crash. The index dropped 80 percent by July 1994.

A decade later, in 2005, the Chinese government announced a scheme whereby all state-owned stocks would become tradable within two years. Investors took this as a signal the government wanted a healthy and higher stock market and ignored the huge supply that was coming—the government had also been introducing other changes to support prices after a bear market that had seen stocks drop by more than half since 2001. The policy changes worked, and the benchmark Shanghai Composite Index rose by a record 130 percent to 2,675 in 2006. Despite further interest rate hikes, the market continued to roar ahead in 2007, with a one-day, 9 percent drop in February a mere temporary setback. Stocks kept on breaking new highs until China's finance ministry announced it would triple tax on stock trades in late May, from 0.1 percent to 0.3 percent. The Chinese government had long used changes in stock trading tax to influence share prices. The stock market lost a total of around 15 percent in the four days following the announcement. Yet again, the bull soon won over. Investors firmly believed the government would want a higher stock market ahead of the 2008 Summer Olympics in Beijing, and the Shanghai Composite Index kept on breaking records till it hit a peak of just above 6,000 on October 16, 2007, up from around 1,200 in early 2006.

There was no clear catalyst for the burst of the bubble. One reason cited was that China was affected by the worsening situation in the US and other world markets ahead of the global financial crisis. In reality, it was probably because the markets had risen too fast and couldn't defy gravity any longer. The speed of the rise had surpassed both Japan's 1989 bubble and America's internet bubble. In April 2008, after China's bubble had burst, the Chinese government cut stock-trading tax to 0.1 percent and announced a series of steps to bolster the sagging stock market. The bear market continued, however, and the Shanghai Composite Index hit around 1,700 in November 2008, a 70 percent drop from its peak just one year prior.

One of the most bizarre bubbles happened in Kuwait in 1982. Tens of thousands of Kuwaitis bought into their stock market, with the total amount invested estimated at $8 billion—more than the country's total oil revenue that year. Most of the trading was on credit, even with interest rates as high as 100 percent. The investors remembered how a few years back, in 1977, when the Kuwaiti stock market crashed, the government spent $500 million to support the market and protect investors. Kuwait was a welfare state: the citizens paid no taxes, food and fuel were subsidized, and almost all services—from education to healthcare—were free.

The most bizarre thing about the Kuwaiti stock bubble, however, wasn't the use of credit, which is a constant feature of all bubbles, but rather how the credit was created and used. Many investors used postdated checks to pay for their stocks! They hoped that the prices of the stocks would rise before the checks were due to be paid. They were literally looking to make millions from nothing. OK, maybe something—if you take into account the cost of the envelope and stamp.

There were a few theories as to why the bubble burst: from the Iran-Iraq War, which turned against Iraq (this was a time when Saddam Hussein was more friendly toward Kuwait than Ayatollah Khomeini (1902–1989) was) to a drop in oil revenue, from a cut in government spending to a sharp rise in interest rates. What we do know is that the panic began in August, when an attempt to cash in a $30 million postdated check was rejected by a bank. The debtor was one of the most prominent businessmen in Kuwait. Word spread, and soon there was a run on the banks. It's estimated that there were close to $100 billion worth of postdated checks at the height of the stock craze. The government was forced to outlay many billions of US dollars to clean up the mess. At the time, the zeitgeist was such that the most treasured and privileged Kuwaitis were seen as having the right to own land and to play the stock market.

Many more bubbles have taken place across the world over the years. Taiwan's stock index broke 1,000 in 1986 and surpassed 10,000 by 1989. It peaked at 12,500 in early 1990 and crashed to 2,500 by October of the same year. The P/E ratio at the peak of the market was variously calculated from 65 to 130. By the end of 2019, the stock index was 12,000, and still hadn't surpassed the height of the bubble 30 years earlier. Over in Pakistan, with aid pouring in from the US after 9/11 to help the country fight the Taliban in Afghanistan, the Karachi Stock Exchange 100 Index rose more than eightfold, from around 1,200 in 2001 to over 10,000 in early 2006. The diaspora also remitted billions of US dollars to help inflate the stock bubble. Saudi Arabia had a big bubble when oil prices rose in the 2000s. The Tadawul All Share Index rose from about 2,500 in March 2003 to over 20,000 in February 2006. By mid-March, it had dropped to 15,000.

But back to today. When you see a bubble, should you watch from the sidelines or should you join in? Bubbles, by definition, have an explosive move in their final phase. Waiting and watching wastes time—the opportunity to make good money passes by quickly. Remember, however, that bubbles usually last for a while. Trying to profit from one isn't for everyone, but with discipline, a clear head, and a regular check on your emotions, it is possible.

A rising tide, as they say, lifts all boats. We know most people make money in a bubble, at least initially, so that gives us confidence to get on the boat. We also know most of these people end up losing more than they make. How does this happen? A typical investor who participates in a bubble usually starts by dipping a toe in. They're skeptical and cautious in the early stages. When a bubble has just started, many people, especially the perpetual bears, give warnings about it. This leads most investors to start small. But once that small investment has turned into a quick profit, the investor's appetite is whetted. The bubble feeds their optimism and provides increasing resources that they can deploy. As the bubble grows, so does the investor's position. The profits get fatter. The investor thinks their growing confidence is justified by their skill and astute investment acumen. Greed slowly takes over. The idea of borrowing to enhance profit comes to mind. When they hear of neighbors, colleagues, and friends making even more than them by using leverage, they throw all caution to the wind. Then the burst comes. Having the biggest position right at the top and using leverage is what kills these investors.

What can you learn from this? First off, never leverage in a bubble. Bubbles are always volatile, as are our emotions. With leverage, our emotional swings are magnified—we lose the ability to make rational decisions. Remember also that greed can turn very quickly to fear. Second, you must have a plan: how much to buy now, when and how much to add on, and when to take a profit. Having a good plan is like using a map and compass to navigate rough terrain in stormy weather.

When signs of a bubble first emerge, it's good to jump in early in good size. This is actually safer than most people think. If the bubble fails to inflate further, your loss will be limited. Only big bubbles have big bursts—small bubbles don't end with a huge drop in stock prices. If the bubble does continue to inflate, you can ride on a big wave and profit handsomely in a relatively short period of time. Having an adequate position lowers the chance of you having regrets later on when the bubble keeps growing. Going in with a small initial position might lead you to increase your size at a higher price and worse time. If you're going to average up on a bubble, your later positions at higher prices must be smaller than your initial position.

Remember as well that bubbles are volatile and there are some big swings along the way. You don't want to be shaken out of your position. The best time to average up isn't when there's a big drop, as you can't be sure whether it's just a correction or whether the bubble has burst. Better timing is to buy at a new high after a correction. Yes, you pay a higher price, but the chance of a bubble bursting right after scaling a new high is lower. You're paying a higher price for better odds that the bubble will continue. Also, when the market is at a new high, your initial position is making more money and gives you a better cushion.

What are the signs a bubble is reaching its maximum size? A chart is probably your best guide—if the price is going up almost vertically, it's about time to get out. You can choose to sell part or all as it's on its way up. You're not going to get everything out at the top, and that's fine. If you sell too early, so be it. It's not realistic to expect to sell right at the top. You can still be proud of yourself for having made and kept the money in a bubble.

BULLS AND BEARS

Bull and bear markets are like summer days and nights—the days (bulls) are long and the nights (bears) are short. But while we know when the sun will rise and set, we don't know how long the bullish days and bearish nights will last. Roughly speaking, stocks are only in the most active phases of a bull market for around 20 percent of the time and the most severe phases of a bear market for around 10 percent of the time. The rest of the time, they either move sideways or undergo minor rallies and corrections within their bull and bear cycles. A bull market takes a long time to reach its peak, but in the last leg, the move quickens. For bear markets, the move to hit the trough is sharper and quicker. The stock market goes up an escalator and down in an elevator.

In our lifetime, we're likely to see many bull and bear markets. In the US, corrections (a 10 to 20 percent drop in prices) happen every one to two years, while bear markets (a drop of more than 20 percent in prices) happen every four to five years. The MSCI Emerging Markets Index, however, has gone through a bear market once every two years since 1994. In general, the average bear market sees a drop of slightly more than 30 percent and lasts about 18 months.

The S&P 500 drops roughly once every five years. In the 2010s, it was down in line with the long term average twice—in both 2015 and 2018. Overall, US stocks have gained more than they have lost, rising by 30 percent or more in 13 individual calendar years and losing 30 percent or more just seven times. In the great bull run of the 1990s, the S&P 500 notched up big gains for five consecutive years, from 1995 to 1999, ranging from 20 to 34 percent. The worst-ever bear market lasted from 1929 to 1933, when the Dow Jones dropped 89 percent, giving it the record in terms of both duration and magnitude. More recently, the Dow Jones lost 38 percent in the internet bubble burst and 54 percent in the great financial crisis.

A bear market is characterized by strong rallies, or "dead cat bounces"—a temporary recovery in share prices. This happened to the S&P 500 when it soared by a quarter in the seven weeks ending January 2009 only to then plunge to a new low. The bear market ended when the index rose to one-third above its March 2009 low in just 60 days. Other resurgences include the 2000 to 2003 bear market in which the Dow Jones saw three rallies over 45 days, with an average gain of 21 percent. From 1929 to 1932, the index saw six false alarms with an average gain of 47 percent. The Nikkei also rose by at least one-third four times in the four years following its peak in 1989. The index saw 10 more false dawns before the 20-year bear market hit its bottom in 2009.

When a bull market has turned, certain stocks and groups are able to defy the general market for a while. In the 1973 to 1974 bear market, the so-called Nifty Fifty was initially bulging but eventually succumbed to selling pressure. When the Nikkei was topping out at the end of 1989, the small-cap companies continued to defy the big-cap. After a few months, however, all stocks headed lower. When internet stocks burst in 2000, the Dow Jones had some big "up" days, while the Nasdaq had some big "down" days as traders switched money from high-flying internet stocks to the old, steady blue chips. As the bear market continued, however, the Dow Jones couldn't stop the pull of gravity and went into a bear market too.

To predict the turn of a bull or bear market is a very complicated task. To buy stocks at the bottom and sell at the top is without doubt more profitable than to hold on to them permanently, and this fact has attracted investors of every generation to try to solve the riddle. It's an elusive holy grail. There are always a few people who call the tops and bottoms correctly and who are celebrated by the media. These people, however, are probably more lucky than skillful, as no one calls it right every time. There's no formula to predict a market turn, but the more signals there are pointing in the opposite direction, the more likely it is a turn's imminent.

The first signal that many investors look at is the economy. This is perfectly logical and sensible in theory but full of faults in practice. First, you have to predict the future state of the economy. This is by no means a simple task, and even economists themselves don't have a good track record when it comes to economic forecasting. Second, the economy doesn't impact the stock market like wind does a sailboat. If the stock market followed GDP growth, China's market would have left the US far behind over the last three decades, but in actual fact, the US stock market outperformed China's. Third, the relationship between recessions and the stock market is a rather erratic one. Some recessions happen without a bear market; some bear markets happen without a recession. Sometimes the stock market continues to fall during a recession; sometimes it turns around. Fourth, what's been important to the stock market historically isn't just whether the economy is growing or contracting but also whether it's getting better or worse. When growth becomes less negative, it's considered good news, and the market responds positively. In short, economic cycles can provide only a partially satisfactory solution to forecasting stock market trends.

Another signal investors watch closely is the valuation of the stock market. A market that's overvalued, with P/E ratios at the high end of the historical range, is a warning sign. The S&P 500 P/E ratio ranges between 10 and 20 most of the time, with an average of 16. When the P/E ratio goes above 20 or below 10, it's believed that the market is near top or bottom.

During a bull market, not all sectors perform equally well. Some lead the general market, while some move lower. The dot-com bubble was led by the internet and technology sector, while the bull market before the global financial crisis was led by banks. The current bull market is led by big, profitable technology companies, such as Amazon, Apple, Facebook, Microsoft, and Alphabet. To some top traders, when a top sector ceases to lead, it's a signal that a bull market is ending. These investors also like to take a cue from the "breadth of market." They look at things like the Dow Jones versus the Russell 2000, which with 2,000 companies represents breadth. If the Dow Jones outperforms the Russell 2000, it's a bearish signal, as the bull market isn't broad. They also look at how many companies are near a 52-week high or a 52-week low. If only the blue chips are near the high and lots of companies are near the low, the breadth of the market is eroding, which isn't a good sign. There are many other variations, but the main idea is that a broad range of companies, both big and small, need to rise for a bull market to be healthy and sustainable.

One signal that a bull's end is near is a hot IPO market. Companies usually rush to list when the market is bullish, allowing them to sell at high valuations and thereby raise more money. These IPOs absorb money that could otherwise be used to buy stocks. As well as looking at the number and size of IPOs in the market, the performance of the IPOs is just as important. When the stock market is red hot, IPO prices can more than double on the first day of trading. The more companies that are listed and the higher the first-day price jump, the more likely the top of a bull is near.

Some people like to use the length of a bull market as a gauge to time the top. They believe that if a bull market has gone long beyond its average, it's "living on borrowed time," and they see this as time to get out. Such a simple rule never really works in the stock market though. Investors who followed this rule in the 1990s and 2010s would have missed a big part of the bull market.

To some investors, technically, market tops happen in two

ways. The first is when volume is high yet prices can't break much higher after a few days. This is an indication that insiders are selling shares to the general public—stocks are being distributed from strong to weak hands. The second is when the market is breaking a new high but on a low volume. This indicates that a new top doesn't have enough support. The bottom of a bear market is a mirror image of its top. Market bottoms happen when the volume is high yet the prices can't break lower after a few days or the market is breaking a new low but on a low volume.

It's hard to generalize, but one of the more accurate indicators that a bear is near the bottom is when increasing good news is ignored by investors. They're despondent because previous rebounds were always followed by a new low. They're skeptical about the good news and don't want to be lured into another dead cat bounce.

The theory that a better profit means higher stock prices seems perfectly logical, but while this is true for individual stocks, it's not true for the overall market. A fresh bull market usually starts while overall profits are still declining. Those who wait till the earnings have turned around are usually too late to the party.

The points above are only some of the signals investors look at in order to make a judgment call on the turn of a stock market. In practice, there are many more fundamental, technical signals that investors all over the world take into account, but whatever combination they look at, no one is able to predict bull and bear markets accurately all the time.

To succeed in investing and navigate both bull and bear markets well, you need to prepare yourself psychologically for both. Don't let greed blind you in a bull market or fear paralyze you in a bear market. Plan ahead, be alert all the time, look for signals, and never follow the crowd blindly.

When the market is bearish, you have to have cash and the courage to look beyond the short term. You need a healthy dose of optimism and have to keep the faith that night is always followed by day, no matter how dark the night is. You need to plan when to buy and at what price. Remember that bear markets are volatile and sentiment swings are wild. When prices are dropping, investors are afraid to catch a falling knife; when prices are surging, they're worried about missing the boat and they jump in to buy. It's important to guard against that emotional swing and only buy on dip, not on rally. It's also prudent to buy in stages rather than all at once. Contrary to what most people believe, having all cash and no stock during a bear market might not be the best scenario. A bounce in a bear market feels like the tide has turned and lures investors in. Investors with everything in cash are scared to miss the boat, but by buying after the market has rebounded substantially, they end up losing out when the market breaks a new low again. If you still hold some stocks, you'll be less likely to chase every turn of the bear and you'll end up doing better than if you have everything in cash.

If a bull market is raging, you have to decide whether you want to lighten your position and prepare for a bear market. Be sure to guard against indulgence in bullish talk and bullish views simply because you have stocks—you don't have to marry the bull. Be alert, but don't be paranoid. There are always people who warn about all sorts of risks and impending bears. If the economy is expanding, they worry about it weakening; if there's a recession, they worry about depression. They're like the crew on Christopher Columbus's (1451–1506) ship the Santa Maria in 1492. Night after night, the sailors were gripped with fear that their ship would fall off the end of the earth. If you worry all the time, you'll never make decent money in a bull market. If you don't make much in a bull market, you'll never make any money in the stock market.

PART IV: OUTSIDE INFLUENCES

INFORMATION

Information has always been king, whether in today's era of big data or in the past. It's sought after and highly prized. If we'd lived in the good old days of carrier pigeons, we could have profited dearly by getting information fast. Nathan Rothschild (1777–1836) did just that, making big money when carrier pigeons brought him the news of Wellington's (1769–1852) victory over Napoleon (1769–1821) at Waterloo. Nowadays, obtaining price-sensitive information ahead of others is illegal —with regulators making stock investing a fairer ground for the investing public, news has to be made available to everyone at the same time.

The internet era is a huge benefit to retail investors. We no longer have to write to prospective companies to ask for an annual report and then wait for days for it to arrive by post. Free, instant information is literally at our fingertips, and financial news channels broadcast 24 hours a day. However, while we're lucky in this day and age to have lots of free information, it's important we get our data from reliable sources.

The amount of information available to us way exceeds our capacity to evaluate it, therefore we have to know which pieces of information are meaningful and which are meaningless. P/E ratios are generally useful, although forward P/E ratios are only useful if the forward earnings forecast is reasonably accurate. We have to filter through the superfluous, sometimes even harmful, financial information. Many commonly watched technical analyses can actually end up doing more harm than good to the average investor.

Of course, it's one thing to possess good information; it's a whole other thing to know how to interpret and draw correct conclusions from that information. Even harder is knowing how to use the information profitably. With information in hand, average investors tend to make a pound of assumptions based an ounce of facts. Few take care that their information and knowledge are adequate enough to form a sound judgment. Such a casual approach can cost investors dearly. It's better to abandon an investment idea than make decisions based on half-truths and misconceptions. Keep in mind that "what everyone knows" isn't necessarily worth knowing. If everyone knows the same information, it's already reflected in the prices and no one can benefit from it.

The ability to skillfully interpret information differentiates the successful from the unsuccessful. In 1991, during the First Gulf War, Iraq was given a January 15 deadline to withdraw from Kuwait. As the deadline approached, most investors preferred to stay out of the markets. They were worried. What if it turned out to be another Vietnam War, which spanned four presidencies? What if Iraq were to fire missiles at Israel, thereby widening the war and driving oil prices up further? As a result, the Dow Jones had its second-worst start to a year ever. The market was eroding steadily in anticipation of a deadline. Some smart investors, however, were quietly picking up stocks. They saw that others were being overpessimistic and that prices already reflected the uncertainties and worries. They knew that many funds were sitting on their highest levels of cash in years. They also thought that the Fed's interest rate cut was enough to withstand a bad situation—even one as bad as a war. They knew that stock markets usually advance before the end of a recession. These investors profited handsomely as a result of correctly interpreting the information and having the courage to go against the crowd at an unnerving time.

When new information comes out, its market significance isn't always instantly recognized. When OPEC started the oil embargo in late 1973, the US stock market actually went up slightly to begin with. In the following days, after the market woke up to the embargo's huge, negative consequences, stock prices went down. They continued to drop for a whole year. When the Britons voted for Brexit in mid-2016, global financial markets were shocked and went into a tailspin. The information was interpreted as being bad for both Britain and Europe, and the expectation was that negative repercussions would spread across the world. Some investors, however, took a different view. They didn't believe the result of the referendum would be bad for financial markets. They bought, and they profited handsomely. The financial markets soon reversed themselves, and the shock result was quickly forgotten.

During the 2016 US presidential election campaign, the market narrative was that Hillary Clinton as president would be good for the market and Donald Trump would be bad for it. Unexpectedly, Trump triumphed over Clinton. International financial markets nosedived before the US opened for trading. By the time the US woke up, however, most of the losses had been reversed, and the US ended up with a positive close. Some investors were able to see the flaws in the argument. Whatever Trump's shortcomings, his infrastructure spending and tax cuts were good for the stock market. These buyers interpreted the information correctly and overwhelmed the sellers. As stocks headed higher, a new narrative took over to explain the rise— Trump was good for the market. More investors turned from sellers to buyers.

Many top traders believe that market reactions to news provide signals as to whether the market is bullish or bearish. If the market shrugs off a barrage of bad news to head higher, it's thought to be showing an underlying, bullish strength. If it's going down despite a flow of positive news, it's considered bearish. If the market moves higher on good news and lower on bad news, it's seen as neither bullish nor bearish. When the war between Iran and Iraq broke out in 1980, the price of gold only increased by $1. A war between two big OPEC members should, in theory, be good news for gold prices. The fact it barely moved was a bearish sign. The market went down sharply soon after. Years later, in the spring of 2009, while the US economy was still in very bad shape following the global financial crisis, the emergence of "green shoots"—promising signs of economic recovery —caused the stock market to jump significantly. This over-reaction to marginally positive news was a bullish sign. Spring 2009 was the low of the bear market.

People, of course, are people, and many only want to hear what they want to hear. If an investor holds stocks, they look for information that suggests the market is bullish, and they ignore bearish information. If they hold cash, they look for market opinions that suggest a bear market is imminent. They've already made up their minds and don't want to be confused by facts! But this approach doesn't work when investing. Investors should guard against the urge to look for information that confirms their view and the tendency to ignore information that goes against it. In fact, they should do the complete opposite. If an investor's position and hypothesis can stand the test of information and facts, that investor is more likely to be right and they'll have more conviction in their positions and strategy.

Some information can be difficult to trade on. Earnings are a good example. They are, however, probably the most important factor when it comes to stock prices. There can be situations where earnings match expectations but the stock price goes down because the outlook is worse than expected. There can even be situations where earnings beat expectations and the outlook is positive yet prices still go down. How? One possibility is that the expectations, which are determined from analyst polls conducted two weeks before the earnings announcement, have risen in the intervening time. The actual earnings end up being worse than the so-called "whisper numbers," which the media and the public don't know about.

How about cases where earnings beat expectations but revenues miss them? It's hard to tell in advance whether a market is more concerned about the top line (revenue) or bottom line (earnings). In some industries, the focus of earnings reports isn't actually earnings. For retailers, same-store sales growth can be more important. A miss on this vital metric can mean a big drop in stock prices, even if earnings are good. Sometimes markets pay more attention to future earnings guidance than they do to past earnings. Sometimes they're too euphoric ahead of an earnings announcement, and even a small miss can cause a big drop in the stock price; sometimes they're too despondent, and a loss that's less than expected can lead to a big rally.

In this age of free-flow information and big data, we would do well to remember Albert Einstein's (1879–1955) quote: "Information is not knowledge."

TIPS. ADVICE. OPINIONS.

Tips to stock markets are like gossip to Hollywood—they'll never die. There are always people in the stock market who aren't just looking for quick money, but for easy money; they're not only looking for big money, but for sure money. What could be better for that than tips? Tips offer opportunities that seem too good to pass up. They're irresistible. It's astounding that many people, some of them highly intelligent, persist in trying to make money by following tips unquestioningly. They're willing to blindly trust others. No one seems to care where the tips come from. They trade on all kinds of tips and rumors—spoken or printed, direct or implied. They want to be specifically told which particular stock to buy, and they have no interest in the general condition of the stock market. They don't want to do any work; they want to get something for nothing.

The tip giver, of course, is always happy to oblige the tip seeker. The tip seeker, always with a ready ear, craves not only to get but also to give tips. The tip and rumor mills always operate at full force. They're not concerned about quality or authenticity. The tip seeker isn't really just after a good tip; they're after any tip, as long as it makes good, easy money! I should double up next time! I've earned my bragging rights! If it doesn't work out, that's down to bad luck—I'll try again with the next tip.

Be aware that most tips and rumors are false. If a tip is correct, it might be insider information, and that can put you in jail. You can bet your last dollar on the certainty that insiders won't share their precious information with the world. Also bear in mind that even good tips can cost you money, especially if they've been circulating for a while. Many unquestioning investors will already have put their money where their mouths are, and the stock price will therefore already have gone up. You might be too late to the party. The risk is that after you buy, you'll end up seeing the price go down due to heavy selling by the early buyers. When there's a raging bull market, most stocks go up—tips or no tips. Tips and rumors just add oil to a raging bull fire.

Inevitably, some investors will learn from tips and rumors causing them to go wrong so often. They'll come to realize the importance of not being influenced by others. They'll learn that while tips might work sometimes, acting on them all is a losing proposition. No one ever earned a fortune by acting on tips and rumors. But for every investor who's disillusioned by tips, there's another new investor who loves them. Tips will never die.

There are some old adages on Wall Street, the origin of which no one seems to know or even care about, but whose wisdom no one questions. To some investors, they're like Bible verses are to the faithful. But not all adages are created equal. Some are wise and timeless, while others are misleading or simply wrong. Investors lose millions of dollars by accepting some of them as semi-official and therefore trustworthy. Don't follow adages blindly.

Take this adage: "Let your profits run, cut your losses fast." It works well for many traders and is widely recommended. It's a good piece of advice, but you shouldn't follow it all the time. It applies more to short-term traders than long-term investors. When you buy a stock for long-term investment, you shouldn't cut the losses too fast on a small correction of 5 percent or less. When you buy a well-diversified fund, you might not even need a stop loss. When you see a quick, substantial profit on a big, stable company, you probably want to run away with the profit before the profit runs away from you.

When I was still an undergraduate, a friend told me a particular company would do well. "Why?" I asked. "Because it's a food business," he replied. "Everyone needs to eat." That was his insight. In 2017, another friend warned me about the coming bear market and kindly informed me that he was selling his stocks and properties. "Why?" I asked. "Have you forgotten the Russian default and LTCM in 1998 and the global financial crisis in 2008?" he retorted. "This bull market has been going on long enough. I tell you, you'd better get out before 2018." We hear such arguments often. People always have investment ideas based on casual, dubious assumptions and logic. We have to simplify this complex world in order to make sense of it but oversimplification isn't going to work in the stock market.

As a young trader at a big, venerable European bank, I was struggling to understand the FX market, let alone make money. The head of the FX desk at the time had a legendary reputation. One story went that he was napping at his desk one afternoon when he suddenly woke up and hit all the voice brokers (the middle men and women who match trades between banks) over the squawk box to sell US dollars and buy Swiss francs. He then went back to his nap. Before he left for the day, he'd covered his positions at a profit.

One day, while I took a miniscule FX position and was keying in my stop-loss and profit-take orders, he took a special interest and asked what was I doing. I told him I'd established my long US dollar position at 1 US dollar to 100 Japanese yen and was placing a stop-loss order at 99 and a profit-take order at 101. The legend said: "No, you don't do that. Your profit take must be twice the stop loss." I duly changed my profit take to 102. Now, if I lost, I would lose 1 yen, and if I won, I would make 2 yen. It sounded like good advice. Days passed, weeks passed, months passed. As sound and prudent as the advice was, it didn't show on my profit-and-loss account. What went wrong? It was prudent for me to listen to an experienced, legendary trader who'd taken the effort to help a young, upcoming junior; it was logical that if the profit was double the loss, in the long term, I should come up ahead. Why was I still losing money? Had I picked the wrong currency pairs, the wrong price, the wrong time, or simply the wrong side?

After carefully studying my trades, I came to realize what had gone wrong. FX trades are mostly short term. To FX traders, holding a position overnight is medium term, and a week is long term. We usually trade intraday, buying in the morning and selling in the afternoon. Most days, currencies don't move too much. The Japanese yen typically moves by just 1 yen or so. For it to move 2 yen is a lot rarer. And that was my problem. I was often stopped out at a loss and rarely took profit. For every 10 trades, I was stopped out eight times and took profit two times. The two times I took profit, I made a total of 4 yen. The eight times I lost money, I lost 8 yen. The net result was a loss of 4 yen. And so, I learned early on that looking at the ratio of potential gain to loss is just part of the calculation—the probability of winning is every bit as important, if not more so.

Jesse Livermore (1877–1940) was a Wall Street legend—a lone wolf who always traded on his own. Percy Thomas was the unusually well-informed "Cotton King." Attracted by Thomas's charm and detailed analysis, Livermore broke his own rule and traded cotton on Thomas's advice. In just one trade, Livermore lost most of his wealth and both of his yachts.

Remember the story I told you about my first investment at the age of 10? When it came to investment advice, listening to Dad didn't work and neither did listening to a legend. Even when a legend listened to a "king," it didn't work. One Wall Street adage that is worth listening to is "seek facts diligently, seek advice no." It's perhaps a little extreme, but you get the idea.

What about expert opinion? Can we trust that? Let's consider renowned global investor Jim Rogers, who urged investors to buy commodities before that became a hot sector in the 2000s, Nassim Taleb, who popularized the term "black swan," and Jeffrey Gundlach, the "New Bond King." Many of them are highly successful participants in the financial markets. The problem is that these gurus' stars usually start to dwindle after a few years, and no one's going to ring a bell to declare that they've turned from hot to cold. There's also no way they've made the right call every single time over the years. Should you follow them or not? If you do, you might find you end up with more questions and problems than you expected.

So, we've ruled out family, legends, and experts. How about listening to and following the best investors? Some of them are eager to share their views and positions with the public. They have great long-term track records, and they put their money where their mouths are. They care about their reputations, and surely they only express their views publicly if they're confident they're right?

On October 14, 1987, in an article for the *Financial Times*, George Soros opined that the Japanese stock market would collapse before that of the US. The following Monday turned out to be Black Monday, when Wall Street saw the biggest daily crash in its history. The Japanese market continued to charge higher and only peaked at the end of 1989. In May 2008, Soros published his tenth book: *The New Paradigm for Financial Markets*. In it, he rightly warned that the financial pain of the time had only just begun. Lehman Brothers went bankrupt four months later. The ensuing crisis became the worst since the Great Depression. Sometimes Soros got it right; sometimes he got it wrong, and he readily admits his ability to forecast events is dismal despite his huge success as a speculator.

Peter Lynch was a mutual fund legend with a fantastic track record at Fidelity Investments. He wrote books to teach lay-people how to beat the professionals on Wall Street: *One Up on Wall Street* and *Beating the Street*. I have great respect for him, and I have no doubt his intentions were noble, but the fact is he's part of the 1 percent. Some investors who read his books may beat Wall Street, but certainly not me. Lynch's main suggestion was that we should keep our eyes and ears open everywhere we go—particularly in the shopping mall. The example he gave was that his wife wore L'eggs pantyhose and his kids loved to shop at Gap. He researched both companies and liked what he saw both on the ground and in the financial reports. He figured out that the companies' earnings could grow. He bought the stocks and multiplied his money. It all sounds very sensible and easy, but when my wife introduced Zara to me way before other women knew this brand, I found out that it was a Spanish company. When I started drinking Nepresso coffee and liked their business model, I discovered that it was part of Nestlé. When I saw everyone was using Facebook and came to understand its "stickiness," I didn't understand its financial reports. When I thought everyone loved Prada, the investors apparently didn't. Lynch's idea is anything but easy to implement in the real world.

Investor and hedge fund manager John Paulson chose to bet big on the subprime mortgage crisis. He won the biggest financial market haul ever, securing more than $10 billion for himself and his investors. His story was told in Gregory Zuckerman's book *The Greatest Trade Ever*, propelling him to fame. Paulson's big win in subprime was a hard act to follow, but just like everyone else, he didn't always succeed. In fact, in the years following the subprime crisis, he was actually wrong more often than he was right. His hedge fund peaked in 2011 at $36 billion. By 2019, it had shrunk to less than $10 billion. After he made his huge killing and rose to stardom, his trades were all well publicized by the media, but he went in too early to buy US and Greek banks, he got it wrong with pharmaceutical companies Allergan and Valeant, and in 2010, he was so bullish in gold that some of his funds were quoted in it. Gold, however, was in the doldrums after peaking in 2011. Nobody got to follow his greatest trade, but many got to follow his losing ones.

Warren Buffett has never written a book, but his shareholder letters, articles, and interviews over the decades have made his investment philosophy, style, and methods widely known. The stocks he buys and sells are all over the news. He's as transparent as any successful investor could be. He's extremely smart and has a photographic memory. He plays golf with CEOs, socializes with the rich and famous, and vacations with his buddy Bill Gates. He reads annual reports with great enthusiasm.

Can we just follow what he buys and sells? Unfortunately it's not that easy. First of all, many companies under his holding company Berkshire Hathaway aren't listed, so we can't buy them. Second of all, for the listed companies he's buying or selling, we always know with a few weeks' time lag, which means that in most cases, we're buying at a higher price and selling at a lower price. In the past, Buffett has famously bought some iconic companies, including The Coca Cola Company and American Express, to hold them "forever," but he's also bought and sold some losers, such as IBM and Kraft Heinz. Maybe someone out there has followed his purchases and sales religiously over the years and has managed to outperform the market, but to follow him now is probably too late. His performance in the last decade is clearly not as outstanding as it was in the past, mainly because he has too much money to deploy and too few big companies to choose from.

How about following his calls to buy stocks? On September 16, 2001, Buffett, together with Treasury Secretary Robert Rubin and famed General Electric CEO Jack Welch, appeared on television to urge Americans to buy stocks. When the markets re-opened on September 17, after having been closed for six days due to 9/11, the Dow Jones fell 7 percent in a day and 14 percent by the end of the week. The bear market didn't bottom until spring 2003. In October 2008, Buffett tried to rally the people again, when he wrote an op-ed for *The New York Times*, titled "Buy American I am." In it, he wrote that he couldn't predict the short-term movements of the stock market but was confident it would go higher, perhaps substantially so, in the years to come. He was absolutely right. The Dow Jones was around 9,000 when the op-ed was published. Ten years later, it had tripled, although those who bought immediately at Buffet's urging needed to ride out the 30 percent down move, which lasted until March 2009.

It's not uncommon to see successful investors offer opposing views. The Little Book of Investing series, published by John Wiley & Sons, is designed to help average people understand various investment topics. Among other titles, it includes *The Little Book That Beats The Market* by Joel Greenblatt—a hedge fund manager—and *The Little Book of Common Sense Investing* by John C. Bogle—the founder of The Vanguard Group. Both authors are extremely successful, respected investors, and both quote Benjamin Graham and Warren Buffett in their books, yet they put forward opposing messages about investing. Bogle strongly believed that passive, low-cost index investing is best, and Greenblatt offers a "magic formula," which he says investors can follow easily to beat the market.

Sometimes a war of words breaks out between the top investors. Occasionally, that escalates into a war of money. Carl Icahn and Bill Ackman, both billionaire hedge fund managers, had an epic fight over Herbalife, a nutritional supplement producer. Icahn was bullish and took a long position; Ackman was bearish and took a short position. The much older, richer Icahn won the five-year-long battle, coming away with $1 billion, while Ackman raised his white flag and exited the trade in 2018.

How about following the most powerful person in the financial markets: the Fed chair? In June 1965, Fed chairman William Martin (1906–1988) gave a speech in which he talked about "disquieting similarities between our present prosperity and the fabulous twenties." The Dow Jones dropped 1 percent that day and 6 percent over the next three weeks. The market hit bottom in July before going on to set a record high in October. In February 2007, then chairman Ben Bernanke told a congressional panel that the weakness in housing had stabilized and wouldn't spill over into the rest of the economy. A year later, Lehman Brothers' bankruptcy ushered in the global financial crisis. In August 2014, Janet Yellen, chair of the Federal Reserve, was worried about high asset prices, especially in parts of the bond market. Carl Icahn chimed in and said he agreed. In the end, there were no major down moves in the markets in 2014 or 2015. Indeed, the bullish stock market kept on roaring for the rest of the decade.

OK, so if we can't follow the most powerful central banker, how about the most powerful man on earth? The day after Black Thursday, in 1929, President Hoover said: "The fundamental business of the country … is on a sound and prosperous basis." Soothing words indeed, but the following Monday and Tuesday, the stock market was blacker than the week before. It went on to drop an unprecedented four years in a row from 1929 to 1932. In July 2002, President George W. Bush claimed "there is value in the market now," but the market only hit bottom in spring the following year. Ironically, the stock markets take the unconventional, erratic President Trump more seriously. His insistence on a strong stock market to prove he's doing a good job seems to make investors more willing to put money in stocks.

What's the lesson from all this? if we follow the successful and powerful in making our investment decisions, the results may not be as encouraging as we had hoped. J. P. Morgan (1837–1913), the most powerful financier of the early 20th century, was asked by a reporter what the stock market was going to do. His reply: "It will fluctuate."

FORECASTS

A week before President Kennedy was assassinated in 1963, Benjamin Graham delivered a speech in which he said: "In my nearly fifty years of experience in Wall Street, I've found that I know less and less about what the stock market is going to do but I know more and more about what investors ought to do; and that's a pretty vital change in attitude." In my much shorter experience in Main Street, I've learned the same: I know less and less about what the stock market is going to do. I've gone from being opinionated about market directions to reactive to market moves. I've evolved from following forecasts to occasionally going against them.

Every day, the media bombards us with all kinds of forecasts and predictions. There are forecasts from multinational institutions such as the IMF and the World Bank, from famous and successful individuals such as Ray Dalio and Jeffrey Gundlach, and from banks and broking houses. The objects of their forecasts range from economic growth to inflation, from company earnings to stock prices, from gold to gas prices, from copper production to cotton demand, and so on.

Forecasters are experts in their fields, with analysts covering companies in the same industry, while some chief economists cover a whole nation. Many are hardworking and smart, but their reports are generally descriptive rather than analytical. There are also sometimes inaccuracies in their reports. Most only repeat what's already common knowledge in the financial community. Nevertheless, they know their fields much better than the average investor does. Being knowledgeable, however, doesn't mean they can see into the future. If it did, every sports pundit would be a millionaire from betting on their predictions.

It's prudent to take financial market forecasts with a pinch of salt—they're not weather forecasts. Financial markets are extremely complicated, with many moving parts. They're tightly woven webs that respond to unpredictable human impulses. Things are always tentative and subject to many different factors and changes. Of course, we understand the economy and markets much better today than we did 100 years ago, but we still have much to learn. We know roughly how they work, but we don't know exactly how they work.

It's important to realize that all forecasts and predictions are based on partial—and sometimes grossly inadequate—information. Forecasters sometimes interpret information incorrectly, as they tend to see things through a biased lens. Regardless of how smart, hardworking, or brilliant they are, they still don't have a crystal ball. It's impossible to predict when and how market participants will make rational or emotional decisions individually or collectively. To complicate things further, change is constant. Look at it this way: if we can't predict the result of a football match with 22 players and one ball, how can we predict financial markets comprising millions of participants?

Even so, forecasts are ubiquitous. Financial institutions employ thousands of economists and analysts to forecast. But if their forecasts are often wrong, why do they thrive? It all comes down to basic economics—supply and demand. Many investors are unsure and confused by uncertainties—and financial markets are always uncertain. Investors look for guidance and a feeling of being in control, and these forecasters provide them with just that. People believe the financial professionals because they look smart and confident on TV, have big titles, and work for reputable banks. Psychological experiments have shown that humans like to follow authority, and these forecasters appear authoritative.

Surely some of them must be good at predictions though? True, some get it right from time to time, but none of them get it right consistently over a number of years. If a forecaster is brilliant, they won't stay in that job for long; they'll use their accurate forecasts to make millions, either for themselves or for a hedge fund. These people make so many forecasts and predictions during their careers that they're bound to get it right sometimes. The ones who get it wrong are quickly forgotten. It's like a game of golf. Average shots aren't reported—only the hole in one is newsworthy. Bear this in mind whenever you look at forecasts —lopsided reporting gives the impression that forecasters are right more often than they actually are.

When a big crowd is asked to guess the number of jelly beans in a glass jar, the average guess is actually very close to the real number. This phenomenon, known as "the wisdom of crowds," was discovered by polymath Francis Glaton (1822–1911) in the early 20th century. It was popularized by *The New Yorker* finance writer James Surowieki in his 2004 book of the same title. So, if that's the case, surely the average forecasts of so many professionals must be better than an individual professional, right? Not exactly. Sometimes they get it right, and sometimes they get it terribly wrong.

In both 2001 and 2008, analysts predicted a double-digit return for the S&P 500. Both years ended with double digit losses— a drop of 13 and 38 percent respectively. Why doesn't the wisdom of crowds work? First, this is a forecast of the future—it's not quite as simple as guessing the number of jelly beans in a jar. Second, unlike the individuals asked to guess the jelly beans, a forecast isn't done independently. The result of jelly bean guesses would be very different if answers were reviewed before being submitted. Analysts speak to their counterparts—ex-colleagues, ex-schoolmates, and so on. They compare notes over a drink. If they don't know each other, they take a look at reports by others that precede their own. Very few analysts want to make an out-of-consensus forecast, as the chance of getting it right isn't high, while the chance of embarrassment is. Finally, when an analyst makes a bold forecast, their report might not even be published because of internal censorship. A large number of analysts are junior and only have a few years' experience. Prior to starting their job, they were students, not experts in whatever field or industry they've been assigned to. Their bosses wouldn't want a bold-but-wrong forecast that could embarrass and tarnish the company's reputation. Analysts are therefore strongly incentivized to make consensus rather than independent forecasts.

Remember as well that forecasts aren't static—it's common for analysts to adjust them when new information comes in. This is the right thing to do. No one should ignore new or important information. What it does, however, is it moves the goalposts. New information comes in all the time. When you're trying to forecast the price of a stock one year down the road, how do you know what's going to happen in the next quarter, let alone the next year?

HSBC, one of the biggest banks in the world, is listed in both London and Hong Kong and is widely followed by analysts. Before the vote on Brexit, newspapers quoted many analysts as saying that HSBC would see its profits drop if the British pound was to fall in the event of a "leave" vote. Actually, this is quite puzzling, as HSBC earns most of its money overseas—the majority of it in Hong Kong. Earnings of a billion Hong Kong dollars would therefore translate into more British pounds if the pound weakened. After a knee-jerk reaction that saw the stock hit a low following the surprising result, the share price then rose for months, and there was no drop of earnings due to Brexit and a weaker pound.

Bank analyst reports on companies usually end with a buy, hold, or sell recommendation. Typically they recommend more buys and holds than sells, though this has changed in recent years, and things are less skewed now than they were prior to 2000. Back then, a sell recommendation was as rare as a panda. Analyst reports were given to clients for free, and stock analysts were often pressured by the banks' management to issue buy recommendations. The banks hoped companies would be pleased with a buy recommendation and therefore give them high-revenue business, such as mergers and acquisitions and bond issues, in return. Stock analysts' salaries and bonuses were paid by these revenues. It was a clear case of conflict of interest. The regulators fined Wall Street banks, including Citibank, hundreds of millions in the early 2000s. These days, the buy-to-sell recommendation ratio is less skewed, but analysts are still wary about issuing a sell recommendation. The company on a sell recommendation may blacklist the analyst and give them less access to the company's management. The banks still pressure analysts against sell recommendations, but these days they do it discreetly and verbally.

Stock price forecasts are usually based on the fundamentals of a company, and the price should move according to changes in those fundamentals. Sometimes, however, the tail wags the dog, and a forecast can move prices. In December 1998, during the dot-com boom, star internet analyst Henry Blodget raised his one-year target price for Amazon to $400. At the time, it was selling at just $240. The market reaction was fast and furious, and the stock surpassed $400 in a matter of weeks. Admittedly this is an extreme case, however reports and target prices from prominent analysts and reputable banks regularly move prices, albeit to a lesser extent.

I'll leave the final words on forecasting to Warren Buffett, who once said: "Forecasts may tell you a great deal about the forecaster; they tell you nothing about the future."

MEDIA

Investors need information to make sound decisions, but understanding how media works and knowing how it can both help and hurt us is indispensable to profitable investing. We have more choices now than ever before—more TV channels, more newspapers (available online), more websites, and more fake news. Investors are bombarded with political, economic, and financial news daily and instantaneously. This explosion of choice and the immediate nature of news in today's internet age is a double-edged sword—it can confuse us or it can clarify things for us. We need to digest daily news correctly and put market moves in their proper context and perspective. If used properly, media can help us see the truth and close the gap between perception and reality. Successful investors use facts—not opinions or forecasts.

Media organizations are generally run as a business, with the aim of making money, or as a mouthpiece and trophy asset for billionaires. Either way, there's an incentive for them to attract readership or viewership. Providing objective news and truth might take a backseat; sensational headlines and dramatic descriptions are commonplace. An analyst once described an unloved sector as "dancing between the raindrops." A daily update on the stock market is always a mix of facts and flavor. Investors must focus on facts, but reporters must write something each day, even when no news of importance presents itself.

Like the ocean, the market is never still, and journalists find logical explanations for even the smallest ripples. Sometimes market moves are completely random and seem to have no explanation. A journalist can't admit they're clueless though, so they'll guess or even invent a reason to satisfy the public's clamorous demand for an answer. When I was a junior FX trader, an equally junior journalist from Reuters used to call me regularly to ask for updates on the FX market. I often had no clue, but I felt obliged to give her some market color. Some of my explanations made it onto the newswire!

Just as all animals are equal but some are more equal than others, all media outlets are biased but some are more biased than others. The media industry is biased by nature. The owners are biased; the journalists are biased; the interviewer and interviewee are biased. In her farewell article for a reputable financial newspaper, one retiring journalist wrote that whenever she published an unfavorable article about a company or a CEO, she would be summoned to "punishment" lunches at smart restaurants, where they lashed out at her. At least it was always a smart restaurant. The point is that it's not easy for journalists to tell the truth. I don't mean to chide the media, and understanding this flaw doesn't mean we should lose all trust in media outlets—exposing the Watergate scandal was one of the industry's finest moments. There are in fact many fine media organizations, of which quality, objective journalism is a trademark—just look at the *Financial Times, The New York Times*, and HuffPost—but we need to recognize that the flaw exists and then filter the bias to get an objective picture.

In the media, there will always be pessimists and naysayers, and there's always a demand, and therefore good supply, of bearish news. Some cynics have shot to fame for calling a bear market or crisis right. Nouriel Roubini, who called the US housing market collapse, is still basking in his fame as "Dr. Doom" a decade later. He's not the only one. Contrarian investor Marc Faber was given the same nickname in 1987. Luckily though, the stock market still has more boom than doom.

If we were to listen to these bears, we'd never pull the trigger and put a dollar in stock market. They jump on any slight bit of evidence as to why a turn is coming and are forever warning of an impending drop. They will, in the end, be right—a bear will eventually come. There's one daily newspaper column by a perpetual bear that I read faithfully. His column is prominently displayed at the top of the page. He's always showing bearish evidence, often with figures and charts. When the market is good, he casts doubts. When the market is great, he warns a crisis is coming. When the market is volatile, he says cash is king. When the market is up, he advises selling stocks and holding cash. When the market is down, he recommends selling stocks to raise cash. When there's a rebound, he says it will be short lived. When there's a correction, he says the worst is yet to come. When the market is calm, he says a storm is coming. When the market is bad, he proudly reminds readers "I told you so." I read it every day because it's informative. He covers a wide range of topics, and lays out many good facts. He also gives me an idea of the market sentiment and what these bears are looking at. Most importantly, since my outlook is generally bullish and my position is long stocks, his articles keep me alert. Most of the time I dismiss him, but one day he'll be right.

Public psychology is one of the most important factors in shaping stock prices. Knowing the wind of public sentiment is a way to profit in the stock market. The media affect public psychology and public psychology affects the media. The media don't just report what's going on though—sometimes they actually shape events. The weekend just before the October 19, 1987 crash, *The New York Times*, the *Los Angeles Times*, *Barron's*, and many other newspapers were all comparing 1987 to 1929. Analysts on television also spoke about the similarities. Without doubt, the media's fear of a crash contributed to it.

The media always promote the fads and fancies of the day. When oil was surging in the 1970s, news outlets loved the oil experts and featured them frequently. During the late 1990s, when internet and technology were in vogue, some analysts, like Henry Blodget and Mary Meeker, enjoyed the fame usually reserved for movie stars. In the 2000s, the acronym BRIC (Brazil, Russia, India, China) was all the rage. In the 2010s, FAANG (Facebook, Apple, Amazon, Netflix, Google) took over and was all over the news.

The media always manage to find a simple, logical narrative to describe financial markets. Some investors accept this as gospel, regardless of whether the story is actually true or not. When enough investors believe something, it can become self-fulfilling. In 1997, the Hong Kong stock market was roaring on the firm belief that both China and the Hong Kong government wanted a strong stock market for the handover. It took a hurricane—the Asian financial crisis—to knock the bull over later that year. In the run up to the internet bubble burst, many investors were led to believe earnings and revenue weren't important for internet companies and that only website views, or "eyeballs," mattered. They soon found out that wasn't the case. During the gigantic run-up of the Chinese stock market in 2006 and 2007, many Chinese investors believed the government wouldn't allow a stock crash ahead of the 2008 Olympic Games in Beijing. The bubble couldn't last until the summer of 2008 though. It burst in October 2007.

Media reports are full of conventional wisdom and popular narrative, but not everything is always as it seems. Prior to the 1970s, economists believed there was a trade-off between inflation and unemployment—if one was high, the other would be low. Stagflation—high inflation combined with high unemployment in the 1970s—proved that theory wrong. In 1998, when Russia was facing financial strain, the common belief was that Russia was "too nuclear to fail" and that the US and its allies would provide financial help to make sure the Samsonite briefcase that holds the nuclear weapon's digital codes didn't fall into the wrong hands. The help did come, but only after investors suffered huge losses—George Soros lost more than $1 billion—when Russia defaulted on both its domestic and international debts.

There are some market "facts" the media "recycle" regularly.

For example, we read again and again a variation of "the stock markets tend to turn three (or six) months before economies do." It's one of those facts that has been repeated so many times and over so many years that no one knows where it originated. Nobody seems to question its truthfulness though.

After the nadir in world stock markets in 2003, both developed and developing countries were recovering nicely, with the developing countries doing particularly well. After many decades fighting one crisis after another, media narrative was that they'd learned their lessons and were strong enough to stand on their own two feet. The day had come when developing countries would "decouple" from the developed countries. But when the subprime crisis hit the US and Europe, the developing countries fared worse than their developed counterparts.

In 1984, Continental Illinois was the seventh largest bank in the US and was winning awards left, right, and center. With its chairman named "Banker of the Year," it was tagged by *The Wall Street Journal* as the "bank to beat." But when oil prices fell, the bank, which had a big loan book to the oil sector, came crashing. It was the biggest bank run in the history of the world. Continental Illinois was bankrupt, and the US government was forced to bail it out.

The bankruptcy of Enron years later wasn't only a sad tale of "cooking the books," it was also a story of media failure. Even after the relentless drop in price from just under $100 to single digits, more than half of analysts still recommended a buy. From 1995 to 2000, *Fortune* magazine even crowned Enron "America's most innovative company."

After Eddie Lampert successfully bought and turned around Kmart, he was dubbed "the next Warren Buffett" by the media. In 2005, Kmart bought Sears. Lampert said that putting the two together was a "transformation." In 2018, after shedding asset after asset and closing down store after store, Sears filed for bankruptcy.

A couple of years earlier, sometime in 2016, there had been

widespread narrative in the press as to why luxury goods weren't doing well. One reason put forward as being obvious was Chinese President Xi Jinping's anti-corruption move. Another reason given was that millennials treasured experiences more than material goods—that they'd rather spend money on a good holiday than a Gucci bag. In the age of Instagram, they needed a lot more new clothes. Zara was in, Prada was out. But by 2017, when luxury goods turned around, Gucci was citing the enthusiasm of millennials over its funky designs as one reason for the explosive growth. Certain human traits never change: the desire to have luxury goods and the urge to show off. A wise man once said: "It is not greed but envy that drives the world." The envy was still there, it had just shifted from the real world to the world of Instagram.

PART V: GET READY

RISK AND RETURN

Risk and return are to investment like patty and cheese to a cheeseburger—they're the crux. You always have to consider risk together with return—like two sides of a coin, they're inseparable. When you look at investment returns, you can't just look at the potential gain; you also have to look at the risk of losing. However, unlike roulette, investment returns don't have a mathematical probability—it's all guesswork. Investors have to make a judgment call on probabilities. When you see a high return, your first question needs to be "what are the risks?" Ideally, this would be as natural to you as breathing in and out —you breathe the return in and breathe the risk out. If you like a stock, how does it compare to a broad-based fund? How much higher is the return? Is the extra return worth the extra risk?

Opportunities are thrown at us every day. You need to compare them all and only commit if the risk and return are favorable and are better than the other choices. No matter how high the return and how low the risk, never put all your eggs in one basket, and never put half or even quarter of your eggs in one stock. Don't be seduced by a high return and thereby disregard the risk of losing all your eggs. Too often, risks that are remote are treated as essentially nonexistent. That's fine if your financial survival isn't at stake, but you can't take the risk that all your financial resources might be completely wiped out. Once you've lost all your money, you're out of the game. You can't invest anymore, and the financial ruin will bring hardship to you and your family.

What are the risks of stock investing? Market risk, or systematic risk as it's sometimes called, refers to the risk of general market conditions on the price of a stock. An interest rate hike from the Fed is a market risk. A terrorist attack is a market risk. Specific risk, otherwise known as unsystematic risk, is the inherent risk in a company's conditions—an earnings report or the departure of the CEO, for example. Liquidity risk relates to the ability to get in and out of a position at a reasonable price and time. Geopolitical risk refers to the interaction of geography, economics, and politics. Tensions in the Middle East and North Korea are recurring geopolitical risks. Inflation risk is the risk of reduced purchasing power, which can cause the stock market to crater. These common risks are easy to understand but hard to quantify. To make a sound judgment, you need to assess each risk objectively and consider its probability. Some people like to give them numbers, such as an 80 percent chance. Just remember that the assessment of risks is more of an art than a science, and it's far from perfect. Getting it wrong can have significant consequences—Long-Term Capital Management (LTCM), a multi-billions hedge fund run by some of the financial world's smartest brains including Nobel laureates, misjudged its risks in 1998 and had to be bailed out.

Investors face multiple risks all the time, whether perceived or real. As Donald Rumsfeld, the US secretary of defense under both President Gerald Ford (1913–2006) and President George W. Bush, once said: "There are known knowns; there are things we know we know. We also know there are known unknowns; that is to say we know there are some things we do not know. But there are also unknown unknowns—the ones we don't know we don't know." MF Global, whose main business was executing and clearing trades for clients, went bust suddenly in 2011. Its clients were stunned; many didn't know this could happen. Their accounts, which were supposed to be segregated and protected, weren't. Many customers were left with uncertainties in the wake of the bankruptcy. Fortunately, two years later, they recouped all the money they were owed. Such risks are real, and you need to manage them well. If your capital is substantial and forms a big portion of your net worth, it would be wise to have more than one investment account. On the other hand, if you worry too much about risks, you'll never invest. Investing is risk taking; you just need to take calculated risks and not reckless ones. Risk management is essential to successful investing.

US government bonds are the most liquid bonds in the world and are considered to be the safest—so safe, in fact, that the interest rates of three-month Treasury bills and 10-year Treasury bonds are thought of as "risk-free rates." Of course, every investment bears some sort of risk, no matter how small that may be, but the concept of risk-free rates is an important one because you can use it as the starting point for each of your investments—it provides a benchmark that every financial investment can be measured against.

Whenever you consider a potential investment, the first thing you need to do is compare the risk and return to the risk-free rate. If the expected return is 3 percent and the risk-free rate is 2 percent, you have to make a judgment call as to whether the extra 1 percent return is worth the extra risk. Alternatively, you can make a judgment about the risks of the investment first and only invest if the return is high enough, say 2 or 5 percent above the risk-free rate. Obviously, the higher the risk, the higher the return you should demand and expect.

What's a realistic long-term investment return? Cash has the lowest return among all asset classes. Bonds also have historically lower returns than stocks. In the US, the average annual return of bonds is about 5 to 8 percent, and the average annual return of stocks is about 10 percent. According to one survey, which covered 32 countries and twenty-five thousand people, 16 percent of investors expect their return over the next five years to be at least 20 percent per year. 31 percent expect a return of 10 to 20 percent. In summary, of those surveyed, nearly half expect to beat the market, some by a wide margin of more than 10 percent. Even the best stock investors—and there are only a handful of them—can only achieve a 20 to 30 percent average annual return over 20 years or more.

If you invested in Warren Buffett's Berkshire Hathaway for the last 50 years, you would have seen an annual return of 20 percent. This might sound like a low figure for the world's top investors, but when it's compounded, the return is staggering. If you can generate a 30 percent annual return for 13 years, you turn $1 into $30. If you can repeat that return for another 13 years, your $1 becomes $900. For anyone who invested in Berkshire Hathaway 50 years ago, $1 turn has turned into $9,100.

For the rest of us, we need to set realistic expectations for our returns, in which the lower boundary is the current risk-free rate and the upper boundary is 20 to 30 percent. If we leave the decisions to others and put all our money in a diversified US stock portfolio, our return will be around 10 percent, while a mix and match of stocks and bonds will give us somewhere between 6 and 9 percent. Remember these numbers—they're useful benchmarks that you need to know whenever you're being asked to buy financial products.

Market wisdom is to go for "high-risk, high-return" trades. It seems logical, however financial markets don't work perfectly all the time. Occasionally, there's an investment that has a low risk and a high return. Everyone will rush for it, making either the return lower, or the risk higher, or both. The low-risk, high-return trade disappears, and the world is back to high-risk, high-return and low-risk, low-return options. Sometimes the low-risk, high-return trade stays for a while. How? When there's a crisis, everyone sells because they perceive the risks to be high and the returns to be low. The investing public assesses the risk as higher than it really is and the expected return lower than the actual return. The market is hairy, and headlines are scary. Investors are fearful. Their gloomy, short-term outlook prevents them from seeing a pot of gold at the end of the tunnel.

VOLATILITY AND LIQUIDITY

Volatility is equivalent to risks, or so some market participants believe. Financial markets generally measure the risks of a stock or asset class by its volatility. The more volatile a stock is, the more risky it's deemed to be. It's a popular measure because the historical volatility of a stock can be measured and quantified easily. The proponents of using volatility believe a stock's previous price movements reflect its risks. It's a neat and elegant way to measure, but it has its limitations.

One problem is that volatility measures both up and down moves. A stock that has big up moves and small down moves is more volatile than a stock that has small up moves and small down moves. The former is considered more risky because of its high volatility, but this doesn't actually make sense. A stock that's heading higher isn't any more risky than one that's moving sideways. Another problem is that the volatility of stock prices is driven more by the sentiment of investors than it is by fundamentals. Yes, sentiment matters in the short term, but it's the fundamentals that will triumph eventually. Historical volatility doesn't help either, as it doesn't provide a good indication of future volatility. Often investors are lured into believing that recent low volatility is going to last. They then panic as it shoots up. The lesson: don't rely purely on volatility when thinking of risks; you should also consider the chance of losing all or part of your capital.

When you buy a stock, you need to be psychologically prepared for volatility in its price. Most of the time, your buying price isn't the low, and you have to deal with an immediate loss. You need a plan to deal with the price swing and not let it turn into a mood swing. This involves looking at the volatility of your individual stocks, funds, and the whole portfolio as a whole. Often you'll find you misjudged your comfort zone. When the market is calm and going your way, you'll be relaxed and feel in control; when the market is heading down and becoming more volatile, you might not have the steely nerves you thought you had. Not many people can sit through a volatile market like a Zen master. Cutting down your portfolio size when the market is volatile gives you a better chance of not panicking at the worst time and ending up selling in the depths of a bear market. When the market is euphoric and rising at a significant pace rather than steadily, it's a good idea to take some profit. Don't let greed blind you. Adjust your position size according to the market's volatility. The more volatile it is, the smaller position you should hold. If you hold too much, your portfolio will swing too far and you'll be at risk of making hasty or bad decisions.

From time to time, when the market is moving up nicely without big down days, we hear warnings that this is the calm before the storm. It's a metaphor everyone understands. Calm, however, doesn't lead to the outcomes many investors assume it will; it can last longer than expected and isn't a good predictor of when a storm will arrive. Since the Great Depression, there have been 20 bear markets in the US. Only nine of them saw low volatility beforehand. In other words, more than half the bear markets had gray, unsettled days before the big storm. In the 1920s, a long period of calm ended in the autumn of 1927, about two years before the crash. In the 1980s, the calm ended in the spring of 1986, 1 1/2 years before the biggest one-day crash of the US stock market. Two thousand and seventeen stands as one of the least volatile years, with a nice, steady uptrend. There were warnings then, however, that clouds were gathering and a storm was coming. The longest bull market ever was still charging at the end of the decade. A calm market as a warning that investors are being lulled into complacency and that a crash is imminent sounds sensible, but it's certainly not always true in the stock market.

When I first read that the stock market has more big up days than big down days, I thought it was a mistake. I was surprised because a bull market tends to be long and smooth, whereas a bear market is fast and sharp. Memory, however, can fool us. We tend to remember the bad things rather than the good things. We remember the crash of 1987, the internet bubble burst, and the global financial crisis. We remember the big, sharp down moves in those bear markets. We forget the days when the markets were making big up moves. True, the biggest-ever move was down—on Black Monday in October 1987—but if we talk about moves of a few percent or higher, there have been more ups than there have downs. On January 3, 2001, the Nasdaq surged 14.2 percent after the Fed surprised the market with a cut in between its scheduled meetings. This jump surpassed the record of 10.5 percent, which had been set the previous December. On October 13, 2008, the S&P 500 jumped 11.6 percent, right after the worst week in its history. The stock market cheered the aggressive plans by governments to guarantee loans and take ownership of banks.

One reason we see lots of big up days during a crisis or a bear market is there's an unusually high amount of short interest in stocks. This can cause a stampede when every short seller covers their positions at the same time. The biggest-ever yearly move in the US stock market wasn't down—it was up. It happened in 1915, when the Dow Jones rose by 82 percent in the midst of World War I.

Since the end of World War II, the US stock market has been up roughly three out of every four years. The intra-year decline per annum, however, has been quite substantial. Since 1980, the annual return of the S&P 500 has been positive 31 out of 40 years, but the average intra-year decline has been about 14 percent. This is significant, as the average annual return is about 10 percent. To enjoy a positive return at the end of a year, an investor needs to sit through some ugly declines. Two years after the 1987 crash, US stock markets experienced a "mini-crash." On Friday, October 13, 1989, the S&P 500 closed 6 percent lower. Market participants were at a loss. Some claimed it was due to the failed deal between UAL Corporation and United Airlines. Others blamed automatic selling by computers, but whatever the reason, the stock market soon recovered.

On May 6, 2010, a "flash crash" saw the Dow Jones free-fall 9 percent in a matter of minutes. This time, the culprit was a trader who wrote an algorithm to spoof the market. Almost as quickly as it had dropped, the market recovered much of the decline. Quick reversals in stock markets aren't a recent phenomenon. More than half a century ago, on May 28, 1962, the Dow Jones dropped 35 points—almost 6 percent. The next day, after sliding another 23 points in the morning, the market changed direction with sudden vigor and gained 27 points by its close. The SEC did a thorough investigation of this "Flash Crash of 1962" and concluded that it was due to "a complex interaction of causes and effects—including rational and emotional motivations as well as a variety of mechanisms and pressures."

According to some academic studies, "low-volatility" companies—those steady, boring stocks that fluctuate less than the overall market—tend to do well over time. The theory is that these stocks are unfairly cast aside by investors who chase the volatile but fashionable stocks and that they'll reward investors in the long run. Some fund managers and academics dispute these findings, but you don't need an expert to tell you such a finding is dubious—you just need to apply some common sense. If only investors could have the best of both worlds—low risks (volatility) and high returns!

When investing in emerging markets—whether stock or currency markets—always keep in mind that they're volatile. On August 27, 1998, the Russian stock market plunged 17 percent to an all-time low. The ruble had devalued 10 days prior, falling from 6.3 to the US dollar to 11. By October 6, one year after hitting a high of 571, the Russian RTS Index hit a new low of 37. In India, when the Congress Party surprised everyone by winning the 2004 election over the incumbent Bharatiya Janata Party, the stock market dropped 18 percent in a day. The fall proved to be just a big dip in India's multi-year bull market. On October 6, 2008, at the height of the global financial crisis, the MSCI Emerging Markets Index fell 11 percent—the biggest drop since records began in 1987. And on August 12, 2019, Argentina's MERVAL index plummeted 38 percent and the peso 15 percent due to a shocking election result. Foreign investors lost 48 percent in dollar terms in just one day!

Understanding and managing volatility is an important aspect of successful investing. Some investors, concerned about the risks that volatility brings, prefer to stick to bonds over stocks. They feel uneasy with the daily movements of stocks and are afraid of a bear market. Without doubt, the stock market is more volatile than the bond market. Investors who choose the stock market have to prepare themselves like a sailor going out to sea; they have to be ready to weather a few storms.

Liquidity in financial markets refers to the ease of buying and selling financial products. A liquid stock is one with many ready buyers and sellers, meaning a big order can be executed quickly and without having a significant impact on the price. The price difference between a buy price (bid) and a sell price (offer) is called the spread. A liquid market has a thin spread, while an illiquid market has a wide spread. The thinner the spread, the cheaper the transaction cost to investors. Most stocks and funds are liquid enough for retail investors, who don't trade in millions of dollars. Financial exchanges are always pushing for more liquidity, which is more relevant to institutional investors than retail investors.

Though the level of liquidity is more than enough for us most of the time, keep in mind that it can quickly disappear if there's a crisis. Buyers either vanish or only appear at a much lower price. While the next bid may be 1 cent lower in normal times, in a crisis, it could be a whole dollar lower. The spread we usually see, say 54.99/55.00, becomes 54.00/55.00. For each bid that has 100 buyers in normal times, it has just one during a crisis.

The most extreme case of poor liquidity I've ever experienced happened in the currency market. July 2, 1997 was a day Thailand will never forget—when the central bank gave up defending its currency after months of relentless attacks by foreign banks and hedge funds. This started a domino effect that spread to Malaysia, the Philippines, Indonesia, Singapore, and even as far away as Hong Kong, Taiwan, and South Korea. Each country's currency began to fall precipitously.

The day before the fateful devaluation of the baht, the Indonesian rupiah (IDR) was trading in a band of around 2,500 to 1 US dollar. In the currency markets, banks trade against each other in millions of US dollars per trade—often tens or even hundreds of millions. The rupiah was no exception, and a standard trade size was $10 million. The liquidity was good, and the spread was 1 rupiah wide, which meant if the bid to buy dollars and sell rupiahs was 2,500, the offer to sell dollars and buy rupiahs would be 2,501. After the baht was devalued, however, the rupiah weakened steadily, and liquidity worsened in the ensuing months as the Asian crisis unfolded. Then came a day, in early 1998, when things reached a point of absurdity. One particular lunchtime, when liquidity was at its worst, pandemonium reigned. The prices were quoted over the squawk box by the brokers.

"10,000, 12,000, in 1." (A bank bid to buy USD and sell 10,000 IDR, and another bank offered to sell USD and buy 12,000 IDR. The spread had widened to 2,000 IDR! The 1 refers to the size of the bid and offer. In this case it meant USD 1 million.)

"12,000 taken!" (A bank panicked and took the offer. Almost certainly, it had hit its stop loss.)

"12,000, 14,000, in half." (This time the size was USD 0.5 million)

"Taken!" came back almost instantly.

"14,000, 17,000, in half."

"Taken!"

I hadn't seen anything like this before, and I haven't seen any-thing like it since—not even the global financial crisis beat it.

GROWTH. VALUE. PRICE.

Stocks can be classified as either value stocks or growth stocks. The term value stock means the price of the stock is lower than its "value." There are many ways to measure values, such as price-to-earnings (P/E) and price-to-book (P/B) ratios. Investors looking for value stocks are those who are seeking a bargain—they want to buy something that has a value of $2 but is selling at $1. It's not easy to find a value stock, and even if you can find a genuine bargain, the degree by which it's undervalued is usually limited. Value hunters believe the values are bound to prevail and that it's just a matter of time before the price moves closer to the value. However, the time it takes for the price to adjust to its true value is usually considerable—it can take years.

Benjamin Graham and David L. Dodd (1895–1988) wrote the bible of value investing, *Security Analysis*, in 1934. Graham went on to write another classic investment book, *The Intelligent Investor*, in 1949 and became to value stock investing what Isaac Newton was to physics. To appreciate Graham's work, we first need to understand the stock market in the years leading up to the publication of the books. At the time, Wall Street was like the Wild West—buying stocks was more like gambling than investing. The investing public had no idea about the value of a company, and they didn't care. The buying of stocks was largely based on tips and rumors, syndicate manipulations, and corners.

Graham's idea was that every company has an "intrinsic value" based on tangible assets, earnings, dividends, and so on. That value, he recognized, is hard to derive and also prone to error, as the factors affecting it are innumerable. He therefore believed that an investor should only buy a stock if there is a "margin of safety," i.e. that the stock is selling at well below the imprecise intrinsic value. Most investors only pay attention to the price of a stock, but Graham believed an investor shouldn't look at investing as buying a piece of paper but rather as buying a small piece of a business.

Graham introduced the allegory of "Mr. Market" to help investors understand that the stock market is sentiment driven, with investors as a whole subject to both euphoria and despair. He believed the stock market is a voting machine in the short term, affected by Mr. Market, and a weighing machine in the long term, reflecting the value of the companies—the market appraisal of a stock can deviate greatly from its value, both on the upside and on the downside, but the gap will close up eventually.

Just as water always seeks its level, stock prices are always seeking a level of values. We know the prices of stocks—that's easy. The hard part is knowing their value. According to Warren Buffett: "Price is what you pay; value is what you get." Novice investors only concern themselves with price, not value. They look at the high and low prices of a stock over the last three months and the last three years. To determine whether it's worth buying or not, they consider its historical prices and maybe add in P/E ratios to satisfy themselves that they're being rather sophisticated.

The definition of whether a stock is "cheap" or "expensive," however, isn't down to its current price in relation to its historical prices; it comes down to whether the company's fundamentals and values are significantly better or worse than the current price. Novice investors have a tendency to attribute true value to the price level. Consequently, when the stock price sinks, bargain hunters rush in to scoop it up, thinking it must now be cheap. What they don't realize is that if the fundamentals are bad enough, the lower price can still be expensive relative to its value. When the price soars, the urge to sell the expensive stock becomes irresistible to many people. This can be a costly mistake because an expensive growth stock can grow for many years, and its stock price can grow multiple times.

The term growth stock refers to any company that can grow fast, whether it's a small company that's growing quickly from a modest base or a big company, such as Amazon or Netflix. Generally speaking, growth stocks have high P/E ratios, while value stocks have low P/E ratios. Growth stocks usually pay little or no dividend, as the companies prefer to plow capital back into the business in order to grow. Philip A. Fisher (1907–2004) was a big proponent of growth stocks. Though not as famous as Benjamin Graham, his influence on Warren Buffett was maybe just as great. His book *Common Stocks and Uncommon Profits* is without doubt a classic, though his methods of picking great growth stocks, which included in-depth research by talking to management, suppliers, and competitors, are obviously not for armchair investors.

Growth stocks tend to be more risky than value stocks because a fast pace of expansion is full of pitfalls and challenges. A high-growth company can trip over many obstacles, some of them fatal—an over-eager expansion, a miscalculation of demand, or a change in economic environment can easily switch an expansion into reverse. Stock prices can drop sharply when the performance of a growth company falls short of rosy expectations.

One reason growth stocks are popular with some investors is they can gain multiple times each decade. They also often sit in new and exciting industries, which attract investors who love to chase fads and fast money. While value investors count on finding a big bargain, hoping stocks will double, they have to sit and wait patiently. In the meantime, growth stocks go up and up.

There are people who believe that buy low, sell high, as logical as it sounds, is wrong. They think that it's a trap to buy low and that the low price is likely to go even lower The momentum of a price going down, they say, will usually cause it to drop further, and the fact that a price is going up is likely to carry it even higher. Such price movements attract momentum traders, whose motto is "buy high, sell higher." Value investors think differently; they're looking to buy low and sell high. Momentum traders love growth stocks. They buy top-performing, growing stocks in the hope those stocks will continue to rise. Stocks that are high and are going higher are a good buy. Stocks that are cheap and getting cheaper don't interest them. They think buying a cheap stock is futile, as it requires holding on to the stock for too long. Momentum traders believe in buying stocks that are moving higher out of sideways bases. They look for stocks with strong fundamentals and technical signals.

As with clothing, there are trends and fashions in stocks. The popularity of value and growth stocks switches back and forth, like the length of skirts and pants. When one stock type is popular, the other isn't. It's hard to predict when market sentiment will switch. Value stocks have been out of favor since the global financial crisis—the patience and beliefs of value investors have been tested repeatedly after many false dawns. At the same time, technology heavyweights like Amazon, Netflix, and Facebook have led the way for growth stocks. While there are indexes to measure the performance of value versus growth stocks, in reality, sometimes it's not so clear which one a company is. Warren Buffett is the face of value investing to the general public. When he looks for value stocks, he isn't just looking for one that's selling at a big discount to the intrinsic value; he's also looking for one that's growing steadily and has a long-term competitive advantage that he terms "moat." He prefers to buy "a wonderful company at a fair price than a fair company at a wonderful price."

PLAN

Planning, in any walk of life, is important. French writer Antoine de Saint-Exupery (1900–1944) got it spot on when he said: "A goal without a plan is just a wish." To win a game of billiards, any decent player has to plan their shots far ahead—they can't just hit the ball before them. Investors have to do the same if they want to win the investment game. Think of a plan as a map and compass with which to navigate the stock market. When you have a plan, you feel confident and assured; your approach is governed more by rules and driven less by sentiment. Plans make you more disciplined and help you make well-thought-through decisions. You know what to do, and you make less mistakes. Without a plan, you're weighed down by uncertainties; you're disorganized, and you fear loss. Emotions like hope and despair cloud your rational thinking and reduce your decision-making capacity. You end up with poor executions, and you don't know what to do. The absence of a plan is the root of many investment problems and mistakes. It can be very costly.

Of course, calling the direction of a stock is important, but it's only part of successful investing—having the right plan for executing the trade is just as critical. It's not uncommon for investors to be right in their bullish views but wrong in terms of price and size. They're shaken out of their positions by a correction, only to see the stock go up later, as they correctly anticipated.

One common problem that plagues investors is they spend a lot of time looking for the right stocks and prices and too little time thinking about how they'll manage their position. Once you've purchased a stock, you can't just sit back and hope for the best—you need to manage the position. You always need to have a stop-loss level—a closer one for short-term trading and a further one for long-term investments. You also need to plan where to profit take or double up.

Planning needs to be done at both portfolio and individual company/fund level. As an investor, you need to have an objective and a philosophy for your portfolio. Is the portfolio for capital growth or is it to generate income? Do you want an active or passive approach or a combination of both? What's for long-term investing and what's for short-term trading? Each company and fund you choose has to fit both the objective and the philosophy. Other standard questions and checklists will help you formulate a good plan. How does this stock compare to a broad-based ETF? Have you looked at the financial report? Are earnings coming out soon? How does the stock fit your portfolio?

A good plan also includes good risk control—you need to make sure the safety of your capital is never in doubt. Remember, AIG and Citibank would have followed Lehman Brothers if the US government hadn't stepped in. For an individual stock, you must have a stop-loss level. Make sure you don't succumb to the temptation of moving it lower though—even the best plan in the world won't work if you don't act on it.

The other type of plan investors need is a contingency plan. If the market is too volatile or too euphoric, you should reduce your portfolio size. You need to prepare for what to do if there's a sudden crash. Consider pilots, who are trained to do "mental flying." In their minds, they go through the routine of checking the plane, taking off, flying, landing, and what to do in an emergency situation. Investors can learn a lot from pilots—"mental trading" is a good habit to get into. Of course, you can't prepare for every eventuality, but you can prepare for a few common scenarios, such as a sideways market, a bullish market, or a bearish market. Through your mental trading, you can work out in your mind what you will do in various scenarios—what to buy, what to sell, how much cash to hold, and so on. This simple exercise will be invaluable, especially when the market is volatile or during a crisis. Investors' bank accounts can improve significantly by either taking advantage of the situation to make good money or, at the very least, reducing mistakes and big losses.

HONESTY

Benjamin Franklin didn't say honesty was about having the best morals—he said it was the best policy. This is good advice for investors. Being honest with yourself is crucial if you're to succeed. It's the starting point and foundation for good investment decisions. You need to take full responsibility for your results. If you aren't honest with yourself, you'll never learn from your mistakes; if you never learn from your mistakes, you won't improve as an investor; if you don't improve as an investor, you'll never be a profitable investor.

It's always tempting—and very easy—for investors to play the blame game. When things are going against us, we like to blame anyone or anything other than ourselves. We like to whine, bitch, and moan. When we lose money, what could be more convenient than blaming someone else or the nameless, faceless, voiceless market? Call it whatever you want, blame things however you like—the market will take everything in silently and without a fight. "The market is crazy!" you might cry, or "The market is stupid!" But getting angry and sore at the market won't get you anywhere. Many investors blame analysts for bad recommendations or friends for dishing out the wrong tips. But if we're honest with ourselves, ultimately we're the ones who are responsible because we made the decision to listen and act.

When we lose money, we like to console ourselves that wealth isn't everything and we still have our health. We tell ourselves that rich people are miserable, living empty lives in big houses, and that they're awful, greedy people. But such consolations don't make us better investors. Looking in the mirror and making an objective assessment of why we lost money is a much better use of time and energy.

All top investors are truth seekers. They have to face the truth, no matter how inconvenient it is or how much it hurts their egos. They know they have to be honest with themselves—there's nowhere to hide in the stock market. Top investors don't pretend to know everything. They know what they know and they know what they don't know. Warren Buffett famously admits he doesn't understand technology companies. He finds it too difficult to figure out their competitive advantages and future earnings. He sticks to what he knows—his "circle of competence." Just like top investors, we need to be honest about our lack of information and knowledge. The investment universe is massive and complex—what we know is just the tip of the iceberg. With so much going on, whether political, economic, or monetary, we can only ever attain an imperfect understanding. We're like the blind men in the story of "the blind men and an elephant," only able to feel a part of the elephant. We have to understand this is just the nature of investing. We know very little, but there's no need to be discouraged by this—investing can be profitable even when you don't know much. The key is to focus on what you do know and never pretend to know what you don't. Pretenders will be punished harshly by the stock market.

We humans can fool ourselves without even realizing it. Our memories can trick us to feel good about ourselves by forgetting our follies and remembering our victories. The long history of the many trades we made fades and becomes distorted. If we were to rely on memory alone, we wouldn't be relying on truth but on warped truth or illusion.

To make sure you're honest with yourself and face the truth, remember to record all your trades and keep a journal on your investment thoughts. A journal might sound trivial or even childish, but it's highly recommended by many top investors. Trade records and journal are the only way to remain totally honest with yourself and not let your memories fool you. It's a discipline that will serve you well—without it, you won't be able to draw objective conclusions. You'll waste all those past experiences and tuition fees spent. There's much to learn from past trades. If a trade was good, remember it and try to do the same again; if it was bad, learn from your mistakes and try not to do it again; if you know why you lost, stop doing what you were doing. Honesty and journaling are indispensable to successful investing.

PSYCHOLOGY

Psychology, temperament, and character—more than intelligence—are critical factors in determining whether an investor can succeed in the stock market. Many aspects of human nature and psychology need to be understood and corrected in order to prevail, and it's likely you'll have to fight a lot of these expensive enemies and demons within yourself. You need to get out of your comfort zone and train yourself to do things that may go against your nature.

Hard work is just as important in the stock market as it is any other field, but working hard on the wrong concepts and ideas isn't going to produce results. There are many ways to make money in the stock market, but finding the right way isn't easy. Some technical analyses and methods can lead investors astray, no matter how hard they work on them, just as hardworking alchemists who try to turn cheap metals into gold will never succeed. Like any endeavor, to reach the top, you need both talent and passion. But for mere mortals like us who want to enhance our wealth, average intelligence, a reasonable amount of work, the right psychology, and common sense are enough to achieve a satisfactory long-term return.

First of all, you need to be sure you really want to invest and trade. Examine your motives, and make sure there are no conflicts of interest. People have different needs, such as making money, protecting themselves from failure, or seeking excitement. These needs can produce conflicts. It's remarkably common for investors to adopt methods that are entirely ill-suited to their personalities. This can lead to internal conflict. For example, an investor who looks for bargains in daily life is buying growth stocks instead of value stocks.

Let's consider different needs and motivations. People assume that a customer in a restaurant is there to eat and that a trader in a stock market is there to make money. However, some customers go to a restaurant for drinks, companionship, or to get away from home. Some stock investors think they want to make money like everyone else, but actually, they're just bored with life and looking for an adrenaline rush. Then there are people who are in the stock market because their friends are in it; they have a desire to join their "comrades" and "fight the market," to talk about war stories over a beer, and to feel like a hero who fell in the line of duty when they lose. There are also people who use the stock market to "escape" from their real-world problems, just like some gamblers and alcoholics. Making money becomes secondary to these people. Sooner or later, they'll find out the stock market is an expensive place for excitement, comradery, and escapism.

One of the most cited reasons for investors succeeding is discipline. Discipline in the stock market is critical and is a prerequisite for effective risk control. An investor who doesn't know where or how to stop their losses will soon find out they have nothing left to stop. Investors also need discipline to apply tested investment philosophies, strategies, and methods. An investor who switches methods on a whim will never make money in the long run. Discipline ensures you follow your own rules, listen to the lessons you've learned, adhere to the dos and don'ts, and consult your checklist. You also need discipline to do your homework before committing to an investment. Have you checked the balance sheet of the company? Have you compared it to the other companies in the industry? When's the next earnings and dividend announcement? The moment you get lazy and sloppy, you'll be whipsawed by the market.

Another important trait for an investor is patience—patience to learn, patience to wait for the right opportunities, and patience to let time work its magic. To be a good investor takes time, just like claiming a black belt in taekwondo. You need patience to learn from your mistakes and experiences; you need patience to understand your own psychology in various economic and stock cycles; you need patience to internalize and change your instinctive behaviors. Investing, just like any practical skill, requires practice for you to become competent and profitable. You can't rush it by reading all the investment books in the library.

The stock market is always moving. There are stocks that jump, and there are stocks that crash. Seldom are all the stars aligned to provide a good investment. Sometimes a company is attractive but the price is prohibitively high; sometimes the price is right but the industry is facing structural changes. There are plenty of opportunities in the stock market, but some simple research or asking a few questions will show that most of them don't offer a good risk-reward. Investors need to wait patiently for a good opportunity to present itself. As a novice investor, I was always tempted by exciting opportunities. A company was in trouble, and its stock looked like a steal; a friend recommended a promising company, and it fit my bill perfectly. I was always eager to put on a position once I liked an idea. My primary emotion was the fear of missing out on a good opportunity. I never had the patience to do more research or to wait for a better price. These good opportunities I was so afraid to miss out on, however, usually turned out to be bad; these good companies I was so keen to buy often ended up being lousy.

Investing is a long-term project and takes years, even decades, to produce a good result. Few investors have the patience to wait a decade or two to see their investment grow—they want it to double or triple in just a year or two. Some even hope to get there in a month or two. These people have unrealistic expectations. Impatience causes them to focus on short-term trades, and they lose their shirts. Building wealth takes time and perseverance; the economy and companies take time to grow; compound interest takes time to work. One of the reasons it's difficult to make money by investing is because it's hard to find someone who's both right and able to sit tight. Jesse Livermore offered this advice: "It never was my thinking that made the big money for me. It always was my sitting. Got that? My sitting tight!"

We humans are social animals. Our nature is to enjoy the comfort of a crowd. When a large number of people are on our side, we delude ourselves into thinking this proves we're right. People want to join the crowd because they're afraid of looking foolish. They fear that if they take risks others avoid, they'll lose money alone and they'll have no excuse for their mistakes. If they make the same mistakes as the crowd, they take comfort that they're not alone. People who are pessimistic and have a lot of internal conflicts are usually crowd followers. When they're under stress, they have a strong need for understanding and control. They watch the news to find out what happened and look for explanations, which they accept without question. Sometimes they choose the simplest solution: do nothing. They freeze like a deer in the headlights.

US army general George Patton (1885–1945) once said: "If everyone is thinking alike, then somebody isn't thinking." In the army, soldiers can leave the thinking to the generals, but in the stock market, every investor has to think for himself. It's a war, and they each have to think and act independently. Investors need to think critically about everything, from market wisdom to adages, from politics to economics, from valuations to correlations. They need to doubt and ask questions. If not, they'll accept a tip or a rumor readily, follow a recommendation blindly, or get easily scared by the media.

Bear in mind that thinking independently doesn't mean you have to go against the crowd all the time. Yes, you should follow the crowd sometimes and profit from the euphoria. However, while you're part of the crowd, always keep an eye out for signs that things are turning. The most important sign is price movement. When prices are going up steeply, it's about time to get out. To go against the crowd, you have to be very sure you're right though. Respect the power of the thundering herd—the stampede can be fatal.

It's easy to imagine that if there was blood on the street, you'd have the courage to face the onslaught of the market and win the battle triumphantly. But imagining isn't enough. If you see something the crowd doesn't, you need to have the courage to act on it. Then you need to stay the course. The reality is even more complicated. In the depths of a bear market, all the headlines are negative, everyone is pessimistic, and the market seems to fall every day. To be courageous when others are fearful, you need to have the conviction that the storm will eventually pass, so draw on your knowledge of financial history and your personal experiences in previous bear markets. You also need to accept that you're not going to buy at a low. More likely, you'll be too early or too late. You have to sit through the storm and wait for it to pass. Most importantly, you need to have cash to deploy. If you were holding your maximum position, you'll be fire-fighting and thinking about selling rather than buying. For investors without cash, the bear doesn't present a great opportunity—it hurts instead.

Ignorance, hope, fear, greed—all these emotions can cost investors dearly, though as investors gain more experience and knowledge, they become less ignorant. Ignorance, however, is like a marathon with no finish line—it doesn't just apply to novices. Investors can keep running, but they're never able to fully leave ignorance behind. Financial markets are so intertwined that knowing finance and economics isn't enough. Every investor needs to know some degree of history, accounting, and management.

Sometimes ignorance causes us to feel fearful, but if you have a good understanding of financial history, your knowledge will help calm your fears, particularly during a bear market. If you judge that a bear market is no worse than the global financial crisis, you can have some confidence that stocks won't fall more than they did then. Another common fear is that of missing the boat. This fear causes investors to make hasty decisions, which they usually regret soon after. When the market turns, the fear of missing out becomes the fear of loss. There are some investors who are always fearful. They keep cash because they fear a bear market, but when the bull market keeps going, they worry that they'll completely miss out. While too much fear isn't good, being fearless isn't great either. Fearlessness leads to overtrading and carelessness. A healthy dose of fear is good, as it keeps us alert.

Investors naturally fear losing money. The irony is that when they're losing money, their overwhelming feeling is hope. When they're making money, instead of feeling hopeful, they're fearful that the profit might vanish. That's why when there's a profit, investors tend to take it quickly, and when there's a loss, they tend to hold on and hope. Try to fight against these natural impulses and instincts. Be fearful when losing and hopeful when winning.

Hope is probably the deadliest feeling of them all. Investors are always hopeful. If not, why would they buy stocks in the first place? When a stock price moves down instead of up, hope of a profit turns to hope of breaking even. We like to win; we don't like to lose. Breaking even means we don't lose and our ego remains intact. When the losses widen, the hope of breaking even turns to hope that the losses will be small. We keep hoping as the stock price keeps heading lower. We hope the market is going to turn, the stock is going to turn, the management is going to buy back, or the Fed is coming to the rescue. When we finally lose all hope, we throw in the towel. Then our hopes come true. The stock finally turns, and now we hope we didn't sell at the low. It's said that hope is the most costly four-letter word to investors.

Greed, one of the seven deadly sins, can also be fatal for investors. When an investor is greedy, they tend to dream of the big returns and forget about the risks. Every investment should be judged on both risk and return, but greedy investors tend to focus on returns and ignore or underestimate the risks. These investors are greedy before they buy the stock, and they worry after they've bought it. The investors who use leverage to turbo-charge their returns are the ones who find out that greed is deadly.

Good investment decisions require confidence. Without it, we become immobilized by uncertainties, second-guessing our own decisions and jumping out of trades at any sign of dis-comfort. Our confidence should be based on our knowledge, experience and track records. Some investors, however, have misplaced confidence and overestimate their capabilities. Just like a great majority of car drivers think they're above average, investors like to think they're smarter than most and able to do better than the stock market average. This overconfidence is a banana peel that causes many investors to slip up. It leads to sloppiness and carelessness, which will be punished by the un-forgiving market. Even if you've enjoyed some winning streaks in the past, be sure to guard against laziness and complacency. If you don't, you'll start making mistakes that could lead to losses or even a major losing streak.

Many people, even the intelligent ones, are bullish because they have stocks and bearish because they have cash. The capacity for rationalization is powerful and it affects everyone—we're all biased. To succeed in investing, you need to be more object-ive and less biased. You need to see the world as it is, not as you want to see it. At any given time, there will always be both bullish and bearish evidence. Try not to cherry pick to confirm your biased view. It's never wise for an investor to fit the facts to their pet theories. Some people go as far as to twist the facts to make them fit, but as Daniel P. Moynihan (1927–2003) once said: "Everyone is entitled to his own opinion, but not his own facts." Look for opposing views instead. When you're bullish, you need to have a certain alertness and watchfulness to look for signs you might be wrong. When you're bearish, you should look for how things could turn around.

Seasoned financial market participants know that regret is a common feeling. When the market goes down, we regret buying too much of a stock. When the market goes up, we regret buying too little. Either way, we regret. We have to learn to minimize those regrets. There's no such thing as the perfect trade. Emotionally, investing is a negative game, even if you're making money. You can always buy and sell at a better price; you can always increase your size and your profits; you can always hold longer to enjoy a bigger move in a stock. The important thing to recognize is that catching part of the move is fine. You should feel perfectly content with far-from-perfect, winning trades. What you should strive for is some consistency, making more winning trades than losing ones and picking only high-probability transactions. Your goal isn't to make perfect trades with the perfect price and size; your goal is to make money in the long run.

The ability to change one's mind is key to successful investing. Dogmatic, rigid investors rarely, if ever, succeed in the stock market. All successful investors are flexible. They understand when a theory works and when it doesn't; they know that following a theory blindly can lead to financial ruin. They're always taking in new facts to reassess and are ready to change their views if warranted; they understand that being too indoctrinated in one's beliefs isn't good for the bank account. George Soros was once asked by a journalist how he could be so rich despite having been wrong so often. "I'm only rich because I know when I'm wrong," he replied. He knows when to change his mind.

A big stock event has the power to shape the collective experience and psychology of investors and continue to influence their investment decisions for years or even decades. What followed the 1929 crash was the Great Depression, which spread and brought hardship to many millions all over the world during the 1930s. Unemployment was higher than 20 percent in the US. Other nations' economies were also contracting, and international trades were being stalled by the Smoot-Hawley Act. Investors all over the world vowed never to touch stocks again. A whole generation feared and loathed the stock market. Few people talked about, let alone bought, stocks in the 1940s and 1950s. The 1950s ended up being a good decade for stocks, but retail investors only started to come back to the market toward the end of it.

The 1987 Wall Street crash gave a new generation of investors a completely different experience. Unlike the 1929 crash, it wasn't followed by a further drop—by 1989, all losses had been recovered. The "mini crash" of October 1989 reversed in a day. The bear market of 1990 was short and barely passed the 20 percent mark. A new bull market was actually born in the midst of the First Gulf War. Investors learned a new lesson: buy on dips. Any dip was a good buy. This simple, newfound strategy was wonderfully successful throughout the relentless bull market of the 1990s.

In the 2010s, the global financial crisis was still fresh in the minds of many investors. Compared to the 1930s, the response from the Fed couldn't have been more different, and stock markets roared back from 2009, marking the start of the longest bull run ever. The crisis, however, had scared away enough investors that the bull run of the 2010s had far less retail investors than that of the 1990s, leading some to dub it "the most unloved bull market." There wasn't much jubilation as the stock market kept scaling new highs. Some investors chose to wait years for another crisis so they could pick up cheap stocks. This is one reason why the bond market, despite its low yields, still attracted money—from these investors.

Mark Twain once said the key to good health was to "eat what you don't want, drink what you don't like, and do what you'd rather not." Twain's advice is just as applicable to financial health. Inbuilt human traits entice people into behaviors that are detrimental to investing. Our natural instincts mislead us when trading, meaning investors have to guard against all sorts of things—most of all against human nature. Always do what you think is correct rather than what feels comfortable.

PART VI: STOCK PICKS

STOCKS VS. FUNDS

According to the book *A Random Walk Down Wall Street* by Burton G. Malkiel, no one can beat the stock market. Malkiel's view is that even the smartest, best-informed investors fare no better in their stock selection than a man throwing darts at the stocks page of the *The Wall Street Journal*. The truth is there are winners who've managed to beat the market over a number of years. Despite their astounding records and close-to-impossible statistics, Malkiel dismisses them as the lucky ones, but to attribute the success of these top investors to pure luck and to ignore their skills is like claiming Michael Jordan's points record was pure fluke. Most investors have rightly concluded that it's possible to pick stocks profitably and beat the market, but it would be wise to always remember Benjamin Graham's warning: "To achieve superior results is harder than it looks."

When a stamp collector first starts out, they get excited easily and buy stamps that they later regret—either the stamp isn't as good or rare as they thought or the price was too high. With years of experience under their belt, however, they'll pass on most stamps they set their eyes on and only buy good stamps at the right prices. Stock picking is a lot like stamp collecting. A stock picker needs to look at many companies in order to gain a discerning eye.

That doesn't mean you have to read every annual report page by page. For the average investor, simplified financial reports, such as balance sheets, cash flow reports, and income statements—which are available for free online—are sufficient. This simple exercise won't take too much time, but its benefits are invaluable. You can cover hundreds of companies in just a few months.

I was promiscuous and fell in love with many companies. Looking at these love-at-first-sight buys now, I wish I'd known at the time that there were even more beautiful companies out there at even lovelier prices.

Getting an eye for truly beautiful companies is just the beginning though. You still need to dig deeper into the companies that attract you. For investors who are driven by fundamentals, reading an annual report is a must, but it's just the starting point. When you pick a stock, remember that you're a "shareholder"—you own a small part of the company and its business. Don't look at buying a stock as just buying a piece of a certificate that has fluctuating prices. Look for a business that can grow its revenue and profits and has competitive advantages that can keep the competition from eroding them. On top of that, you need to buy at a reasonable price, or better still, at a price that's lower than the intrinsic value. Remember McDonald's in the 1970s—a great business at the wrong price is still going to hurt the shareholders. This method is essentially the one that Warren Buffett sticks to.

It's also important not to look at a potential buy in isolation. You need to compare the stock with other stocks in the same industry as well as with the general market. Simple comparisons of P/E and P/B ratios aren't enough. Some investors will stop right there and conclude that one company is a better buy than another because it's cheaper and has lower P/E and P/B ratios. In reality, it's not so simple, and investors need to look at the fundamentals of the various companies in the same industry. If this sounds too difficult, there is an easier way. You can choose instead to look at the price action of all companies in the industry, especially during a bear market. Most investors want to buy the company that has dropped the most, as they think it's a bargain and that it will rebound more than others. This is usually the wrong choice. The company that drops the most is almost always the weakest, and it may or may not recover. A better option is to buy the company whose price dropped the least.

This company is the strongest and will often scale new heights in a bull market. Another way to pick a company—though a less reliable one—is to look at how individual stocks react to significant good or bad news in the industry. If the news is bad, the company that reacts in the least negative way is the one you want to buy. If the news is good, you want to buy the company that reacts most positively.

That's not all though. Even after filtering through numerous companies and deciding on one you want to buy, you still need to conduct a final test and compare the stock with the country's benchmark index ETF—the S&P 500 in the US, the FTSE in the UK, the Nikkei in Japan, the BOVESPA in Brazil, the Hang Seng in Hong Kong, and so on. How does the company's P/E ratio compare to the index? Is the stock offering a higher or lower dividend yield? Do you expect the earnings to outperform the index? If you come to the conclusion that the stock is only marginally better than the index, it's not a good buy.

You need to set a high hurdle when choosing a stock over the index ETF, as a lot of things can go wrong with individual stocks. An index ETF offers good diversification and simplicity. It's not easy to manage a portfolio of 20 to 30 stocks (for sufficient diversification) on your own. Your portfolio will have both winners and losers, and the losers will cause you to worry about the winners' profits evaporating before your eyes. Many people end up selling the winners to guarantee a profit while keeping hold of the losers. This will almost certainly affect your portfolio negatively.

With any big portfolio, there are lots of decisions to make. When there's a bull or bear market, which stocks should you sell first? What price should you sell at? Market price? Or should you leave a limit order to sell? Should you cut your portfolio by half, or should you cut it altogether? Should you cut all 20 stocks by half or sell 10 selected stocks? Should you sell before or after earnings and dividends? There are many more questions, but you get the picture. No matter what you do, you're bound to regret one action or another. You might sell the wrong stocks; you might sell too early; you might sell too late. When a market's volatile, you'll realize that a portfolio of 20 or more stocks might be too much on the plate of a part-time investor.

If you want to have a well-diversified portfolio, it makes sense to buy a fund. It's cheaper and much easier to manage than a self-selected portfolio—you only have to make buy and sell decisions on one fund instead of 20 separate stocks. The more decisions you have to make, the more mistakes you could make. A fund reduces stress and makes life a lot simpler.

Does this mean you shouldn't pick individual stocks at all? Not really. You can still pick stocks, just keep the number small— the maximum I suggest is 15. The sticking point with this is that academic studies show we need 20 to 30 stocks for good diversification, so how can you diversify well with just 15 stocks? First, make sure all your stocks are diversified across various industries. Second, on top of individual stocks, you must have funds.

If even professional stock pickers struggle to beat the market in the long run though, what chance does an average investor have? Peter Lynch argues that retail investors actually have advantages over professional investors. But how can that be? Professionals spend more time and have more resources than us; they have $24,000-a-year subscriptions to Bloomberg's Terminal and all kinds of support from their institutions; they also have contacts in company management as well as access to competitors and suppliers. The issue is that they always have to do something. The advantage you have is that you can be patient and choose to do nothing. Professional investors' mandates require them to invest nearly all the money. Generally, they can only hold 10 percent or less in cash. When the market is too volatile and uncertain or the prices are too high, you can choose to hold a big amount of cash and wait for some new information or a market development. They must hold on to stocks regardless of the market conditions or their views.

Another big advantage you have as a retail investor is the

flexibility to invest in any product or market you see fit. Professional investors are restricted by their mandate as to what they can buy. A US fund can't buy foreign stocks; a technology fund can't buy utilities. Professional investors are constantly under pressure from their bosses to perform, and their bosses are under pressure from the ultimate bosses—the funds' investors. These pressures can cause them to make mistakes. Regular folks, on the other hand, only answer to themselves. Professional investors live and breathe the market every day. Their jobs, networking, and social lives revolve around financial markets, meaning they're prone to herd mentality, but for the average retail investor, stock investment is a part-time endeavor. Just like Warren Buffett, living far from Wall Street is an advantage for us, not a disadvantage, as some believe.

The advantages average investors have over the professionals can, however, be a problem for some, and the flexibility of being able to hold 100 percent cash results in many people holding too much and missing the long-term uptrend of the stock market. Having the flexibility to invest in more products and markets can also lead them to spread their time, effort, and expertise too thin. Some investors become disorientated by the plethora of choices, which can make picking the winners difficult. They can't offset this with a true in-depth company study, as they don't have the necessary resources or access to company management.

Some investors like to pick companies from the IPOs—the young and exciting companies. Studies show, however, that buying all new companies and holding them for years doesn't beat the return you can get from a broad index like the S&P 500. More new companies lose than gain over the years. Groupon was listed in 2011 and dropped almost 90 percent by 2019. Other companies that did well on the first day but drifted lower than IPO prices include Zynga, GoPro, and Snapchat. The few winners that did extremely well attracted a lot of investors.

Benjamin Graham was always wary of IPOs. Why? First, IPOs

have special salesmanship by the underwriters, meaning investors need to have special resistance. Second, most IPOs are sold under "favorable market conditions"—favorable for the seller but unfavorable for the buyer.

Of course, the young, exciting company might eventually succeed, but as time goes by, original investors become impatient and end up dropping out or selling at a loss. One example is Facebook's IPO in May 2012, which didn't start well. There was controversy about the high, aggressive pricing. The price went below the IPO price of $38 on the second day and hit a low of $17.58 in September—a 55 percent drop. The market was worried that Facebook wasn't moving fast enough from computers to mobile devices, and the end of the six-month lock-up period saw an avalanche of shares on sale. Those who sold out during the big drop were to regret it deeply later on; those who held on profited handsomely.

On the flip side, when a market is bubbly, IPOs can be a fertile ground, and they offer one of the best risk-rewards to short-term investors. During the internet boom and when China's stock market was hot, IPOs became a lucky draw. Those investors who were allotted shares and could sell on the first day made a big profit—sometimes more than double the IPO prices. Those who missed the draw just wasted time and small fees. In 1999, during the dot-com boom, a total of 23 IPOs ended the year trading at at least 10 times their original offering price, while in 2009, when ChiNext (China's Nasdaq) was launched with 28 companies, the average price doubled on the first day.

The risk to investors trying the IPO lottery is that the market can turn suddenly and the stocks they've been awarded may never trade above the IPO price. In this situation, they must cut their losses fast to avoid a short-term lottery trade turning into big, long-term losses. However, while the risk is indeed real, investors can sometimes make enough money early on to cover sudden losses—they just need to remain alert and not overstay the game.

As with anything in life, stock investing is, of course, subject to a degree of luck. How much does luck come into it? The unlucky man believes in luck, and the lucky man believes in skills. When you pick a stock, even if you do all your homework and make the correct judgment, you can end up losing money if something unexpected happens. That's just bad luck. But if you keep doing the right things and making sound decisions, in the long run, you're bound to be profitable. If you have the right skills and buy good companies, luck can only affect you in the short run and not in the long run.

TECHNICAL ANALYSIS

In addition to fundamental analysis, technical analysis is one of the main disciplines of the investment world. While fundamental analysis uses information such as economic data and earnings to forecast prices, technical analysis employs price, volume, sentiment, and technical indicators. The theory is that by looking at historical market data such as price and volume, usually using a chart, you can forecast the future price.

Generally speaking, technical analysis comes in two forms. One is price patterns, which we can see from charts. A famous price pattern is "head and shoulder"—a chart with three peaks, the middle of which is higher than the other two. The other form of technical analysis is indicators—algorithms that take each aspect of price movements and put them together to form analysis and ratios. There are all kinds of interesting and exotic names in technical analysis—Fibonacci, moving average, relative strength index (RSI), and so on. Practitioners believe that technical analysis and chart reading contain the secrets of the market. They think the charts speak to them—all they have to do is figure out how to understand the language. Many caution, however, that technical analysis isn't a simple case of following a set of rules and applying the outcome indiscriminately—they see the interpretation of charts as more of an art than a science. There are some faithful who spend most of their lives trying to unlock the secrets and find solutions to the market's many puzzles, in search of the holy grail. Some succeed phenomenally, but most get nowhere.

The most common terms used in technical analysis are support and resistance. The support price is lower than the current price. It's a base price, which is supposed to hold and attract lots of buyers to "support" it. The resistance price is higher than the current price. It's a "ceiling" price, which is hard to break above, as there are lots of sellers at that level. Many investors like to use recent lows and highs to place their buy and sell orders, turning these lows and highs into support and resistance. Trend lines are another common form of support and resistance.

It's very difficult to tell in advance how well a support or resistance can hold. Once broken decisively, a support can become a resistance and vice versa. The support level that attracted lots of buyers now becomes a resistance level that attracts lots of sellers. The buyers knew they were wrong in thinking the support would hold, and now they're eager to sell at where they bought to get out even.

A lot of technical analyses are self-fulfilling. The more people believe in a support level, the more buyers and less sellers it attracts. The support is therefore more likely to hold. One famous, influential technician, whose views can move markets, is Tom Demark. His followers believe in him so strongly they make some of his calls come true. Demark has advised a number of top fund managers over the years, including George Soros.

A particularly important part of technical analysis, and one all serious technical followers watch closely, is volume. In fact, they watch it as closely as they do price. Technical analysts believe that an up move should be accompanied by big volume to make it more meaningful and sustainable. They also believe that when a stock is consolidating after a big up move, a low volume is a bullish sign, as it means recent buyers who accumulated the stock don't want to sell. The few investors and traders who saw the October 1987 crash coming cited the record volume of the previous Friday while prices were on the downside as a reason. In 1929, the Black Thursday before the crash of October 28 and 29 was also a big down day with a record volume. However, when it comes to illiquid stocks, the volume can be so low that technical analyses probably aren't going to work

—there's just not enough data from such stocks to make any meaningful technical reading. Volume is easily available information that's worth paying attention to.

Moving average is a type of technical analysis that's often cited in the media and is widely followed by investors. The two basic moving averages are the simple moving average, which is the simple average over a period of time, and the exponential moving average, which gives greater weight to more recent prices. Moving averages lag behind the current price, and the longer the time period for the moving average, the greater the lag. 50-day and 200-day periods are the most commonly used moving averages, with 200 having a bigger lag than 50. Shorter moving averages are for short-term traders, and longer moving averages are for long-term investors. Moving averages are considered a support line in an uptrend and a resistance in a downtrend. Any break above or below a moving average is considered a significant signal that a trend has changed direction. When a short-term moving average crosses above a long-term moving average, it's a bullish sign, and when a 50-day moving average crosses a 200-day moving average, this infrequent occurrence (about once every year or two) is an important signal to followers to either buy or sell. Its track record, however, is dubious.

Another popular technical indicator we always see on the financial news is the RSI. RSI ranges from 0 to 100. A high RSI number of above 70 is considered overbought, while a low number of below 30 is considered oversold. RSI works better as an oversold indicator. An oversold stock usually lasts just weeks before a sharp snapback occurs, partly due to short sellers covering. RSI doesn't work very well as an overbought indicator because stocks can remain overbought for a long time.

Trend following is also an oft-used technical strategy. The basic idea is that when a trend is established, the momentum will carry it further until the trend has exhausted itself. The beginning of a trend is hard to follow because we're not sure if it's going to be a trend or just a sideways drift. The end is usually volatile, with the wind changing direction. The middle move is what most trend followers are looking for. Some people write computer programs to try and catch a trend. Others look at charts and use discretion to decide when to buy and sell. As trend following grows more popular, it becomes more difficult to make money from it. Dow Theory was created by Charles Dow, the joint creator of the Dow Jones, more than 100 years ago. It's a mechanical method, meaning practitioners buy and sell according to signals. It worked well from 1898 until 1933, when it became too popular to give good results. Right now, there are still people who use Dow Theory, but they no longer use it mechanically.

One pattern that's very popular among traders is breakout. When a stock trades sideways in a range for a long time and suddenly breaks the upper boundary on heavy volume, traders expect it to continue the move. This isn't always the case though —after breaking higher, some fall back to the previous range. When consolidation in a range is observed by many speculators, the breakout is likely to be a false one. To have a higher chance of success, it's best nobody understands why the breakout happened. If there's an obvious reason, or a widely expected one, the chance of a false breakout is higher. If the breakout on the top side occurs when the general market is flat, that's a good sign. If the market's down, that's even better.

Most investors prefer to buy stocks at new lows rather than new highs. According to most technical analyses, that's exactly the wrong thing to do. The risk is that when a stock or market has scaled a new high or a new low, it's more likely to continue that move than not.

Critics of technical analysis think it's a rather questionable art. Jim Rogers claims he has never met a rich technician. Peter Lynch, however, who is a fundamental and value investor, does pay attention to technical analysis, looking at statistics such as how many stocks went up versus how many went down.

The fact is some investors and traders make money in the long run from technical analysis. There are even people who failed to make money using fundamental analysis and only found success after switching to technical. Marty Schwartz, a famous technician on Wall Street, was quoted as saying: "I used fundamentals for nine years and got rich as a technician." There are enough cases and evidence to show that technical analysis can work by itself or that it can be used to complement fundamental analysis. Some investors employ both methodologies successfully, using fundamentals as the reason to buy a stock and technical analysis as a tool to choose the right time and price.

Despite the fact that some technical analyses work, in reality most don't. To find a technical analysis that works requires a lot of hard work and a significant time investment. It's probably beyond most of us, with our limited time and knowledge. Many of the successful technicians are great with computers, statistics, or both. If you want to learn about technical analysis, there are seminars, courses, and books that try to teach it. The first question anyone who's interested in learning about technical analysis needs to ask: if the technical system is as good as the promoters claim, why are they selling it—surely they could have made millions using it themselves? Any technical system will fail to work if too many people are following it. The promoters are killing the goose that lays the golden eggs by selling it.

Some quantitative and technical hedge funds like Renaissance (its founder Jim Simons was a Cold War codebreaker) and D. E. Shaw (which employed Jeff Bezos without knowing what job to offer him because he was so brilliant) make billions for themselves and their investors. They're extremely secretive and go to great lengths to protect their golden goose—the employees have to sign nondisclosure forms.

Even assuming the technical system you're being sold is a good one, it may not fit your personality, and you may not have the confidence to follow it without second-guessing yourself. Say the system you buy has big stop losses. You end up finding the losses too much to bear and stopping yourself out before the system's stop-loss level. The market then turns around to show the system was right. The next time you follow the system religiously, it might give you repeated wrong signals and test your faith. Essentially, it takes a lot of time and a great deal of effort to develop your own technical system—there's no short-cut here.

TIMING

"October: This is one of the peculiarly dangerous months to speculate in stocks. The others are July, January, September, April, November, May, March, June, December, August and February." Mark Twain's wit and wisdom on timing the stock market is on point. Investors like to put their fingers on the pulse of the market and decide when to buy and sell. The urge to time the market is irresistible. If you choose to be a long-term investor instead of a short-term speculator, it's easier to be correct in your infrequent judgement calls. You also don't have to spend as much time and energy as short-term speculators. In today's fast paced world, timing the stock market is still as popular as ever—maybe even more so. Some high-frequency trades involve buying and selling stocks within milliseconds.

Some academic studies say timing the market is futile. If you're of this opinion, you should invest regularly instead. You may choose to invest monthly from your salary or annually from your year-end bonus. The idea is to ignore the performance of the stock market and invest a predetermined, fixed amount. When the market is bullish and stocks are expensive, your fixed dollars buy you less stocks or funds. When the market is bearish and stocks are cheap, your fixed dollars buy you more stocks or funds. This is known as dollar-cost averaging. It puts your investment on autopilot. This way, you avoid the negative effects of bad timing but you also give up the chance to buy at a good time. The key to successful dollar-cost averaging is a strong commitment come rain or shine. You can't come up with excuses as to why you shouldn't invest. You need to have the courage to stick to your plan when the markets are bearish and the news is full of end-of-the-world headlines. You need the patience to let your plan work over a long period—at least 10 years, but preferably more than 20.

Another similar concept is the scale-in, scale-out method. When you decide to buy or sell, it doesn't have to be an all-or-nothing decision. Instead, you can scale in and out in stages. If you win the lottery or come into a large inheritance, it's prudent to spread your investment out over a few years. This way, if the market sees a severe decline during this period, you'll have purchasing power to take advantage of it. If the market is heading higher instead, your initial winnings will provide a cushion in case a severe decline happens later. The gains on your earlier purchases should largely offset the declines on your more recent ones. No severe loss of capital will be involved, and your timing won't be subject to pure luck. You'll never catch the top with this method, but you'll never catch the bottom either. You won't regret missing the boat or showing your hand right at the top.

If you invest all at once and then find a bear market arrives shortly after, you'll inevitably feel uncomfortable. This discomfort can then turn to panic when you see your investment drop further. You might decide to get out at the worst possible time. Spreading your investment over a long period of time gives you the chance to invest and learn about your psychology while the market is moving up and down. It's a good way to ease yourself in, and it helps improve your trading and investment skills.

Scaling in and out can also be deployed on a short time frame. If you decide to buy a stock or fund, you can buy half or quarter at current market price and then wait a few days or weeks to buy the rest. Momentum traders would choose to average up, while value investors would average down. There's no contradiction here. As long as you choose a method that matches your personality and a stock that matches your style, either approach can work and be profitable.

Say you're one of the most unlucky stock investors in the world, having put in $1,000 at the peaks of the last three bull markets (which borders on statistical impossibility). After investing in the Dow Jones when it peaked at 2,722 in August 1987, you broke even in two years' time; after the index hit 11,722 in January 2000, it took six years; after the top of 14,164 in October 2007, you made your money back in five years. For most of us, who need to work for about 40 years, six years isn't that long. What happened to the $3,000 that you invested at the tops? By the end of 2019, the Dow Jones reached 28,538. The $3,000 you invested at the worst possible times in the last three decades turned into $14,934—almost 400 percent profit.

What if you put $1,000 in at the bottom of each bear market over the last three decades? How did you do? The Dow Jones had dropped to 1,738 by the close of Black Monday in 1987. In March 2003, it bottomed at 7,286, and in March 2009, it hit 6,547. By the end of 2019, the $3,000 had turned into $24,696 —more than 700 percent profit. This best-case return is 65 percent better than the worst-case scenario.

Let's look at a more realistic yet still unachievable scenario. Say you didn't time it perfectly and were off by 10 percent each time. You bought 10 percent above the bottom and 10 percent below the peaks. The difference between the best-case scenario of buying 10 percent above the three bottoms and the worst-case scenario of buying 10 percent below the three peaks was 35 percent.

For the millions of long-term investors who tried to time the market over the last three decades, these results are striking. The difference of buying at three rock bottoms and three summits was just 65 percent. At 10 percent above the bottoms and 10 percent below the peaks, it was just 35 percent. Many studies have shown that when investors try to time the market, their results are worse than if they buy and hold. Investors tend to sell into weakness and buy into strength. Many investors who are worried about buying at highs should take comfort in these results—if they hold stocks for decades, it doesn't make that much difference.

One of the most tempting propositions for stock investors is to profit take a stock with the intention of buying it back later at a lower price. Some investors want to sell simply because the price has gone up; some want to sell because they worry about a large profit shrinking; some think a stock that's gone up a lot has used up most of its "potential;" some want to sell because they look at P/E and P/B ratios and conclude that the stock is "overpriced." They're all worried about a market top and an impending correction. In their minds, if they sell now and buy back later, they could "save" some money in the coming correction.

Say you're certain a bear market is coming soon and you think there's going to be a 30 percent drop. It seems irrational and irresponsible not to save the 30 percent. But what's your chance of getting everything right? Your view of a 30 percent drop has to be correct. Your timing of selling and buying has to be perfect. In the real world, a lot of things can go wrong. In a good but improbable scenario, you sold and bought 5 percent too early and saved about 22 percent. Most likely, however, your grand plan didn't work out. In some cases, you sold too early and the stock never came down enough to give you any meaningful savings. Quite possibly, you sold without buying back, as the price drop fell short of the reentry price. Refusing to chase the market, you ended up watching from the sidelines as the price advanced. People don't realize how hard it is to get back in. In other cases, when the share price was approaching your target, the sentiment was bad and fear took over you. You either changed your mind about buying back or you lowered the buy price. Investors who sell stocks to wait for a more attractive price to buy the same stocks back seldom attain their objective.

For those who can't resist the temptation to sell now and buy back later, you can scale in and out of your positions. It's important to take action to address your emotional need to do something. When there's a profit, you might want to sell a quarter or half of your positions to lock in your gain then try to buy the position back later. If you miss buying back, at least you still have half or three-quarters of your position. Some investors find trading around positions highly beneficial. It satisfies their urge to profit take, it helps them to hold on to a position better, and it reduces their portfolio size and the risk of sentiment swings.

If a stock price has already risen quickly, it's better not to chase, or at least not to buy all at once. Most of the time, fast moves are due to speculations and euphoria, making them prone to quick reversal. The exception to this rule is when a company announces surprisingly good earnings or there is some sort of good news that will have a lasting, positive impact on the company. If you've identified the next Amazon, you want to bite the bullet and buy the stock despite a big up move. If a good company's stock price has dropped a lot, say 30 percent, but the fundamentals haven't changed, you want to act fast. The key here is that the stock is a good one and the price drop isn't due to worsening fundamentals. Of course, these are general rules, and investors can make their own as they gain experience.

Eighteenth century British nobleman Baron Rothschild was credited with saying: "The time to buy is when there's blood in the streets." The baron, you may remember, was the one who made money out of a carrier pigeon from Waterloo. This is one of the most famous quotes on contrarian investing. It's always a tempting proposition for some to be contrarian. Some people enjoy being different; some like to go against the herd. Contrarian investing has a heroic appeal, but going against the crowd can get you trampled on by a stampede. Everyone knew the stock market would open much lower after 9/11. Contrarian investors who bought that day at 7 percent lower were catching a falling knife that would keep falling for another 18 months. Alan Greenspan was fearful when others were greedy and warned of "irrational exuberance." But the thundering herds kept on charging for another three years. Anyone who was contrarian and sold short during this period would die a thousand deaths. When you decide to go against the general trend of investment thinking, you must be very sure you're right. You need to read the situation correctly and have irrefutable logic. Most importantly, you need to get the timing right.

Investors use many indicators to time the market. Some sound sensible and have a degree of success, but the market is too complex for any indicator to work well most of the time. If an indicator works well, the market will discount it and make it less effective. These indicators are to investors like a patient's temperature, pulse, and other vital signs are to a medical doctor. You can't just rely on one and ignore the rest.

One of the simplest indicators is based on general market P/E ratios. Since 1900, the US stock market P/E ratio has ranged between 10 and 20 most of the time. Investors buy when the S&P 500 P/E ratio is less than 10, and they sell when it's more than 20. The five times the P/E ratio dropped below 10 in the last century produced a 100 percent success rate. The problem is if you wait for the P/E ratio to drop back below 10 again, you'll be out of the market too long. This simple indicator doesn't perform as well as a buy and hold. In the last decade while interest rates have been very low, the S&P 500 P/E ratio has often been above 20. Those who sold above 20 would have missed most of the latest bull market.

Some indicators are based on the sentiment of investors. This could come from a survey to canvass the views of professionals or it could be based on the amount of cash they hold. Only sensible, logical sentiments matter though—remember that market moves are the aggregate of millions of investors' emotions. Sentiment indicators don't work well over time. This could be due to time lags, or there may be inaccuracies in their capture. According to one sentiment indicator, early August 2008 was a good time to buy stocks. The previous five out of six times this indicator had shown a buy signal, the results were excellent, and the remaining one still produced a small, positive return.

Anyone who chose to follow the great past record of this indicator at that particular moment would have bought right before a severe plunge, in the depths of the global financial crisis.

Another popular indicator comes in the form of fund flows. The theory is that funds are managed by professionals who have lots of information and abundant brainpower—they're the "smart money." There are all kinds of reports on fund flows—flows in and out of mutual funds and ETFs, big-cap and small-cap, developed markets and emerging markets. Investors take particular note when the flows are very large or when they break a record. However, just like sentiment indicators, fund flows face the same problem of time lag—the numbers reflect what happened in the past and can be weeks old. The assumption that more funds flowing into a market means it's bullish can be wrong. What happened in the past isn't always a good indication of the future. Fund flows are fluid by nature, and they can change direction fast.

Some investors consider insider buying a good guideline for timing the market. If many insiders are buying, it's a good sign, and investors might want to join them. Insider selling, on the other hand, isn't usually significant. It's common for insiders to sell regularly to pay taxes and expenses or for diversification, but if insider selling is heavy and the P/E ratio is high, be careful —you probably want to avoid the stock.

One not-so-well-known indicator is dividend dip. If a significant number of companies announce an increase in dividends, this is a signal to sell. The logic is that companies are usually hesitant to increase dividends because if they were to subsequently cut them, the shareholders wouldn't be pleased and the share price would plummet. In most cases, companies only decide to increase dividends after the economy has been in good shape for a considerable period. This is the time to put on a contrarian trade by selling. It doesn't work all the time though.

Some smart investors look at magazine covers and the tallest buildings as reverse indicators. If a magazine cover has a bullish heading like "Dow at 100,000!," sell; if the heading is "The death of stock market," buy; if the CEO of a company appears on *Time* magazine's cover, the stock is near its peak. When the tallest building in a country is topping out, watch out for a bubble burst. The theory is that when a city or country is building the tallest skyscraper, it's a sign of boom and hubris. Investors should look to sell and run for cover. Supermodel Gisele Bündchen famously declared in late 2007 that she wanted to be paid in euros, as she feared the US dollar would continue to weaken. The euro peaked a few months later and never saw that height again.

The indicators we've looked at are just some of the many tools an investor can use to time the market. It's clear that alone they're not sufficiently reliable to form the basis for good timing. Better is to look for tendencies. In conjunction with other considerations, this can yield a more positive result—the more indicators there are pointing in the same direction, the more likely you are to be right. Remember, however, it doesn't have to be an all-or-nothing decision. You can always time with part of your portfolio.

The media always like to cite another potential indicator: historical statistics, but just how useful are these statistics in reality? A typical one may be: "If the opening five days of the year are up by more than 3 percent, the stock market has an 80 percent chance of a positive year." First of all, the sample size is too small to make it statistically significant—there haven't been too many years when the stock market has been up 3 percent in the first week. Yes, the beginning and end of the year are important, but such simple statistics miss out what's happening in between. The intra-year swing of the stock market is wider than most people realize, and the predictive power of backward-looking statistics is dubious, as they completely ignore the context of the numbers. It's impractical to use these statistics to trade profitably, as you have to wait years before there's one such signal to buy. You then have to sit through the intra-year swing and hope this isn't the year that loses 20 percent.

Another thing to be wary of when looking at historical statistics is "averages." Stock market averages are usually derived from a small sample based on a wide range, which makes them pretty useless to a statistician. The average time from the peak to the trough of a bear market, the average length of a recession and a bull market—if you rely purely on averages for your investments, you can be wrong in both timing and price.

The phrase "sell in May and go away" is as popular now in finance as it has ever been. Every year, without fail, we see this "wisdom" in the media. Sure, there's some truth in it, as historically, the most "productive" six months in stocks are November to April. However, this "fact" is so well known nowadays that it would be crazy to think you can make money by following it.

Benjamin Graham once said: "I insist, which will always maintain some interest in common stocks regardless of how high the market level goes." Contrary to what many people think, having some stocks all the time is prudent rather than dangerous. You can't afford to keep all your capital in cash, regardless of market levels. Cash is a sure way to lose the value of money through inflation—it's a slow death. Granted, it's right to be cautious and reduce some stock holdings when you see signs of a bubble. However, even in times like that, hold on to some stocks because no one can predict how much further prices might advance before the crash. Those who got out totally during the global financial crisis would have missed a big part of the V-shaped recovery and likely felt compelled to buy back at higher prices. When everything looks bleak and hopeless in a bear market, don't panic and sell everything. If you're totally out of stocks, you're likely to chase the volatile market in and out at the wrong time.

PICKING BOTTOMS

Picking bottoms is always popular among investors. Buying on weakness appeals to human nature. It's a natural inclination and a comfortable approach for most people to buy a stock near its low—we all like a bargain; we're all attracted by big sales in a store. With stocks that have come off a lot from their highs, say 30, 50, or 80 percent, a normal sale seems to turn into a great sale and then a fire sale. But while merchants on sale are exactly the same before and after, stocks on sale can become a completely different company. The assumption that the company is the same—same business, same management, same dividend —is wrong. In many cases, the drop in price is a reaction to a deterioration of company fundamentals. The sale is only true if the price has changed while the intrinsic value hasn't. Bottom pickers only look at price; they don't consider values. A company that has seen its stock price drop by 50 percent but has earnings of 90 percent is actually more expensive now.

When you buy a stock after it's dropped from a peak of $100 to $50, you feel great—you've got a good bargain. If the stock turns out to be a big loser and drops further to $1, even though you bought at a 50 percent discount, you still lose 98 percent. It's not much better than the 99 percent loss of someone who bought right at the top. Say you've learned that a 50 percent discount isn't enough. Now you'll only buy at a 90 percent discount, but there's nothing stopping a stock from dropping from $100 to $10 and then to $1. How much do you lose if you bought at $10? 90 percent! You could have lost 90 percent on a stock that you bought at a 90 percent discount!

If you think this can't happen, I once bought a stock worth

$7,425, Now it's worth $3. Another company I tried to bottom pick had seen its share price plunge 65 percent the previous year and 44 percent the year before that. The great bargain attracted me. After I bought, it collapsed even faster, losing another 80 percent in six months. Picking bottoms is a dangerous game. The lows can go lower, and the loss can easily balloon. Sure, if a company goes down 90 percent or more, there are usually some strong rebounds along the way—often more than double—but they tend to be due to temporary, positive news that forces panicking short sellers to cover their shorts. The fundamentals of the company haven't actually improved, and soon it will test new lows.

I once read that a successful investor said some of the most attractive long-term buys come from the "fallen angels"—companies that fall more than 90 percent and yet still survive for years. A long time ago, I read about a company that fit this description. It had peaked more than 10 years earlier and was still surviving. The balance sheet looked pretty strong. I bought the stock with high hopes that it would be my angel. After a few years, not only had the company not turned around but it continued to lose money. My fallen angel kept falling. The consolation for me was that I got out before it became much worse.

Jesse Livermore, the legendary trader who was immortalized in Edwin Lefèvre's (1871–1943) book *Reminiscences of a Stock Operator*, warned against trying to buy at bottoms and sell at peaks: "The last eighth or the first. These two are the most expensive eighths in the world." (Stocks were quoted in eighths in the early 20th century). One reason why so many investors try to pick tops and bottoms is they want to show the world how smart they are. But remember: you're not going to make a perfect trade. Indeed, far-from-perfect trades can still make you good money.

We know that some companies bounce back strongly after facing near death. One of the most famous cases is Apple. Other big companies that came back from their deathbeds include

Chrysler and Delta Airlines. Bill Ackman, a high-profile activist hedge fund manager, bought General Growth Properties—a real estate investment trust that owned shopping centers across the US—during the depths of the subprime crisis. The company's stock price had plunged from $60 to just $0.30 when it couldn't roll over its debts. Ackman knew that if the company could restructure its debt through bankruptcy, the stock price would shoot up because the assets were worth more than the liabilities. The company's stock price recovered to $23. It's stories like this that attract investors to buy companies in trouble —they hope to strike it big with small capital. Yes, there's sometimes good money to be made by picking a turnaround company at rock bottom prices, however bottom picking is full of pitfalls. The possibility that investors might win big blinds them from looking at the probability. For every successful turnaround, there are many more failed ones.

Warren Buffett isn't interested in turnaround companies because they seldom actually turn around. Peter Lynch, on the other hand, was keen on turnarounds, and wrote about this in his book *One Up on Wall Street*. He made a killing when Chrysler turned around in the 1980s. While he acknowledged that many turnarounds never happen, he felt the few winners were big enough to pay for the many losers. He was cautious when it came to buying purely on hope, however, and advised that investors should wait for evidence that a turnaround was working. This meant investors buying not at the low but possibly at more than double the low. Turnaround companies' share prices are very volatile though, and most people find it immensely difficult to buy something that has doubled in a matter of weeks or months. It's tough to master the skills of turnaround and do it frequently enough to have the big winners cover the losers. You have to follow each company closely, as there are bound to be lots of twists and turns. If you find you still love a turnaround despite its difficulties, it has a distinct advantage—its ups and downs are hardly related to the general market.

Generally speaking, companies with high margins are better buys than ones with low margins. When an industry is facing a headwind, it's the company with a high margin that survives. But in a situation where the low-margin company survives, the stock price can rise more than that of high-margin companies. Say two companies produce an identical product. Company A has a high cost of $2 per unit, while Company B has a low cost of $1 per unit. If the selling price is $1.50, only Company B survives. If the selling price is $2.50, Company A is making $0.50 per unit and Company B is making $1.50 per unit. When the selling price rebounds to $4, Company A's profit jumps from $0.50 to $2 (four times) while Company B's profit is up from $1.50 to $3 (two times). The bigger jump in profits for Company A means its share price moves up more than Company B's. With turn-arounds, a low margin can reward the bravehearts better; for buy-and-holds, a high-margin company is the best bet.

When you bottom pick, one of the questions you need to ask yourself is whether the company is in a dying industry. Type-writers, for example, were dominant for so long that even as it became clear that personal computers would take over, investors were still willing to buy Smith Corona all the way down to zero. Kodak and Fujifilm were duopolies in camera films, just as Boeing and Airbus are in commercial jetliners. Kodak invented digital cameras in the 1970s, but selling films was such a good cash cow that the company's management chose not to go into the new field, as they didn't want to cannibalize themselves. When digital cameras started gaining popularity, Kodak went into terminal decline and went bankrupt in 2012. Fuji-film, on the other hand, used the money it earned from camera films to diverge and went into other related businesses. It managed to survive.

When a stock price is going down a lot while the general market and its industry are holding up well, it's a sale you'd be better off not buying. The drop in price isn't due to sentiment change, as the industry and the general market aren't going down. Check out the company's bond prices. Bondholders are usually vigilant and know more about a company than its shareholders do. If the bonds are selling at 20 cents for a dollar, there are some serious problems in the company. Only buy the stock if you have good reason to believe the drop in price is just a sentiment change.

Some investors are attracted to absolute low prices. According to them, a $1 stock is better than a $100 stock. They believe the lower the absolute price, the higher potential for it to grow. They see the downside as being limited. They're wrong. A $100 stock can grow to more than $200,000 if the company is Berkshire Hathaway. An extreme case, yes, because the company never had a stock split, but all other fast-growing companies split their stocks again and again. These investors question how much lower a $1 stock can go. The truth is that a $1 stock can just as easily go to $0.10 as a $100 stock can go to $10. In fact, a $1 stock is more likely to drop 90 percent, as penny stocks are more likely to be companies in trouble. And for those who think absolute-low-price stocks are less "dangerous," that's only true if you buy with less capital. If an investor has $1,000 to invest, whether they chose to buy 1,000 shares at $1 or 10 shares at $100, the capital at risk is exactly the same. Buying $1 stocks isn't any less dangerous.

Remember that you always need to prepare yourself, both financially and emotionally, for a bear market—one will inevitably come. You'll need both cash and courage to buy some good companies and funds while sentiments and headlines are terrible. Enter the market prudently with determination to hold on for a long time. Don't be disturbed by fluctuations—bear markets are volatile, and no one can be sure of the best time to buy. Sooner or later the panic will spend its force and the bull market will be back. During the last two bear markets, in 2000 and 2008, the S&P 500 dropped about 50 percent. The bear market that began in 2000 lasted around three years, while the 2008 bear lasted around 18 months. Always remember: look for the companies that drop the least in their sector, not the most. These companies are much more likely to scale new heights than the laggards. Investors who are decisive and have sound judgement, capital, and courage will be rewarded handsomely if they buy in times of depression and wait patiently for a general revival of businesses and the stock market. Be fearful when others are greedy, and be greedy when others are fearful.

ROTATION

From time to time, we read about a sector outperforming other sectors or the general market by a wide margin. It would be perfect if we could switch from one sector to another, catching the top and bottom in the process. Banks and brokerages pick and recommend their favorite sectors. The media and analysts all have their opinions about each sector too—which is hot, and which is not. They have reasons and explanations for why we should buy this sector and sell the other. There's no doubt that different sectors outperform and underperform one another. This doesn't just apply to sectors though. Sometimes it applies to developed versus emerging markets; sometimes it's emerging versus frontier markets; sometimes it's big-cap versus small-cap; sometimes it's local versus foreign stocks. There are many combinations and possibilities.

The temptation of rotation is that it seems obvious and therefore appears easy. When the economy is recessionary, we should buy defensive sectors, such as utilities and consumer staples—this should help us lose less or even make money in a bear market. When the economy is expansionary, we should buy financial and consumer discretionaries. When interest rates are cut during a bear market, we should buy utilities and real estate investment trusts. On the face of it, it seems easy to move money from one sector to another and make a profit. Examples of this working—like the utilities sector being up 40 percent in 2000 when the Nasdaq was crashing—are often touted as why sector rotation can work. In practice, however, it's a lot harder than it first appears.

The stock market has ceaseless ebbs and flows. It's easy to have hindsight, but to make money, you need foresight. In 2000, it wasn't so clear that utilities would perform well, as the Fed was still hiking up interest rates at the time. In 1994, when the Fed had increased interest rates unexpectedly, utilities had fallen more than 30 percent in eight months. It's very hard to pinpoint in advance the turning point of an economy or the cycle of interest rates, and the time lag between economic and interest rate cycles and the effect they have on a sector isn't clearly defined. It's even harder after buying and selling one sector correctly to follow up with more good timing and prices in another sector. Sometimes the correlations between sectors break down, sometimes they last longer than usual, and sometimes the correlations simply change. What seems simple in theory is actually extremely complicated and difficult in practice.

To be successful in sector rotation, you not only need to understand the different sectors well but you must also be aware of the current financial community's appraisal of the various sectors. You must constantly probe to see if the appraisal is more or less favorable than the fundamentals warrant. These appraisals can change slowly without being noticed or suddenly without giving you ample time to react. You can end up jumping around from one sector to another, taking a small profit here or a loss there. Chances are your active approach of sector rotation will end up doing worse than buying and holding a broad-based fund. Charlie Munger, the vice chairman of Berkshire Hathaway, once said he'd never met a rich sector rotator.

Of course, there will always be some hot sectors that are promoted by the media. Usually, this is only after the sector has already performed well for a considerable period of time. By the time investors are keen on the sector, it might be too late. There are also times when a hot sector has performed so well there are repeated warnings. FAANG is a good example. As early as 2014 and 2015, there were warnings about the rise of FAANG, but these stocks continued to defy gravity and headed higher after each correction over the next few years. Investors who are keen in the technology sector should note its unique feature—it is not homogeneous. Companies in retail, energy or finance are pretty similar to one other, but not technology companies. This diversity makes understanding and investing successfully in technology even more challenging. It takes a lot more effort to get to grips with than say a bank or an airline.

When a sector is turning really big and is dominating the market, it's probably a sign that its top is near. Historically, a dominating sector is eventually replaced by another one. Energy stocks, for example, rose 68 percent in 1979 and 83 percent in 1980, making up 28 percent of the S&P 500 by the end of that year. The following two years, the energy sector underperformed the S&P 500, falling by about 20 percent in both 1981 and 1982. At the end of 1999, technology stocks made up a quarter of the S&P 500. The five largest technology companies at the time—Microsoft, Intel, Cisco, Dell, and Sun Microsystems —accounted for a third of the value of the Nasdaq, which then comprised over four thousand companies. The Nasdaq's peak came the following March. In 2007, the financial sector made up more than 20 percent of the S&P 500. It was the hardest-hit sector during the global financial crisis in 2008. The technology sector came to life again after the crisis and dominated the S&P 500 at the end of the 2010s. By the end of 2019, the five biggest technology companies—Apple, Amazon, Google, Microsoft and Facebook—made up 18 percent of the S&P 500.

Global investors are constantly searching further and further from home for stock investment opportunities, and as emerging markets become more advanced and future returns begin to look less attractive than they did before, a new class of markets is gaining popularity: frontier markets. Frontier markets include countries like Sri Lanka, Nigeria, and Vietnam. Their stock exchanges and currency markets are too small or underdeveloped to be classified as emerging markets—there needs to be "at least some" openness to foreign ownership and "at least partial" ease of capital flows for that.

Due to their limited financial links with other countries, frontier markets are less correlated with global stock markets than emerging markets are. They're also less correlated with one another than emerging markets are. Frontier markets can be volatile by nature, although a basket of frontier markets is less volatile than a single one. This fact attracts an inward flow of money. Day to day, the correlation of frontier markets to global markets is less than that of emerging markets, though both frontier and emerging markets dropped about half during the global financial crisis. The risks that come with investing in frontier markets are considerable, including debt default, currency devaluation, and capital controls, but for the adventurous investor, there are ETFs that invest in individual countries or in baskets of frontier markets. Some of these ETFs have low AUM and low liquidity.

SIZE

Most investors pay a lot of attention to price and tend to over-look size. Whether for long-term investing or short-term trading, very few think about what the right position size actually is. They forget that the right size may, in actual fact, be more important than the right price. Investors usually seek advice to find a good entry level and look at charts to decide what price to buy at. Their default position usually ends up being too large and beyond their comfort level. They think that in order to maximize their return, they need to maximize the size of their position. Thoughts of fantastic returns stop them from considering the risks. If the price starts to go down, their position size will weigh on them; the larger their position size, the more likely their trading decisions will be driven by fear rather than good judgement; they're likely to exit a good trade on a small adverse price move, and they'll find themselves whipsawed by the market, with too many losing trades. A much better plan is to have a smaller position and a wider stop loss instead.

Amateur investors usually like to decide the size of their position first, then work out the stop-loss amount and the stop-loss levels. A professional trader, on the other hand, will decide the stop-loss amount first, then the stop-loss level, and lastly the position size. They usually base their stop levels on technical indicators like support levels. Controlling position size is one of the most undervalued traits in investing.

Bear in mind, however, that while an oversized position is clearly undesirable, a small position can be problematic too. A small position of a company in your portfolio may be due to a partial fill or odd lot given as a dividend. Many people tend to neglect a small position until one day they realize it lost them more money than they thought possible. They're affected more than they expected, and this distracts them from paying more attention to their other, bigger positions. If you keep a small position because at the back of your mind you hope it might be the next Apple, then you're gambling rather than investing. If the stock is good, you should have a bigger position. If it's not good enough, you should sell it. Investing is complicated enough—you should never have a small position in your portfolio.

OK, so if neither too big nor too small is recommended, what is the right size? First, you have to look at the position size versus your portfolio. You need to diversify to reduce the companies' risks. If your portfolio consists entirely of individual stocks, financial planners and academics recommend holding around 20 to 30 companies, with 20 probably being better than 30. Having less companies makes you more selective—you tend to only include good companies and exclude the marginal ones. The other thing to bear in mind is that managing a portfolio of 20 companies is time consuming enough, let alone 30. If your portfolio is entirely in funds, having a few well-diversified funds will suffice. Second, and just as important, is your own psychology. No one can give you a magic number or formula to measure your risk appetite. You have to put your money at work to find out for yourself. Whether it's an individual stock or your entire portfolio, the test is whether you can sleep soundly with its size. If not, "sell down to a sleeping point." It's sage advice. As you become more knowledgeable and gain more experience, you'll become more comfortable with a bigger position size.

PROFITS

"You never go broke taking a profit!" This sounds like perfectly sensible advice, and investors who believe in it eagerly take profit whenever there is one. This adage, however, only mentions the head of the coin and completely ignores the tail—the losses. When there are winners and losers, believing in never going broke by taking a profit can be dangerous. Investors who take many small profits but don't take small losses will end up going broke. Eagerness to lock in a profit limits the profit potential, and those who fail to take losses fast will only see them get bigger. Overall, investors who follow this adage win small and lose big, and that's how they go broke.

The right approach, according to many top traders and investors, is to "let your profits run, cut your losses fast." They believe the higher payoff on the winners should more than offset the small losses on the losers. Being too eager to lock in a small profit is a sure way to ultimate failure. After prices have doubled, there's no reason why a stock can't double again. That's how Apple and Amazon turned into the biggest companies in the world—they doubled and doubled many times. These big winners are able to pay for small losers. But "let your profits run, cut your losses fast" is a difficult rule for most of us to follow because it goes against human nature. When we're winning, we become risk averse and timid—we want to lock in the profit before it slips away. When we're losing, we become stubborn —we're more willing to accept the risk of further decline than lock in the loss. This instinct, while completely natural and normal, is one of the most dangerous indulgences in investing.

Having many wins and very few losses under your belt is, naturally, good for the ego. The number of wins versus losses isn't as important as most of us believe, however; it's much more important to make money in the long run. Some top traders have a low win rate—way less than half. But when they lose, they keep their losses small; when they win, they swing their bats hard to hit a home run. It's a winning strategy—lots of small losses that are more than outweighed by a few big winners. If you'd prefer to have a high win rate, you have to be more patient and selective though. You should only buy companies you think have a high probability of winning.

OK, so we know it's a bad idea to lock in small profits, but should you take a substantial profit of more than 50 percent or hold on for a 500 percent gain? I'd say it's advisable to lock in any substantial profits, unless you're extremely confident that a particular stock will go up many times and you've based this on good information and sound reasoning. There aren't many companies that can go up multiple times in just a few years. Most of the companies you pick are likely to go up and down, so you probably want to sell some of your stocks into strength. It's not uncommon for blue chips and funds to move up and down as much as 30 to 50 percent in a year. More often than not, substantial profit is lost rather than gained. If you're unsure whether your stock will grow a number of times, a compromise would be to sell part of the position and take a partial profit.

How about taking quick, substantial profits? There were times I got lucky, when the stock prices moved in my favor soon after purchase—perhaps 10 percent in a day or 20 to 30 percent in a few days or weeks. If I didn't take a quick profit, the stocks inevitably had a large correction soon after, and my profits turned into losses. Now, I have a rule to always take a quick, substantial profit. The important thing to stress here is that the profit needs to be both quick and substantial—it can't be quick and small. The exceptions to this advice are those stocks that you've identified as having the potential to go up multiple times in the coming years. In this case, it's not a wise move to take a 20 to 30 percent profit for a stock that could double or even triple.

Some investors regard familiarity with contempt. They think that to make good money, you have to buy something new, or exciting, or both. But size and success aren't a hindrance to further success, as many inexperienced investors are inclined to think. If you were to miss Walmart for the first 10 years after its IPO in 1970, which saw the price go up 20 times and the store count rocket from 38 to 276, you could still have made a whopping fiftyfold profit over the next 11 years. Warren Buffett bought The Coca-Cola Company in the 1980s when it was already 100 years old and went on to make 10 times his investment in as many years. Anyone who bought Boeing shares near the low in 2009 was also rewarded with a tenfold return in as many years. The giant airplane maker really can fly.

There are, of course, cases when the price of a stock has gone up to the point that you view it as expensive and overvalued. In these instances, you won't buy any more of the stock at the current price, but should you take a profit? Charlie Munger was quoted as saying: "Psychologically, I don't mind holding a company I like and admire and I trust and know that it will be stronger than now after many years. And if the valuation gets a little silly, I just ignore it. So, I own assets that I would never buy at their current prices but I am quite comfortable holding them."

The other thing to understand when it comes to profits is the concept of averaging up—the act of buying additional shares in a company you already own at a higher price than you originally paid. Averaging up has a better reputation than averaging down. Some would even say it's heroic. If an average up is executed according to plan, you buy half at market price and the other half if the market price is moving in your favor. This is perfectly fine. Momentum traders never average down, but they regularly average up because they believe a price movement in their favor increases their odds of winning. Sometimes, however, investors average up because they're swept up in euphoria.

When they see the market is moving in their favor and their profits are growing, greed takes over and they regret having not bought more earlier. They correct the mistake by averaging up. The results are usually unfavorable. When the market is euphoric, it's sentiment driven and often sees a quick reversal. This hurts those who averaged up. My own past experiences offer good examples. As prices dropped, the misplaced confidence I had when I averaged up vanished quickly. My greed turned to fear as my profit turned to loss. I found that I'd misjudged my comfort level. I became alert and concerned and was in two minds about selling or holding. My procrastination usually ended with me selling into further weakness, and I lost good positions that I would have held on to if I hadn't averaged up.

LOSSES

As investors, we have to accept losses, both in an intellectual sense and on an emotional level. Of course, you want to reduce the number of losses you have as well as their magnitude, but you can never eliminate them altogether. You have to embrace them and think of every loss as a tuition fee paid for a valuable lesson. Dealing with losses is one of the most difficult parts of investing, but if you can't bear to take small losses, you'll end up taking big losses. Big losses will impede you from taking advantage of good opportunities. You'll end up using all your mental energy fighting fires and won't be able to see the opportunities in the market. Getting rid of the losers provides a clear mind. All successful investors handle losses well. A good exercise to carry out is to think of the worst case scenario—knowing it can be liberating.

If you're really struggling with the idea of taking small losses, you might want to think of them as a premium paid for insurance—the losses "insure" you against financial ruin.

Sometimes after buying a stock, we quickly realize it was a mistake, and we promptly make another one by holding on to it, as our purchase shows a loss. One reason for this is that we're taught to be consistent. Once we're committed to an investment, we feel pressured to keep going with our strategy, even when it's contrary to our own interest. Buying a stock and selling it fast is inconsistent. Consistency in sticking to tested investment philosophies and methods is commendable, but consistency in sticking to a trade you know is wrong is plain folly.

Is paper or unrealized loss a real loss? For those who answer "no," ask them if paper or unrealized gain a real gain. They'll hesitate. Some may say yes, but it's illogical to treat paper gain as real and paper loss as unreal. They're both real. Look at it this way: You buy a stock at $10 and it goes down to $8. This position is exactly the same as if you sell the stock at $8 to realize the loss and immediately buy back at $8 (assuming you can buy and sell at the exact same price and there's no transaction cost). The $2 loss, whether you realize it or not, is real. If you buy a stock at $8 now instead of $10 earlier, everyone agrees that the saving of $2 is real, so logically, the $2 loss has to be as real as the $2 saving. As Jim Rogers once said: "There is no such thing as a paper loss. A paper loss is a very real loss."

Despite this, many investors prefer to treat paper loss as unreal. It's psychologically comforting. When something isn't real, you can relax about it; you don't have to deal with it; you can just chuck it in the drawer and hope for the best. These investors argue that as long as they still hold on to the stock, it can rebound, therefore the loss isn't real. They treat the possibility of a rebound as if it were a certainty. But no one can be sure whether the stock will rebound or whether the loss will widen further. You don't want to get confused and blinded by paper loss and refuse to take a loss when it's actually the best course of action.

For those who love to get out even, just think a minute. A stock price that has dropped 20 percent requires a 25 percent advance to break even. A 50 percent loss requires a 100 percent advance, and an 80 percent loss requires a whopping 400 percent gain to make your money back.

Would you place a bet with a maximum profit of $10 and a maximum loss of $90? No? But this is exactly what most people are doing when they hold a losing position and declare "I'll get out when I'm even." Let's say you buy a stock at $100 and it drops to $90. Unwilling to take the $10 loss, you decide to wait until the stock bounces back to $100 to get out. At the same time, you don't set a maximum loss. You limit your subsequent maximum gain to $10, while your loss, in the worst case, is $90.

Averaging down is a very tempting proposition because we're loath to take a loss and we think it will give us a better chance of avoiding one. Let's go back to our example. You buy a stock at $10 and it goes down to $8. This time, refusing to take a loss, you decide to double your position at $8. In a masterstroke, you've lowered your average purchase price to $9, and the share price only needs to go up by $1 rather than $2 for you to break even. Often, however, those who like to average down ignore the other side of the coin. If the stock price subsequently goes down to $5, you're losing $8, as you've doubled the size of your position. It's a grave mistake to think that what goes down must come back up. It's not uncommon for an out-of-favor stock or a bad company to see its share price on a big decline. It doesn't matter how big the company is; sometimes they never come back—just think of Kodak, Lehman Brothers and Sears. Some just keep drifting lower for decades, like General Motors and General Electric. Occasionally they rebound, but only after a number of painful years in which you hold on and miss out on other better stocks. In general, averaging down is a bad idea. It's better to cut your losses, move on, and live to fight another day.

OK, then. If averaging down is such a bad idea, why does Warren Buffett do it? Whose approach is right? Traders who don't average down are usually momentum, technical traders, who have good reason to argue against it. Warren Buffett is a value investor. If he thinks a company's intrinsic value is $10 and he bought at $8, he'll buy more if the price drops to $7. For most average investors, following the momentum, technical traders will probably serve them better. When a stock price is going down, it's usually not a bargain—it's a trap. Warren Buffett knows how to value a company; most regular people don't. If you don't know the intrinsic value or if you work the value out wrong, buying more as the stock price goes down is dangerous.

That being said, if you want to buy a stock and you're not sure whether the price and timing are right, you can plan to average down. You can buy half at current market price and the other half at, say, 10 percent lower. This is totally acceptable. By getting just half at today's market, you don't completely miss the up move. It's unlikely that the original price you pay is going to be the lowest in the coming weeks or months, and averaging down allows you to accumulate your full position at a better price than buying all at once.

While we know that averaging down can be dangerous for individual stocks, it is a good idea for some funds. Out of the thousands of unleveraged stock funds that only invest in listed stocks, I'm not aware any that have gone bust, even though funds can drop as much as 90 percent or more. Study funds carefully before you choose to average down on them. Look at historical figures, and use your common sense. Between an industry fund and a broad fund, the former is more volatile. Between an emerging-market (EM) and a developed-market (DM) fund, an EM fund can drop more. When there's a crisis in an emerging market, both the stock and currency market can drop drastically at the same time. Don't be too eager to average down on a 5 or 10 percent retracement. Most funds are volatile enough that a 15 to 20 percent drop is warranted.

In psychology, the term "anchoring bias" describes the common human tendency to rely too heavily on one piece of information when making decisions. When we buy a stock at $10, the purchase price becomes our anchor. We establish in our minds that the price must represent the stock's true value and that it's worth at least what we paid for it. We attach too much importance to it. No one knows we bought at $10, and no one cares. If we were able to sell above $10, even with a small profit, we'd be happy because it would be a "win." If the price were to dip below $10, we'd probably prefer to wait and hope. Our ego doesn't want us to admit we're wrong; it's just too painful to take a loss—even a small one. This unwillingness to "fail" can turn into an unconstrained loss, until the position is dangling by a thread. The atmosphere and sentiment around the bottom of declines are always very pessimistic. When we finally throw in the towel with a big loss, ironically, we feel relief—no more uncertainties. The loss is locked in, and it can't get bigger. It all started with us attaching too much importance to our anchor price.

Anchoring bias also affects the price at which we sell our stocks. If we sell a stock with the intention of buying it back on a correction, we base the buyback price on our selling price. This seems to make sense. If we sold at $50 and want to buy back at 20 percent lower, we set our target price at $40. But very rarely do we sell at the high and see a correction immediately follow. If a stock goes on to hit a high of $60 before a correction, most people still stick to their $40 buy price. Now the price needs to retrace one-third instead of one-fifth to hit $40—a much more unlikely event. This is one reason why people who like to profit take and then buy back on correction rarely end up actually buying back. The recent high of $60 is significantly more important than their selling price of $50. Everyone who monitors the stock knows the recent high was $60, but no one knows or cares that they sold at $50. Most people are blinded by their anchor price and focus wrongly on $50 instead of $60. If they want a realistic chance of buying back, they have to admit they sold too early and raise their buy price. If they sold way too early and way too low, they might even have to buy back at higher than their selling price. It's difficult psychologically, but if you really like a stock, you just have to do it.

Sometimes after we take a painful loss, we're eager to make another investment to "win it back." This is one of the surest recipes for failure, as a vengeful investment is done hastily without a good thought process or proper plan. Good opportunities aren't going to present themselves just because we want to win back. Never force a trade unless the risk and reward are favorable. After making big losses, it's a better idea to take a break, clear your mind, and get your emotional balance back.

Of course, dealing with losses is never pleasant, and we all try to avoid unpleasant things. Among the many weaknesses I have, one of them is a tendency to delay making difficult decisions when a stock is going against me. I hope that I won't have to make a stop-loss decision in the end. One way to deal with this weakness is to set a mechanical limit, like sell at 10 or 20 percent loss no matter what. This isn't easy to execute because it requires discipline to stick to it. When my stop loss approaches, I naturally hope for a short covering or a white knight to appear. These unrealistic hopes have in the past led me to move my stop loss lower—to allow more time for Lady Luck to come to my rescue. I could've saved a lot of good money if I'd applied a mechanical stop loss and stuck to it.

In my experience, whenever there's surprise bad news, the best thing to do is sell immediately, no matter how big the loss is. It's not easy to do, but it's in the best interests of my bank account to "just do it!" If you don't learn from your losses, a loss is just a loss. If you do, you turn your loss into a tuition fee and you turn yourself from a losing investor to a winning one.

MISTAKES

We all make mistakes, whether in life or in investing. It's never a comfortable feeling knowing you're wrong, but mistakes are inevitable. Warren Buffett readily admits his mistakes in his annual shareholder letters, and Ray Dalio positively embraces his mistakes. Making mistakes isn't a problem in itself, but never learning from them is. As you gain experience in the investment world, try not to repeat the same mistakes time and time again.

Since the industrial revolution, there have been a number of technological breakthroughs. Railroads, electricity, automobiles, airplanes, radio, telephone, television, and computers—these industries were exciting and full of promise when first put to commercial use. Investors often wrongly assume that a fast-growing industry means fast money for shareholders, but history has shown us otherwise. Generations of investors who put money into these high-growth sectors, expecting high returns, were disheartened when they faced losses instead.

At the beginning of the 19th century, there were hundreds of automobile companies in the US. By 1929, three-quarters of US cars were made by the "Big Three"—General Motors, Ford, and Chrysler. The Great Depression killed off most of the remaining independents. The majority of investors who bought into automobiles—an exciting and fast-growing industry at the time—lost money. More recently, millions of investors were attracted by the unlimited potential of the internet and eagerly snapped up internet companies. Unfortunately, lots of these companies folded, leaving many investors loaded with losses. Peter Lynch likes a boring industry—when competitors close down, the survivors can do very well. In *One Up on Wall Street*, he mentions that a carpet company, after emerging as a survivor from a declining and boring industry, gave him a big return.

Some investors' favorite hobby is looking for a bargain, which they strictly and simply define by price. The way they tell it, a stock is cheap only because it hasn't gone up yet. They believe in the fallacy that laggard stocks will go on to see their day in the sunlight. They make the mistaken assumption that stocks that haven't yet made their move provide more potential upside and less risk. They subscribe to the delusion that all stocks go up about the same amount. They think the one that's already moved up a lot won't rise much further, while the one that hasn't moved yet is due to catch up. Nothing could be further from the truth. A great stock can rise a lot more, even it has already gone up. What matters is whether the fundamentals have improved—or will improve in the future—to justify the higher price. Bargain hunters can miss the best stocks because they can't bring themselves to buy a stock that has already gained substantially. A lousy stock, on the other hand, can stay low and go even lower if its fundamentals are bad and getting worse. The fact that a stock has or hasn't yet moved in the last few months or years is of no significance in deciding whether it should be bought now.

When an industry is making a big advance, there are some leaders and some laggards. Many investors prefer to buy the laggards and leave the leaders alone. By way of illustration, say the banking sector is making a good run, with an index that measures all the banks up 10 percent in a month. If JPMorgan is up 20 percent and Citibank is up 5 percent, the "buy-the-laggard" investors will scoop up Citibank stocks. They believe that Citibank will catch up with JPMorgan. Often, when a stock is lagging behind, it's for good reason—perhaps the earnings aren't strong, the balance sheet is weak, or the dividend might be cut. Instead of catching up, when the wind changes direction, you'll find the laggards finally running fast—in the opposite direction.

After the global financial crisis, a few friends mentioned their regret at not having bought Citibank. I never heard anyone talk about buying JPMorgan. During the crisis, Citibank plunged 98 percent from $55 to $1, while JPMorgan slumped 55 percent from $52 to $23. Those who bought JPMorgan during the crisis, or even at the peak, would definitely have made money by now, while investors who preferred to buy Citibank would almost certainly have made a loss. JPMorgan scaled new heights in 2013 and stood at about $140 by the end of 2019. Citibank, on the other hand, finished the year at around $8 (all Citibank prices quoted are based on before it combined 10 shares into one in 2011). I know what you may be thinking: if calculated from the low, a Citibank shareholder could have seen an eight-fold return, while JPMorgan's price only went up six times. This logic, however, ignores the fact that all JPMorgan shareholders made money while only those Citibank shareholders who bought near the low made a profit. Remember that investing isn't just about the maximum return you can achieve but also the probability of returns. For a Citibank shareholder to have made eight times, they would have had to buy at the low and then perform the heroic act of holding on to a scary, volatile stock for years. An investor who bought JPMorgan at the low doesn't need to be a hero to hold on to the stock. JPMorgan didn't require a bailout from the government and was clearly a strong bank with its survival never in doubt. It also maintained its dividends. Investors who bought Citibank at the wrong time and price are likely to still be holding on to a loser 10 years later, while all of JPMorgan's shareholders are making money regardless of the time and price they bought at.

Some people think of the stock market as their fairy godmother. They wish for it to pay for their dream cars and holidays immediately. This is one of the most prolific sources of investment loss. When investors set out to make the stock market pay for a sudden need, they're merely hoping and gambling. They focus on the potential return and run greater risks than they normally would. They reach for trades instead of patiently waiting for good ones to present themselves. When they think of investment gains and losses in terms of just monetary implications, their ability to make good judgments and decisions is impaired. Though all investors want to make money, to treat the stock market as an ATM isn't going to work.

As the highest-paid writer of his time in the US, Mark Twain not only lost his fortune on bad investments but also that of his coal heiress wife. He didn't lose his humor though. "There are two times in a man's life when he should not speculate: when he can't afford it, and when he can," he advised. If your capital is too important and you can't afford to lose it, you'll be doomed to a number of errors. You'll miss out on some good opportunities because they'll often be too risky for you; you'll be too quick to take a small profit because of your concerns about the market taking it away from you; you'll get out of a perfectly good position prematurely if there's an adverse price movement. Fear of losing, ironically, makes you hold on to a loser longer than you should. You indulge in hope. All of these emotions, magnified by "scared money," will cloud your decision-making and guarantee failure. The old Wall Street adage "scared money never wins" should be added to an investor's long list of "don'ts."

Some investors have money saved up and can afford to lose in the stock market. This can make them careless and reckless. They prefer to follow wild rumors and hot tips; they tend to pull their triggers quickly without much thought, as they look for quick and easy money; they prefer exciting trades with a chance of a multiple returns, even if that chance is slim; they think they're fearless, and they like to joke about their losses nonchalantly and project an air of coolness in adversity. Their losses don't hurt them, and that's their biggest problem—they need to feel the pain so that they become more alert and careful, or they could end up losing what they can afford to.

OK, so don't invest when you can't afford to lose, and don't invest when you can afford to lose? Should we resign ourselves, like Mark Twain, to the notion that we should never invest? Not quite. Both extremes are destructive. As the ancient wisdom of Buddhism goes: the middle way is constructive. Never invest with a "can-afford-to-lose" mentality; you need optimism and fear in equal measure. The money you use for investing should be true surplus money. Don't use every dime you have left over after your everyday living expenses—you still need money set aside for rainy days, sufficient to take care of illnesses and other unexpected situations, and for specific future purposes. It's only after all these matters are taken care of that you can invest the surplus money comfortably.

Some speculators don't require a great deal of encouragement or instruction to jump into a trade. They're willing to invest in a heartbeat, and they share a weakness for get-rich-quick schemes; they're constantly dabbling in the stock market on tips and rumors; they have a compulsion to be in the thick of the action and to "do something"—they're incapable of doing nothing. These investors treat each day of trading as if it were their last. Their overwhelming feeling is the fear of missing the action; they always have a "sense" of where the market is heading and an opinion on why it should go up or down. They don't want to think or work much—they just want to make quick money so they can buy fast cars. When they have a position on, they check it frequently, feeling despair if the prices are down and elated if they're up. They actively look for excitement. These speculators won't last long before their capital drains on them. The stock market is an expensive place to look for adventure—a bungee jump is a much cheaper option. No one can have enough information to interpret things correctly all the time and make a daily trade an intelligent one. Only buy when opportunities are available, not just because they happen to be desired or needed. Jim Rogers has some good advice about not overtrading: "I just wait till there is money lying in the corner, and all I have to do is go over there and pick it up. I do nothing in the meantime."

Abraham Lincoln also had a good piece of advice for investors: "Give me six hours to chop down a tree and I will spend the first four sharpening the axe." All too often, investors are overly eager to chop down trees without a plan or preparation. They overlook the need to learn and practice. It's unrealistic to think you can be a profitable investor without putting effort in and doing your preparation work. Even as a part-time, non-professional investor, you need to spend time learning the stock market and studying the companies. You need patience to give yourself time to sharpen your investment skills. Benjamin Franklin's wise words come to mind: "By failing to prepare, you are preparing to fail."

Opinions are rife in the investment world. It's common for investors to argue over beers and in investment forums about where the market is heading or which stock is the best buy. Most people have the courage to fight for their opinions, but few have the courage to abandon them. Obstinate investors don't live long in the market. People who win an argument always think they're right. They congratulate themselves on how smart they are. But in the end, their opinions, even logical, convincing ones based on lots of data and facts, mean nothing in the market.

It doesn't matter how many arguments you win or how good your opinion is, the market doesn't know, and it doesn't care— it will go where it is going. The smart, opinionated people may feel sure they're right, but that doesn't mean the market has to agree with them. They shouldn't let their opinions and views cloud their ability to make objective observations. They should always keep an open mind and accept that they could be wrong. Indeed, they should look for evidence as to why they actually may be wrong. As a young FX trader, I liked to have opinions, but I learned over the years that my opinions made me no money. They did however, lose me plenty. It took me years to understand Bruce Lee's (1940–1973) philosophical quote: "Be water, my friend."

Quite often, our opinions and forecasts are based on fuzzy, dubious facts. They rely on our impression of the facts rather than the actual facts. They're also shaped by our emotions. If we're afraid and downbeat, we project that feeling with a pessimistic forecast; if we feel buoyant and upbeat, we make an optimistic forecast. In short, our own forecasts are just as dubious as those of the experts. Often I hear logical arguments as to why the market is bearish or bullish, along with a few assumptions. When these opiners talk about their theories, they readily admit that they are indeed based on assumptions, however they speak and think about them as though they're hard facts. Good logic with the wrong assumptions and facts can still produce a logical conclusion—it's just the wrong one.

Novice investors tend to focus on making money, as it's more enticing to think about winning than losing. They fantasize about how wins can boost their egos instead of focusing on how losses can hurt them. Nobody, however, wins all the time. Whether we like it or not, losing is a big part of the game. Focusing on the losing trades and reducing them is just as important as making winning trades—maybe even more so. Losing money doesn't just hurt us financially, it also affects our psychology. Fire-fighting drains our energy. It stops us from putting on or reducing the size of a good trade. For the first few years of my career, my only focus was looking for winning trades. Many turned out to be losers. When I started to pay attention to losses, I cut down the number of losing trades as well as the magnitude of my losses. This enabled me to spend more energy looking for good trades than fighting bad ones. My overall results improved drastically.

One common mistake investors make is to judge an investment decision solely on its result. We equate making money with good investments and losing money with bad ones. This isn't always the case, however. When investing, there's always an element of luck. A losing investment need not be bad, just as a winning investment isn't necessarily always good. Say someone challenges you to a bet about the toss of a coin. Heads you win

$2, tails you lose $1. Would you take the bet? Of course you would. It's a good trade. If it turns out to be tails, the trade is still good despite a poor result due to bad luck. If you're able to make this trade and place the bet many times, you'll end up making money. It's what investing is all about—looking for investments with a good risk-reward. You might lose due to bad luck in the short run, but if you only invest when the odds are in your favor, you'll come out ahead in the long run.

Many investors make investment decisions based on possibility rather than probability. They don't recognize the difference between the two. This is one of the biggest sources of loss in the financial markets. The investors are attracted by a possible but improbable high return. I term this "lottery mentality." Just like gamblers buying lottery tickets, they know the odds are against them but they still bet because the reward is big and they hope to get lucky. Lottery mentality is rife in the financial markets. The billions of dollars made by star managers like George Soros and Ray Dalio over the decades for their lucky investors attract people to put money in hedge funds in the hope of investing in the next superstar. Of course, most hedge fund managers don't come close to matching Soros or Dalio's records. Lottery mentality is also common in the IPO market, where a few high-profile, high-return IPOs have given investors hope that they can stumble across the next Amazon or Google. Apple's success in coming back from the brink has also convinced many investors that there's a pot of gold in turnaround companies.

Truth be told, the actual lottery can be a better bet than the "stock lottery." Investors with lottery mentality fail to see the important difference between the two. In the lottery, the prize money is fixed and the time to collect the winnings is short. In the stock lottery, the prize money fluctuates and there are always huge temptations to collect small "prize money." It requires a lot of patience and courage to be able to collect the big winnings. An investor who bought Amazon at its IPO in 1997 would have turned a $1,000 investment into more than $1 million by 2019. This mouthwatering return whets the appetite of those eager to win big. But how many people would have been willing to wait more than 20 years to get the prize money? How many would have been able to resist collecting a fiftyfold return in 1999 when *Barron's* published an article titled "Amazon.bomb?" When the internet bubble burst, Amazon lost 95 percent in less than two years. How many people would be able to hold on during an onslaught like that?

Working out the probability of an investment return is more an art than a science. There's no exact probability attached to an investment—it requires subjective judgement and guesswork. You need to make an intelligent guess and not base your decision on an unrealistic dream. Often the information we have to hand isn't enough. Sometimes its's too confusing or just too hard to understand. In this case, it's best to give up. Mr. Buffett and Mr. Munger, as intelligent and successful as they are, have a "too hard" tray, which they often put investment ideas in. You should do the same.

Some investors like to watch the prices of stocks they've sold recently more closely than the prices of those they still own. They feel elated if they sold near the high, but they're full of regret if it turns out they sold too low. If the sole purpose of watching a recently sold stock is curiosity, they should just move on and avoid that emotional swing. The only good reason to watch a sold stock is to learn something dispassionately and rationally from the sale—to improve future timings and price-to-sell decisions.

While this chapter has listed some of the common mistakes average investors make, the list is by no means exhaustive. Learning from our mistakes is important, but it's not all that straightforward. When we make a mistake, time elapses before we realize our error, and even more time goes by before we realize the implications. It's amazing how one trading mistake can lead to a cascade of others. Successive mistakes can be spiritually deflating. Once you've made a mistake, it's vital to be alert so you can avoid following it up with yet more mistakes. While you shouldn't allow mistakes and losses to upset you too much, you also shouldn't allow them to pass by lightly. It's important to analyse any mistakes from a detached, objective standpoint. Review and study mistakes with care so that valuable, correct lessons are learned. Implementing those lessons isn't easy though—human nature often holds us back. We might fail to resist the temptation to take a small profit or be too scared by poor market sentiment to place a buy order. We repeat the same mistakes again and again. Recently, after thinking I'd learned enough over the years to avoid making silly mistakes, I duly made a careless schoolboy error. A wise man learns from his mistakes, but a fool never does.

PART VII: MAKE YOUR MOVE

FREE LUNCH

There are free lunches to be had in the financial markets. Credit cards are one. Banks and payment companies make money from merchants and card users who don't pay their bills in full each month, while credit cards users whose annual fees are waived and always pay on time get to enjoy all the convenience and benefits of a credit card without paying a single cent. Their free lunches are the points they can exchange for airmiles or other products and services.

Back in the introduction, I promised you a free lunch too. Here it is: it involves options—financial derivatives, the value of which is derived from an underlying asset. A stock option's value is derived from that stock's price, just like gold's option value is derived from the price of gold. In many countries, options are used before the completion of a property transaction. A buyer of an option pays a premium to the seller. An option has an exercise price, also known as the strike price, and it has an expiry date. The buyer has the right but not the obligation to exercise the option. There are two types of options: call options and put options. Call options give buyers the opportunity to buy the underlying asset at an exercise price, while put options give the buyer the opportunity to sell the asset.

The math surrounding options has lots of Greek names—delta, gamma, vega, and so on. Options strategies also boast interesting names, such as butterfly, condor, strangle, and straddle. It all sounds—and can be—very complicated, but for your free lunch, you only need to know the basics: premium, exercise price, and expiry date.

The free lunch idea is simple, and so is its execution: it involves selling an option.

The concept of selling an option probably needs some explanation. When you sell an option, think of yourself as an insurance company selling a specific travel insurance policy that only covers flight delays. You collect the premium upfront. If the flight is on time, the premium is your profit. How much the premium costs depends on a few factors. A customer who wants to be compensated for an hour's delay has to pay a higher premium than a customer who will only get compensated for a two-hour delay. The exercise price of options works the same way: An investor who wants cover for a year has to pay a higher premium than one who only wants cover for three months. The premium varies according to the expiry date. If the "flight" is delayed, you need to pay compensation to the insurance buyer. In the case of selling stock options for your free lunch, the "compensation" comes in the form of either buying or selling stocks.

When you want to buy a stock at less than market price, you can place a limit order. Alternatively, you can sell a put option at an exercise price the same as your limit order price. Say you want to buy Apple stock at $280 and the current price is $300. Without using an option, you simply place a limit order to buy at $280, and you wait. Your other choice is to sell a put option with an exercise price of $280 to earn a premium of $3 with a one-month expiry date. If the price drops below $280, the buyer of the put option exercises it and you end up buying the stocks at $280. Whether by limit order or put option, you buy Apple stock at $280. In either case, if the stock price doesn't move below $280 within one month, you don't get to buy Apple at $280. The result is the same. However, if you choose to sell a put option, you earn a $3 premium—your free lunch—regardless of whether you buy Apple stock at $280.

Unlike placing a limit order to buy a stock, selling a put option creates real-time profit and loss in your margin account. If the stock price goes up, your margin account shows a profit. If the stock price drops, your margin account shows a loss. As your account has enough money to buy the stock, you're unlikely to face a margin call. Your risk is similar whether you buy the stock with a limit order or you sell a put option.

When you want to sell a stock at more than market price, once again, you can place a limit order. Alternatively, you can sell a call option at an exercise price the same as your limit order price. Say you want to sell Apple stock at $320 and the current price is $300. Without using an option, you simply place a limit order to sell at $320, and you wait. Your other choice is to sell a call option with an exercise price of $320 to earn a premium of $3 with a one-month expiry date. If the price goes above $320, the buyer of the call option exercises it and you end up selling the stocks at $320. Whether by limit order or call option, you sell Apple stock at $320. In either case, if the stock price doesn't move above $320 within one month, you don't get to sell Apple at $320. Once more, the result is the same. However, if you choose to sell a call option, you earn a $3 premium—your free lunch—regardless of whether you sell Apple stock at $320.

Unlike placing a limit order to sell a stock you own, selling a call option creates real-time profit and loss in your margin account. Make sure you have money there. If the stock price goes down, your margin account shows a profit. If the stock price moves higher, your margin account shows a loss. You might face a margin call if you don't have enough money in your margin account.

Remember: you sell a put option if you want to buy a stock and you sell a call option if you want to sell a stock. If you want to buy or sell the stock at market price, you can't use options to earn a free lunch.

Generally speaking, buying options is safe and selling options is dangerous. The options buyer can't lose more than the premium. The profit, in extreme cases, can in fact be as much as hundreds of times the premium. This possibility of a small premium turning into a multiple return attracts those retail investors with lottery mentality. On the flip side, an option seller's profit is the premium, and their loss is the buyer's profit, which can potentially be big. This is why selling options has the reputation of being a dangerous game. You need to be careful with options and remain prudent with your size.

But if selling options is so dangerous, why am I suggesting you might want to consider it? The answer is it's safe under certain conditions. Only sell a put if you want to buy a stock with cash (no leverage), and only sell a call if you want to sell a stock you own. To be clear, never sell an option if you don't want to either buy a stock or sell a stock you own. This way, the risks of selling an option are similar to the risks of buying and selling a stock. Selling an option becomes dangerous if it's sold "naked"—in other words if the put seller doesn't have enough money to buy the stock and the call seller has no stock to deliver.

If this really is a free lunch, why isn't everyone doing it then? First of all, many investors misunderstand financial derivatives such as options and futures. Most of these derivatives have built-in leverage, which makes them appear "dangerous." To some people, the issue is that the premium involved is too small for them to take the trouble. Option premiums depend on several factors. One is the "time value"—the longer the expiry, the higher the time value and the premium. For example, for the same exercise price, the premium of a one-month expiry option could be $1 and that of a three-month expiry option could be $2.50. The other factor in determining the premium is the volatility of the underlying asset. The more volatile it is, the higher the premium. When the underlying asset is volatile, the chance of an option hitting its exercise price is high, therefore buyers are willing to pay a higher price and sellers are only willing to sell at a higher price. This means the premium that can be earned isn't as small as some believe. A one-month option can earn a premium of about 1 percent for stable stocks and 3 percent or more for volatile stocks—and those are non-annualized rates. Say you have $10,000 in your account and you want to use it to buy 1,000 shares of a company at $10 each. You sell

10 one-month put options at $0.30 (in the US, one option can exercise 100 shares). The premium you earn is $0.30*10*100= $300. That's a 3 percent return in one month for your capital of $10,000.

Another concern for some investors is that short-option positions also carry a margin requirement—usually 20 percent of the exercise price. Some people don't like the idea of too much money being tied up in a margin account; others don't like worrying about meeting a margin call. Some investors are unwilling to learn and try new things—they consider options to be too complicated.

Occasionally, when selling a put option, the stock price will have temporarily dropped below the exercise price before then rising and staying above it until expiry. Conversely, when selling a call option, there may be cases where the price temporarily went above the exercise price before then dropping and staying below it until expiry. In these unlikely cases, you'll fail to buy or sell at your target (exercise) price, even though the market price has reached it, and you'll earn the premium without buying or selling your stocks. When this happens, you can either sell another option to earn a premium or buy/sell the stock at market price.

When you place a limit order to buy and sell stock, you have the flexibility to change the price. Once an option is sold, however, you can't change your exercise price. What you can do is buy back the option at a gain or loss before the expiry date and sell another option with a new exercise price.

The premium of an option will steadily move higher ahead of an earnings result because the volatility is likely to increase when the result is announced. Selling just ahead of an earnings result allows the seller to get a higher premium. However, if the result is a big surprise, it's possible for the stock price to move more than 20 percent in a day and go well past your exercise price. The extra premium earned might not be worth the risk. Always remember to check the earnings calendar to avoid selling an option just before an earnings result or having an expiry date just after one.

It's true that options prices are, by nature, much more volatile than the underlying stocks; it's not uncommon for a stock price to move a few percent and the corresponding option price to move a few hundred percent. Don't be tempted to become an options buyer. Most options expire worthless, which means most buyers lose money. The occasional wins aren't enough to pay for the frequent losses. For the average retail investor with limited time and effort available, options are simply too complicated and too difficult to trade successfully, both in the short and the long term.

You may feel after reading all this that options trading is too difficult. So how else can you get a free lunch? If the company you've invested in offers shareholders cash or scrip as dividend, you might get a small free lunch. The way it works is the company states the price at which the scrip will be given and shareholders are given a period of time—usually a few weeks— to choose between cash and scrip. If the stock price is higher than the scrip price, you should sell the number of shares you're entitled to from your shareholding and then opt to get the scrip to replenish what you've sold. Beware though—this exercise is only worth the effort if your dividend is substantial and the price difference is more than 2 percent, as you have to take transaction costs into account. Why would a company offer you stocks instead of cash as a dividend? Sometimes they want to conserve their capital. If the shareholders don't opt for the stocks, their shareholdings are diluted by more shares being issued.

GAME PLAN

With the knowledge you've gained, it's now time to put a practical game plan into play. It's all well and good understanding the theory, but that's of no use unless you turn it into specific actions. There are many ways to make money in the stock market. Your job is to establish which method matches your chosen investing philosophy, style, and personality. It's a case of each to their own. Investors who are always looking for value, whether when searching for a holiday or buying groceries, will probably want to look for value stocks. For investors who are impatient and like excitement, momentum and growth stocks may be a better fit. There are many other choices described in this book to suit different people—technical analysis, dividend stocks, turnaround companies, and so on. You're free to choose whatever you fancy and as many methods as you like. However, it's not advisable to use too many strategies at the same time. I hope this book has helped you understand the challenges and difficulties of each option so you can avoid some of the more common mistakes investors make.

As an investor, you will fit into one of three groups according to the capital you have. First are those with a lump sum to invest; second are those who save regularly to invest; third are those who have both a lump sum and regular savings to invest. Remember the buffet meal in the introduction? Whichever group you belong to, make sure you have the signature dish—a low-cost, broad-based, passive fund, whether that's a mutual fund or an ETF. A good example is SPY—an ETF that invests in all 500 companies in the S&P 500. Both Warren Buffett and John Bogle strongly recommend it.

Of course, as Mark Twain, that great writer but hopeless investor, once wrote: "The secret of getting ahead is getting started." To kick-start your long investment journey, begin by buying a low-cost, broad-based index fund in your country. If you're in the US, start with the S&P 500. If you're in the UK, look at the FTSE. Have some faith in Mr. Buffett and Mr. Bogle, and put at least 10 percent of your investable capital in a broad-based, passive fund. That's not a recommended amount; it's the minimum amount you should invest in this way.

In fact, the amount you should invest in the fund ranges from 10 to 100 percent of your capital. Warren Buffett's recommendation to his wife was to put 90 percent in an S&P 500 fund. The proportion of capital you decide to put in your chosen fund depends on how convinced you are that a broad-based fund is superior to active investing and how active an investor you want to be. If you're not convinced at all and would prefer to manage your investment actively, put 10 percent in. If this 10 percent underperforms, it won't hurt your overall return too much; if it overperforms, it won't improve your overall return much either. 10 percent is insignificant enough that you're much more likely to commit to it for decades. Meanwhile, this commitment to a broad-based, passive fund allows you to see and feel for yourself while the stock market does what it does best—fluctuates. If a sudden storm comes along, the capital committed to a broad-based, passive fund can contribute much to your peace of mind—you know this fund won't disappear, and you can be sure that it will come back in time.

The most important thing is to put your money to work—it's the only way to learn about both the market and yourself as an investor. Get behind the wheel of the race car—not the simulator. You can't rely on a risk-appetite test—the only way to discover the limits of your comfort zone is to invest with your hard-earned money. There's no other way.

Remember, however, that other than committing at least 10 percent to a broad-based passive fund, there's no need to rush and commit all your capital in a short period of time. You're playing a long game that lasts decades. While you may be excited about opportunities and returns, you always need to remember about risks and luck. I would recommend taking at least a year—preferably a few years—to fully commit your capital. You need to be emotionally comfortable and only take further risks when you feel ready to do so. If your commitment to a passive fund is 10 percent, you can put it all in at once, or you can choose to invest half now and the other half a year later. If your commitment is more than 10 percent, you want to spread it over a few years.

When it comes to active investing and trading, remember that your capital doesn't have to be limited to individual stocks. There are thousands of ETFs in the US to choose from, which you can buy and sell exactly like a stock. Whether you choose stocks, ETFs, or both as your active investment vehicle, you should put your capital to work slowly as your skills and comfort zone expand. The golden rule, whatever combination of active versus passive funds you choose, is that your exposure has to match your comfort level.

While you're trying both passive funds and active investing, remember that you need to make sure you record all your trades and keep a journal. If your active investments outperform your passive funds, the question you need to ask is whether that's due to skill or luck. During the internet boom, many people thought they had innate skill, as they made easy money. Some even quit their day jobs to become traders. But a rising tide lifts all boats. When the tide went out, many of those new traders found they were swimming naked, and while they'd put their wins down to skill, when they lost, they thought it was just their bad luck.

When you've been investing for a few years, either your passive funds or active investments will be doing better than the other. Your results and experience will lead you to move more capital accordingly. More than likely, you'll move more into passive funds. If you want to persist in active investing despite an inferior result, there's nothing stopping you, but you might want to try other ideas and strategies, or you might need more time to hone the skills required for your current approach. Your skills will grow over time, and you might eventually outperform the market. If your active investments are underperforming your passive fund yet you're reluctant to put all your money in the "boring" option, it's alright to keep 10 percent in active investments. This can keep you more committed to the broad-based funds and allow you to have some fun.

If you're the type of investor with regular savings, unless those savings are substantial—say more than $1,000 per month—you'll need to commit more than 10 percent of your capital to a passive fund. Say your monthly savings are $200. You need to put at least a quarter or even half of it in a passive fund, as one share of an S&P 500 fund costs about $50 (e.g. SWPPX), with some costing as much as $300 (e.g. SPY). The positive side is that because you're buying regularly and adopting dollar-cost averaging, you avoid the problem of timing. This makes it more likely you'll commit to the fund in the long term. Just like those with one lump sum, you can manage the rest of your savings actively using whatever ideas and strategies you fancy.

For the last group of investors—those with both a lump sum and regular savings—the pace at which you put your lump sum to work can be quicker than that of investors who only have a lump sum to invest. You still shouldn't invest all at once though —spread it out over a year or two. If the market is heading lower while you invest your lump sum, your regular savings are able to take advantage of the lower prices.

Some people are skeptical about whether passive funds work, as they firmly believe that only hard work can produce good results. Surely buying something now, doing nothing for the next 20 years, and ending up with a good result is impossible, they argue. They reason that working hard means trading hard; they think they need to read the financial pages, listen to the opinions of the movers and shakers, follow Twitter, and watch

CNBC. It's not true. All the evidence proves that a simple strategy of buying and holding a broad-based, passive fund works in the long term. As Charlie Munger said: "The harder you work, the more confidence you get. But you may be working hard on something that is false."

Whichever method you begin with, make sure you keep developing and fine-tuning your investment philosophy and style, which will take a considerable period of time to form and mold. It will be tested along the way, and when verified, it will give you the confidence to stay the course through the difficult times. Investing is a dynamic process and needs to be refined and revised regularly. Adapting your philosophy and style as you learn will stand you in good stead in the years ahead. After a few years, your financial situation will change, your risk appetite will change, your psychology of investing will change, and you'll gain knowledge and experience. Remember this, and review your portfolio at regular intervals.

As suggested in the title, this book is about "investing." That means long-term investing, not short-term speculating and trading. Your game plan will take a few years to implement, and the satisfactory results might take a while to show. Your patience will be tested along the way. In today's fast, modern world, we're so used to seeing instant results. Investing isn't fast. These days, everyone is living longer. Be patient—time is your friend.

CONCLUSION

The stock market is full of ironies, paradoxes, and contradictions. Making money seems easy to some people, yet they still lose it. Investors rush to sell when prices are low and to buy when prices are high; those who try to get high dividends get dividend cuts; those who try to time the market are experts of uncannily bad timing; people who look for value stocks fall into value traps. Speculators turn a losing stock into an investment; investors turn a winning stock into a speculation. Investors blame the market when they should actually blame themselves. They dream of profits when they should worry about losses; they focus on returns when they should concentrate on risks. Investors need to be both fearful and fearless. Good news is bad news, and bad news is good news. Market wisdom isn't wise. Investing is simple, but it sure isn't easy.

As you begin your journey, you'll most likely find that active investing is hard. You'll have to fight many enemies within yourself. You'll need to be honest with yourself and learn to accept mistakes and losses. You'll need to be disciplined, patient, independent, and confident. You'll have to rely on and yet be wary of media. Common sense will help you judge what methods and strategies work, what's right and what's wrong, what to do, and what not to do.

Amid all the challenges and difficulties, some investors enjoy great success. The Market Wizards book series offers some good explanations as to why they succeed while many others fail. These top traders trade FX, futures, options, stocks, bonds, and commodities. They can be pure fundamentalists, pure technicians, or somewhere in between. Their time horizons range from intra-day to years. They are different, and yet they're the same. They all love what they do; they embrace mistakes and always strive to do better; they understand that losses are a part of the game and they control them; they're confident yet wary of overconfidence; they're flexible and never argue with the markets; crucially, they take full responsibility for their actions.

There's an old Chinese saying: "In the books, stand a golden house." I found a golden house in Jack D. Schwager's Market Wizards books. They showed me a path in the dark investment forest. I read them again and again, each time learning new wisdom from the top traders they featured. My book may not be in the same league, but it is a culmination of my decades-long investment journey, trying dozens of methods, reading hundreds of books, and making thousands of trades and mistakes. The range of topics covered in this book is probably the widest of any stock investment book out there. For most of you, it's probably worth your time to read it through again, and then maybe once or twice more. You'll find you missed this point or that point when you first read it. As you gain experience, however, you'll read it in a different light. You'll find the time you invest in it is all worthwhile.

Investors are an optimistic lot. Successful investors are realistic optimists—they're not dreamers. After all, despite all the setbacks, difficulties, challenges, natural disasters, cold wars, trade wars, and world wars, the world economy keeps growing and the stock markets keep scaling new heights. The Dow Jones was below 100 at the beginning of the 20th century. By the end of 2019, it had reached more than 28,000. The FTSE started at 1,000 in 1984 and rose to more than 7,500. The Hang Seng was launched in 1969 at 158 and was around 28,000 by the end of the 2010s. Will these indexes continue to break new highs in the future? No one has a crystal ball, but I wouldn't want to bet against it.

In a game of tennis, professionals try to win by hitting their best shots. When the amateurs play against each other, they shouldn't hit the ball with maximum power or try landing it in the corners—most of the time, these attempts will just send the ball into the net or out of play. An amateur needs to play safe shots. The winner will be whoever makes less mistakes. If you're reading this book, you're an amateur investor. That's why in your game plan, you must have broad-based, passive funds. It will keep your game simple, defensive, and less prone to mistakes. It doesn't matter that you're not a professional— you can still love the game and play it well. If you keep putting in the time and effort, keep learning from your mistakes, and keep improving, you may never win a grand slam but you could end up as a local—or even national—champion. Some of you will win by playing it safe and simple. The more competitive and talented among you may keep on winning and eventually become investment champions.

DISCLAIMER

This book is intended to be used as a guide to managing your money and achieving your financial goals. It is for educational and informational purposes only. The past performances of stocks, stock markets, and funds mentioned in the book are not a guarantee of future return, nor are they necessarily indicative of future performance. Your use of the information in this book is at your own risk. Content contained or made available through this book is not intended to and does not constitute legal advice or investment advice. You should never make any investment decision without first consulting with your own financial advisor and conducting your own research and due diligence. It is important to do your own analysis before making any investment, based on your own personal circumstances. All investment decisions have inherent risks. The value of your investment will fluctuate over time, and you may gain or lose money. In the worst case, you may lose all your capital. You are responsible for your own choices, actions, and results. While best efforts have been used in preparing this book, the author disclaims any and all liabilities in the event any information, commentary, analysis, opinions, advice, and/or recommendations contained in this book prove to be inaccurate, incomplete, unreliable, or result in any investment or other losses. The author is not held liable or responsible to any person or entity with respect to any loss or incidental or consequential damages caused, or alleged to have been caused, directly or indirectly, by the information or recommendations contained in this book.

RESOURCES, REFERENCES, AND RECOMMENDED READING

A Bull In China: Investing Profitably in the World's Greatest Market, Jim Rogers, ISBN 9780812977486

Adventure Capitalist : The Ultimate Road Trip, Jim Rogers, ISBN 9780812967265

A Gift To My Children: A Father's Lessons for Life and Investing, Jim Rogers, ISBN 9781400067541

A Man For All Markets: From Las Vegas to Wall Street, How I Beat the Dealer and the Market, Edward O. Thorp, ISBN 9781400067961

Amsterdam: A History of the World's Most Liberal City, Russell Shorto, ISBN 9780307743756

Anatomy of the Bear: Lessons from Wall Street's Four Great Bottoms, Russell Napier, ISBN 9781906659356

A Random Walk Down Wall Street: The Time-Tested Strategy for Successful Investing, Burton G. Malkiel, ISBN 9780393330335

Beating The Street, Peter Lynch with John Rothchild, ISBN 9780671891633

Big Mistakes: The Best Investors And Their Worst Investments, Michael Batnick, ISBN 9781119366553

Business Adventures: Twelve Classic Tales From the World of Wall

Street, John Brooks, ISBN 9781497644892

Charlie Munger: The Complete Investor, Tren Griffin, ISBN 9781511337250

China's Stock Market: A Guide to its Progress, Players and Prospects, Stephen Green, The Economist Series, ISBN 9781861976659

Common Stocks and Uncommon Profits, Philip A. Fisher, ISBN 9780471445500

Contrarian Investment Strategies: The Next Generation, David Dreman, ISBN 9780684813509

Deng Xiaoping and the Transformation of China, Ezra F. Vogel, ISBN 9780674725867

Devil Take The Hindmost: A History of Financial Speculation, Edward Chancellor, ISBN 9780452281806

Fifty Years In Wall Street, Henry Clews, ISBN 9781511383424

Frontier: Exploring the Top Ten Emerging Markets of Tomorrow, Gavin Serkin, ISBN 9781118823736

Guns, Germs and Steel: The Fates of Human Societies, Jared Diamond, ISBN 9780393317558

Hedge Fund Market Wizards: How Winning Traders Win, Jack D. Schwager, ISBN 9781118273043

Hot Commodities: How Anyone Can Invest Profitably in the World's Best Market, Jim Rogers, ISBN 9780470014981

How Legendary Traders Made Millions: Profiting From the Investment Strategies of the Greatest Traders of All Time, John Boik, ISBN 9780071468220

If It's Raining In Brazil, Buy Starbucks: The Investor's Guide to Market-Moving Events, Peter Navarro, ISBN 9780071433198

In An Uncertain World: Tough Choices from Wall Street to Washington, Robert E. Rubin and Jacob Weisberg, ISBN 9780375757303

Investment Biker: Around the World with Jim Rogers, Jim Rogers, ISBN 9780471961260

Leonardo da Vinci: Flights of the Mind, Charles Nicholl, ISBN

9780143036128

Liar's Poker, Michael Lewis, ISBN 9780393338690

Maestro: Greenspan's Fed and the American Boom, Bob Woodward, ISBN 9780743205627

Market Wizards: Interviews With Top Traders, Jack D. Schwager, ISBN 9780887306105

More Money Than God: Hedge Funds and the Making of a New Elite, Sebastian Mallaby, ISBN 9780143119418

My Life, Bill Clinton, ISBN 9781400030033

Once in Golconda: A True Drama of Wall Street 1920–1928, John Brooks, ISBN 9780471357520

One Up Wall Street: How to Use What You Already Know to Make Money in the Market, Peter Lynch, ISBN 9780743200400

On The Brink: Inside the Race to Stop the Collapse of the Global Financial System, Henry M. Paulson, Jr., ISBN 9780446561938

Outliers: The Story of Success, Malcolm Gladwell, ISBN 9780316017930

Poor Charlie's Almanack: The Wit and Wisdom of Charles T. Munger, Charles T. Munger, ISBN 9781578643660

Practical Speculation, Victor Niederhoffer and Laurel Kenner, ISBN 9780471677741

Precious Metals Trading: How to Profit from Major Market Moves, Philip Gotthelf, ISBN 9780471711513

Principles For Navigating Big Debt Crises, Ray Dalio, ISBN 9781732689800

Reminiscences Of A Stock Operator, Edwin Lefèvre, ISBN 9780471770886

Sam Walton: Made in America, My Story, Sam Walton and John Huey, ISBN 9780553562835

Security Analysis, Benjamin Graham and David L. Dodd, ISBN 9780071592536

Soros On Soros: Staying Ahead of the Curve, George Soros, ISBN

9780471119777

Stock Market Wizards: Interviews With America's Top Stock Traders, Jack D. Schwager, ISBN 9780066620596

Street Smart: Adventures on the Road and in the Markets, Jim Rogers, ISBN 9780804141147

Tap Dancing To Work: Warren Buffett on Practically Everything, 1966–2013, Carol J. Loomis, ISBN 9781591846802

The Age Of Turbulence: Adventures in a New World, Alan Greenspan, ISBN 9780143114161

The Alchemy of Finance, George Soros, ISBN 9780471445494

The Art Of Speculation, Philip L. Carret, ISBN 9781614272380

The Battle For Investment Survival, G. M. Loeb, ISBN 9781617200557

The Essays Of Warren Buffett: Lessons for Corporate America, Lawrence A. Cunningham, ISBN 9781611637588

The Everything Store: Jeff Bezos and the Age of Amazon, Brad Stone, ISBN 9780316219266

The Go-Go Years: The Drama and Crashing Finale of Wall Street's Bullish 60s, John Brooks, ISBN 9780471357544

The Greatest Trade Ever: The Behind-the-Scenes Story of How John Paulson Defied Wall Street and Made Financial History, Gregory Zuckerman, ISBN 9780385529945

The House Of Morgan: An American Banking Dynasty and the Rise of Modern Finance, Ron Chernow, ISBN 9780802144652

The Intelligent Investor: The Definitive Book on Value Investing, Benjamin Graham, ISBN 9780060555665

The Little Book of Common Sense Investing: The Only Way to Guarantee Your Fair Share of Stock Market Returns, John C. Bogle, ISBN 9780470102107

The Little Book That Beats The Market, Joel Greenblatt, ISBN 9780470624159

The New Paradigm For Financial Markets: The Credit Crisis and

What it Means, George Soros, ISBN 9781921372483

The Prize: The Epic Quest for Oil, Money & Power, Daniel Yergin, ISBN 9781439110126

The Wisdom Of Crowds, James Surowiecki, ISBN 9780385721707

This Time Is Different: Eight Centuries of Financial Folly, Carmen M. Reinhart and Kenneth S. Rogoff, ISBN 9780691152646

Trade Like Jesse Livermore, Richard Smitten, ISBN 9780471655855

What Goes Up: The Uncensored History of Wall Street as Told by the Bankers, Brokers, CEOs, and Scoundrels Who Made it Happen, Eric J. Weiner, ISBN 9780316066372

Winning On Wall Street: How to Spot Market Trends Early, Which Stocks to Pick, and When to Buy and Sell for Profit Peaks and Minimum Risk, Martin Zweig, ISBN 9780446672818

www.ingramcontent.com/pod-product-compliance
Lightning Source LLC
Chambersburg PA
CBHW030611220526
45463CB00004B/1254